HP

Richmond upon Thames Libraries

Renew online at www.richmond.gov.uk/libraries

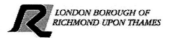

"While the focus is on women in this book, King is not blind to others facing barriers too – men themselves who deviate from the Don Draper model, for example, and others who are perceived as not fitting in. Fixing the workplace to help women will lead to fixing the workplace for all because, King concludes, 'it is the only way companies will survive the inevitable changes to come'."

Financial Times

"A passionate, practical roadmap for addressing inequality and finally making our workplaces work for women."

Arianna Huffington

THE FIX

Overcome the Invisible
Barriers That Are Holding
Women Back at Work

MICHELLE P. KING

SIMON &
SCHUSTER

London · New York · Sydney · Toronto · New Delhi

First published in the United States by Atria Books, an imprint of
Simon & Schuster, Inc., 2020
First published in Great Britain by Simon & Schuster UK Ltd, 2020
This edition published in Great Britain by Simon & Schuster UK Ltd, 2021

1 3 5 7 9 10 8 6 4 2

Simon & Schuster UK Ltd
1st Floor
222 Gray's Inn Road
London WC1X 8HB

www.simonandschuster.co.uk
www.simonandschuster.com.au
www.simonandschuster.co.in

Simon & Schuster Australia, Sydney
Simon & Schuster India, New Delhi

The author and publishers have made all reasonable efforts to contact
copyright-holders for permission, and apologise for any omissions or errors in
the form of credits given. Corrections may be made to future printings.

A CIP catalogue record for this book
is available from the British Library

Paperback ISBN: 978-1-4711-9306-4
eBook ISBN: 978-1-4711-9305-7

Interior design by Timothy Shaner, NightandDayDesign.biz
Printed in the UK by CPI Group (UK) Ltd, Croydon, CR0 4YY

For any woman who feels like they are not good enough, I hope you read this book and realize just how truly exceptional you are.

Contents

Foreword

As women, the message we often receive is that we need to try harder if we want equality. We need to lean in further, do better, and juggle with greater dexterity. We need to change how we look and change how we feel. This can leave us with the inaccurate perception that it is *us*, not the workplace, that needs fixing.

The truth is that the world of work wasn't designed for women. It was shaped around a predominantly male workforce that historically (and often currently) wasn't recognized as having caring or parenting responsibilities. As a result, it doesn't meet the needs of us as women, nor ironically the needs of the men that so often still dominate it. As women, we want equality, but we want equality in a system that is designed to meet the needs of all of us as we really are—whatever our race and gender.

In *We: A Manifesto for Women Everywhere*, we laid out a path for individual transformation that would enable us to come together to shape our world for the better. Individual transformation and systemic change are intimately linked. And, as Michelle King so powerfully lays out in the pages that follow, the world of work is ripe for some very profound changes.

It is not enough to pay lip service to equality. Tokenism and bolt-ons to our existing systems won't work.

The solutions we seek must look beyond a point of gender parity to one where our society, economy, and workplace are designed to meet the needs of all of us as humans—real, rounded, flawed, complicated human beings. Not ones that need to pretend to be perfect or pretend not to need, fear, desire, hurt, and care. Ones that recognize that we are not human doings but human beings and that our current me-first culture has endangered the threads that bind our communities and nations together.

Our binary system of first-past-the-post winners and losers serves none of us. Real, meaningful success isn't about accumulation and reaching the finish line first. It's about acknowledging that we are all connected and ensuring that we are all okay—wherever we are born, live, and work. It is time for a way of measuring our progress that isn't based on our economic worth but on our collective well-being and our planet's. Happiness can't be bought, sold, or manufactured. Real happiness is a by-product of right living. And, at the heart of right living is the knowledge that we are all humans of equal worth and value. Together we can, will, and must change our world to make sure it reflects that.

—Gillian Anderson and Jennifer Nadel

Introduction

It's Not a Woman Problem, It's a Work Problem

It was a hair clip and reading glasses that stood in the way of Sarah getting her promotion—only she didn't know it. Sarah was a white, forty-something senior manager who worked in the same large multinational company that I did. I was working in human resources, supporting the chief operations officer (COO) with managing and developing his team. Sarah was smart, capable, experienced, well-educated, and one of the best leaders I knew. Every year, as part of my role to facilitate the COO with his succession-planning process, I would help his leadership team decide who to promote. And every year Sarah's name came up. And every year, the suggestion for her promotion was denied. I never agreed with the final decision, but it was inspiring to see Sarah's resilience and determination, even after she had been given the news of "not this year."

The first year Sarah was passed over, she accepted the rejection and used it as an opportunity to get feedback, put in the work, and do whatever she could to become the next vice president. After all, that is what all the leadership books told her resilient and successful people do. Sarah stayed late at work, read all the popular books on women in leadership, and attended development training for women executives. Sarah applied everything she was taught, by being more assertive, speaking up more in meetings, not apologizing as much, and asking for what she wanted. Sarah even perfected her handshake.

The second year, again, her direct manager was the bearer of bad news, this time he acknowledged Sarah's efforts, but gave her the corporate script, saying something like, "Management doesn't want you to think your initiatives have gone unnoticed. Quite the contrary. Keep doing what you're doing. You just need more time in your role to round out your experience and judgment. You are just not quite ready."

Sarah was more than ready for a promotion; it wasn't her judgment or experience that was holding her back. Unbeknownst to me, "just not quite ready" was corporate speak for workplace sexism. After all, I had spent my entire life believing the cardinal rule of meritocracy. Whether in school or work, our achievements are rewarded with accolades like verbal praise, high honor role, outstanding performance appraisals, promotions, and raises. The harder we work, the more we are rewarded. Somehow, as a woman, this formula wasn't working for Sarah, but this didn't stop her from trying—yet again. Sarah found a mentor and hired an external executive coach. She doubled her efforts at work, often spending more hours in the office than at home. She took on extra projects and participated in every work-related social event. She attended women's conferences and spent hours networking internally to ensure she was on good terms with all the senior leaders. To further her expertise, Sarah enrolled in a master's program at a university, which she undertook part-time so as not to disrupt her working life. Sarah did everything she could to be perceived as a leader—she even changed the way she dressed by adopting the pantsuit.

Finally, after three years of being considered and then passed up, Sarah's performance was so outstanding she could no longer be overlooked for a spot on the leadership team. Sarah was overdue the promotion, especially as the company was supporting candidates that had nowhere near her capability.

At the annual succession-planning meeting, her manager made the obvious case, with me to support him. We thought we had it. Sarah was finally going to become a vice president, making her the only female leader in the department. That is what I had been hired to do after all—ensure the best people got promoted.

"I nominate Sarah," I said confidently in the boardroom that held about twelve senior executive leaders—all middle-aged white men. Everyone nodded but remained silent. Then my eyes fell on the COO—the final decision maker. He wasn't nodding. He was scratching his head and looking concerned. Then the others looked at him. After what seemed like forever, the head-scratcher finally spoke. "Sarah is good, but I don't know . . . she isn't quite right."

Here we go again. "What do you mean, 'not quite right'?" I asked.

"I don't know; she just doesn't fit," he answered. "She has those glasses and she wears that clip in her hair. *You* know."

I nodded. I did know. Sarah did not fit in. But it wasn't the glasses and it wasn't the clip. Nothing Sarah ever did to fix herself and prove her worth would change the fact that she didn't fit in because she wasn't the problem. If I'd have known then what I know now, I would've told Sarah, "It's not you, it's your workplace."

Fixing Something That Isn't Broken

If you are reading this book, it is likely Sarah's story sounds familiar, whether it has been your personal experience, or it happened to someone you know, or you've been in a decision-making position where you have passed on a candidate as qualified as Sarah. While I was still working in corporate human resources, I wanted to understand what women needed to do to advance at the same rate as men, because it was my job to develop and support them. I wanted to be able to support women like Sarah, not discourage them. This was a topic that hit very close to home. I too had countless qualifications, many years of experience, and high-performance ratings, yet when I became a manager, I started to notice male peers who didn't have these credentials and accolades progressing at a faster rate than I. It didn't make sense. Just like Sarah, I began to believe that I was the problem. I needed to do more or be more to succeed. When Sarah responded in defeat—"I don't know what else to do. I don't understand"—I needed to find the answer. I wanted to give Sarah practical solutions to the challenges she faced, because at the time, I didn't have any.

For years I had worked in the private sector, where I facilitated numerous leadership-development programs, workshops, networking events, and mentoring programs, all with the sole purpose of increasing the number of women in leadership positions. These initiatives were the solutions most companies adopted, because it was assumed that women were accountable for their lack of representation in leadership positions. Women were not networking in the right way, speaking up, asking for a raise, asserting themselves, accessing mentors, supporting one another, or leaning in enough.

In recent years, companies have been under tremendous pressure to advance the representation of women in leadership positions. Ever since the 1964 Civil Rights Act made discrimination illegal in organizations, companies have been working to reduce any potential discriminatory practices to manage the associated legal and financial risks. Workplaces installed formal recruitment, training, and promotion processes in the 1960s and 1970s, which then progressed to formalized diversity management programs, which included things like anti-harassment training, diversity targets, flexible work practices, and maternity leave.[1] These efforts ensure that companies comply with the law and do the bare minimum to increase the representation of minority groups by helping them fit into existing organizations.

But none of it is working. Most diversity programs are not advancing equality; workplaces do not value men and women equally. Despite existing efforts, women remain underrepresented in leadership positions. We all know the statistics, like the fact that women account for only 4.6 percent of Fortune 500 CEOs, 8.1 percent of top earners, and 16.9 percent of Fortune 500 board seats—despite the fact that women hold 52 percent of all professional-level jobs, according to the nonprofit firm Catalyst, which seeks to help companies increase women in leadership positions.[2] The situation is far worse for women of color who continue to remain underrepresented in every level of leadership in corporate America. To add to this injustice, women also continue to work longer hours[3] than men in both developed and developing countries, as they are primarily responsible for unpaid domestic duties and dependent care. All the while, women continue to earn less.

These statistics remain poor despite the increased number of diversity and inclusion programs in corporations today. Research by the Corporate Leadership Council published in 2015 found that only 43 percent of human resource executives think that current approaches to increasing gender diversity in organizations—including employee resource groups for women, mentoring, networking, unconscious bias training, coaching, increased maternity leave, and flexible work options—are effective at all.[4] Even if women make it to the top, it doesn't guarantee that anything will fundamentally change. For example, since 2009, only three women succeeded the twenty-four female CEOs of S&P 500 companies who left their positions. The rest were all replaced by men, according to 2018 data on executive departures compiled by the recruitment firm Spencer Stuart.[5]

So, I made it my mission to understand what women needed to do in order to not only advance at work but to thrive in organizations. While still working in human resources, I went back to school and pursued a doctorate specializing in gender in organizations, where I began to investigate specifically what women could do to succeed in them. As the years passed, my desire to answer this question turned into a bit of an obsession. I spent twelve years at university, to complete five degrees. At the same time, I worked for major corporations before ending up at UN Women—the United Nations entity responsible for progressing gender equality worldwide—where my job was to advance women in innovation and technology. My sole aim with all of this was to find out what women needed to do to advance at the same rate as men and ultimately lead—how women could finally fill the void that has been holding them back. It almost became my hobby. I interviewed hundreds of high-profile women and men on this topic for numerous publications—this included thought leaders, celebrities, academics, and world leaders. I even started a podcast called *The Fix* to share these stories. I conducted research studies on organizations for free just to get a better understanding of the challenges women face. I spoke at numerous conferences and volunteered at countless women's initiatives. I read every book and academic journal article I could find on the topic. After all this effort, I came to realize that I wasn't alone—we are all a bit obsessed with trying to fix women.

There are countless books and programs designed to help women fix themselves to get ahead. Maybe you've read some of these books or tried some of these programs. But why weren't they shifting the numbers? These programs and trainings tell women they need to upskill themselves, join women's groups, find a mentor, attend conferences, learn to negotiate, speak up, ask for a pay rise, and own their power. Women undertake all of this effort to ensure no one is ever in any doubt as to why they have a seat at the table. They've obviously done the work to earn it. Not only do women need to work harder than their male counterparts to demonstrate their capability in order to advance, but they must continuously expend insurmountable physical and mental energy to prove they are simply worthy of doing the job.

So, what's the problem? During the first two years of starting my PhD, I became increasingly frustrated. I kept finding studies that didn't align with what I was looking for, but instead highlighted the many ways that workplaces were set up for women to fail. Research study after research study pointed to women's different experiences of working life, resulting from workplace cultures that are unsupportive of women and include things like sexist jokes, blatant discrimination, male favoritism, and a lack of opportunities to advance. And that was only the beginning. It never occurred to me that women might have everything they need to succeed. Like most people, I believed women were the problem—after all, that's the story I'd been told. My research helped me realize that the idea that women need to be fixed is built on the assumption that women are not as capable as men. To succeed, women need to manage their differences by fixing themselves to fit into organizations never designed for them in the first place. This is simply accepted as fact, with absolutely no grounds or statistical evidence to support this sexist belief.

For example, there is a commonly held belief that women are not paid the same as men because they can't negotiate and simply don't ask for a pay rise as frequently as their male colleagues. But research published in the *Harvard Business Review* in 2018 finds that women ask for a pay raise just as often as men, but they are less likely to be given one.[6] Like many women, however, I wasn't aware of this. I assumed the dominant "fix yourself" narrative was correct. If we could just find the key skill or trait that women were lacking, which was holding them back, we could correct the problem. So, I forged ahead to find the solution for women, who, like me, still didn't feel quite good enough. But I certainly wasn't the first person to try.

What surprised me the most was discovering that women already have everything they need to succeed at work, and then some. Women are outstanding leaders, they are communal, democratic, innovative, collaborative, and supportive. I should have been happy to discover countless studies highlighting all the ways that women are exceptional workers but instead I felt deflated. All those years I had spent writing, speaking, researching, and delivering initiatives to "help women" were wasted efforts. I was fixing something that wasn't broken. Women are skilled, talented, and educated enough, just as they are. So, why have so many women like me been encouraged to believe anything different?

Now, with nearly two decades of experience working in human resources in the private sector, two undergraduate degrees, an MBA, a master's in industrial psychology, and a PhD on the topic of gender inequality at work, I have uncovered the true root cause of—and the antidote to—workplace inequality. My solution is not just for women; men have a tremendous amount to gain from more equal workplaces. The answer has nothing to do with fixing people, improving them, developing them, or helping them acquire skills. The truth I've uncovered saves organizations from expensive, time-and-energy sucking, futile attempts at equality that ironically tend to backfire. In fact, all the books and philosophies on leaning in, swimming with sharks, breaking glass ceilings, and getting people to like you will never solve the problem of workplace inequality.

Why? Because women are not the problem. When it comes to gender inequality, we have been looking at women, all the while ignoring the many ways workplaces are broken. If the current solutions we have in place worked, we wouldn't have the gender inequality problem that exists in workplaces today. It's worth repeating: We are trying to fix something that isn't broken. We needed to look at the workplace itself. So I did.

It took me three years of reviewing more than three thousand journal articles—as part of a PhD literature review—to persuade even myself that the current initiatives designed to advance women had a marginal impact at best. Organizations were never created with women in mind. So, from the beginning, women have had to change to fit into the established world of work.

The years we have wasted *fixing women* in the name of gender equality is simply time spent ignoring the inherent design flaws in most corporations. Instead, we need to look at the blueprints of our workplaces, to understand how the policies, processes, structures, employee behaviors, leaders, and culture all enable a very small number of people to succeed.

Like me, a lot of women buy into the idea that they need to be fixed, and this belief is reinforced every time women walk into their offices. Workplaces devalue women and their contributions, which reinforces the message that they are simply not good enough. For example, the Pew Research Center's findings from a 2018 study reveal that only 38 percent of women who work in male-dominated environments feel they are treated fairly when it comes to pay and promotions.[7] Also, 25 percent of women feel they have to constantly prove themselves at work just to be respected by their coworkers. Workplaces simply don't work for women and men in the same way.

My research has revealed that from the moment women start their careers up until their last working day they will have to navigate what I call "invisible barriers," which are challenges inherent in workplaces that prevent women from thriving at work. These are the design flaws in the workplace blueprint. We don't see them because we've been trained to believe that fixing ourselves is easier than fixing a corporation. That's why identifying the invisible barriers women face, which are built into the structure of the modern-day workplace, will be a game changer.

By becoming aware of these barriers and understanding how they work we will begin to see all the ways workplaces enable a limited number of people to succeed, while also preventing the majority of women from advancing. This happens throughout a woman's career: when she first enters the workforce, when she balances the dual roles of manager and caregiver (to children or elderly relatives), or when she's navigating a high-level leadership position in a man-made world of work. I didn't see these barriers until I really examined the narrative highlighting the so-called shortcomings of women, but calling them out one by one is the groundbreaking and critical first step to overcoming them and finally removing them once and for all. Whether you're a woman, man, or corporate leader who wants to bring about change in your organization, *The Fix* will help you focus on the true cause of gender inequality—the system itself.

We need to call time-out on the women-fixing epidemic. It is sexist, unfair, and damaging. *Fix-the-women* approaches are inherently misogynistic because by telling women they need to *do more* or *be more* than men to succeed, we are in fact telling them that they are not good enough to start with. This sexist message slowly chips away at women's confidence, which makes fix-the-women solutions even more compelling. But—as you'll see throughout the pages of this book—solutions aimed at fixing women are built on a lie. Women are not broken. Women are exceptional. Women are innovative. Women are transformative. Women make for great team players. Women are remarkable leaders. The more we try to fix women, the less effort we all dedicate to the real issue of gender inequality in workplaces. That's why sharing this message is so incredibly important.

I draw on my personal research over the last five years to shine a spotlight on the invisible barriers and share the many varied and nuanced experiences women have throughout their careers. This includes seventy-two interviews with men and women from two major corporations—one from the financial services sector and the other from the energy and resource sector—as well as two surveys with more than a thousand participants. I have also included interviews with world leaders, academics, CEOs, and thought leaders, as well as a full review of the latest research, case studies, and leading practices related to advancing women in workplaces.

This book is divided into three parts. Part I shares how we got here. It outlines why workplaces were rigged from the start and how they don't work for everyone in the same way. Hint: they were never designed with "difference" in mind. This section dispels common myths about meritocracy, patriarchy, feminism, gender bias, and the idea of the corporate ladder. It also reveals the truth about gender inequality—we are in denial that it exists. This encourages us to accept the inequality women experience at work as the way things are and then hold women accountable for fixing it. We are all in denial of the challenges women face at work. Awareness is the key. Only by becoming aware of the real problem we need to fix can we ever hope to solve inequality.

Part II will guide you through the three career phases women experience throughout their working life—from the early idealistic years of entering the workforce, to the middle years when women have to endure the constant balancing act of managing work and home life, to the veteran years when women want to meaningfully contribute and make a difference but find their leadership is constantly undermined in male-dominated environments. I will introduce the seventeen most common barriers women are likely to encounter throughout these three phases, which limit women's advancement and fulfillment. Part II is your road map. A way for every woman to understand their work environment and ultimately navigate it. Beyond exposing the seventeen hidden barriers, this part also reveals the many ways you have overcome these challenges without even realizing it, which really makes you remarkable.

Part III is your invitation to take action and fight to remove the barriers women face at work. We all have a role to play in this, because workplaces don't really work for any of us. This section opens up an important dialogue about how hidden barriers within our organizations also create challenges for men, and what employees—particularly leaders—can do to fix workplaces so they work for everyone.

This is something that we need to do together. Both women and men stand to benefit from workplaces that value difference and give employees the opportunity to be themselves. But ultimately, organizations need this even more than employees do. To thrive in the future, organizations need employees to innovate, problem solve, create, and share their unique ideas. We need environments that encourage employees to use all their talents, to share their experiences, and to work in cultures in which they not only *feel* free to contribute but *actually* are free to do just that. The thing that makes great minds so great is that they don't all think alike. If workplaces want employees to share their unique perspectives, expertise, and talents, then they need to not only value these differences, but also create the right environment, culture, and infrastructure that enables them to thrive.

If you don't identify with feminism or are disenfranchised with the white feminist rhetoric because it erases the challenges women of color face, this book is for you. If you are a woman starting out in your career who has been told to fix yourself to advance, I wrote this book with you in mind. If you are a working mother or part of the "sandwich generation" struggling to reconcile your dual identities as caregiver and employee, then I implore you to read this book. If you're a woman leader fighting for a spot on the executive management team who needs to decide just how much of yourself you are willing to sacrifice to lead ... before you decide, please read this book. And if you're a man who feels unsure of your place in the gender-equality movement or who struggles with feeling good enough at work, please continue to turn the pages.

This book is an introduction to the numerous invisible barriers all women face throughout their careers because organizations are not designed for difference. And that's a true problem, because our differences are not barriers to be overcome, they are what make us remarkable. We deserve the freedom to be ourselves at work and to be appreciated for this. This is equality. It's also freedom. Gender inequality at work is a problem for all of us. This means that your fight is my fight. Equality is not about women, and it is not about men; it is about making workplaces work for everyone.

Part I
AWARENESS

We can't tackle inequality if we are in denial it even exists.

1.

Who Broke the Workplace?
A Brief History

Growing up, I was severely nearsighted, but no one knew it. I didn't even know it because when vision deteriorates it happens slowly and over many years. For me, this continued until I was twelve, at which point my vision was so poor that I couldn't see my own reflection in the mirror. I literally couldn't see myself. It probably comes as no surprise that because I couldn't see, I struggled in school. I couldn't spell or do math. I was disruptive in class and talked too much. I also had braces, freckles, pale skin, and one of those 1970s bowl haircuts, which didn't help. Over time, I began to feel as though I was the student teachers didn't want in their class—I also began to believe that I wasn't good enough.

Then one day my favorite teacher, Ms. Anderson, realized the problem was that I couldn't see, so I was talking a lot in class to try and understand what was being written on the board. I had managed to get by for so long relying on memory alone. The day I finally got glasses, I didn't care that my classmates teased me for wearing them, because now I could see. The downside was now I could see that '70s bowl haircut, which came as

17

a bit of a shock. But I will never forget those first few days. I just stared at all the details around me. The leaves on the trees. The handwriting on the board. I could see everything. I could even see myself.

This experience is a perfect metaphor for gender inequality at work. We don't see things for what they are, which makes it impossible to truly understand why there are so few women in leadership positions. We have been looking at women for so long because we believed that they are the problem that we have not seen all the ways workplaces do not value or serve them. This has made us blind to the inequality both women and men experience in workplaces today.

It has also made us blind to how capable women are. In 2003, researchers Alice Eagly from Northwestern University and Linda Carli from Wellesley College conducted a review of more than 162 studies on leadership and found that women's leadership style more closely aligns with contemporary views of good leadership, as they are collaborative, democratic, and communicative.[1] The name for this leadership style is transformational, and it is associated with greater organizational success compared to traditional command-and-control leadership styles. When it comes to managing employees, women tend to be empathetic, supportive, and good at building relationships—all of which are important skills for leading.[2] As managers, on average, women tend to foster inclusion, collaborative problem solving, and team cohesiveness. Ultimately, women lead in a way that puts the team's and organization's interests ahead of their own, which is good for business.

It is not just an issue of leadership or interpersonal stylistic differences. Often women are more qualified. As of 2016, women held more advanced degrees than men. The number of young women enrolled in tertiary education currently surpasses that of young men globally.[3] We raise young women to believe that if they work hard they can do anything, and clearly based on this research they have the capabilities to do just that. So, the question then remains: What's holding women back?

Gender inequality exists because organizations are set up to enable one type of worker to succeed, and this tends to be a white, middle-class, heterosexual, able-bodied male. Importantly though, this male prototype is also known for making work the number-one priority and engaging in behaviors that are dominant, assertive, aggressive, competitive, and even exclusionary, to get ahead. The more closely employees align to this ideal, the more likely they are to succeed, which is why workplaces work better for some men. But how did this happen? Who broke the workplace, making it systematically challenging for women?

To answer these questions and give context to our unequal and outdated organizational cultures, we need to understand where this all started. Once we understand how we got here, it becomes easier to see that workplaces are not only "gendered"—that is, dominated and favoring one gender and set of behaviors over the other—but how and why workplaces became gendered in the first place. It's like putting on a pair of glasses that will finally reveal the missing details. We need 20/20 vision to truly see why typical corporate diversity programs fall short, and finally fix the workplace once and for all—instead of placing the onus on women to fix themselves.

How Patriarchy Handcuffs Men and Women

Remember Sarah from this book's introduction? She was the incredibly competent, intelligent, creative leader I incessantly tried to have promoted to manager status. She was continually passed over by the senior executive team, led by the COO. All the managers in the room agreed with the arguments put forward to promote her. After three years of self-improvement, working longer and harder hours, and evolving her leadership capabilities with compelling results, Sarah had earned a seat at the leadership table. Yet even with a large consensus, Sarah needed the COO's endorsement—he was the unofficial patriarch of the company. He was expected to have the last word—no matter how ludicrous or unfounded—and every leader in the room would accept his decision without argument or pushback.

Patriarchy—the belief that women are less valuable than men—is everywhere, and this is the foundational belief underpinning most of our workplaces today. It isn't something most of us intentionally do or are even aware of. It is, however, ingrained; it is insidious, and until we can peel back the layers of its traditional underpinnings, we won't fully understand how gender inequality works or what we need to do to solve it.

Where did the patriarchal belief originate? In his book *Sapiens*, author Yuval Noah Harari outlines a brief history of human life. He describes how through collective myths and stories, humans learned to cooperate with one another and advance. Shared beliefs enabled humankind to collaborate because they were all working with the same value system. While there isn't an exact date for when patriarchy took hold, it is clear that at least since the Agricultural Revolution (which occurred at different times in different regions of the world) most societies have held the pervasive belief that men and masculinity are more valuable and important than women and femininity.[4]

When humans moved away from their hunter-gatherer lifestyles and began adopting agriculture as an additional way to obtain food, this created a hierarchical division of labor. Women took care of the children and the home and men worked in the fields to farm and produce food. You might be thinking that men and women assumed these different roles because of biological sex differences—men had the strength to work the fields and women were natural nurturers on the home front. But research actually reveals that boys and girls are socialized to perform gender roles linked to their sex.[5] Gender is an integral part of our identities. As young girls and boys spend more time with their same-sex peers, they learn what behaviors are acceptable and expected. This determines not only how we interact but also the interests we pursue. For example, boys might be encouraged not to play with dolls or girls might be encouraged not to be superheroes. Adhering to these gender-appropriate behaviors is how children come to understand what it means to be a girl or a boy—and eventually women and men. It is important to note this creates tremendous challenges for any person who does not identify with the binary gender roles. Gender roles are set early in life and determine the expectations we hold for women and men. For example, even today women are assumed to be involved in housework and childcare. Men are encouraged to provide for their families.

These gender roles took hold as agricultural work became monetized and valued. Society placed a premium on men because the work they did was given a monetary value. In contrast, managing home life was never monetized and so "women's work" wasn't exactly prized. Patriarchy emerged from a division of labor and the value we associate with it. Men were able to undertake tasks associated with status and power, which further reinforced their higher social standing. Not only were men given the opportunity to do work that was deemed valuable, but without childcare and domestic responsibilities, they were free to establish themselves as leaders in nearly every aspect of society.

Over time, men and traditional masculinity became synonymous with power and leadership. Workplaces and systems were built by men to reinforce men's power. At best, these work environments are blind to the needs of women, and at worst, they function to uphold the belief that men are supreme and women are simply not as valuable. This is patriarchy. It is a system that works to maintain men's privilege, which leads to power, and reinforces the message that women are not as worthy as men.

The patriarchy may be taken for granted as the way things are, but not all societies function in this way; gender-egalitarian societies have existed before. While men and women in these societies differ in terms of their influence and power, there is no gender hierarchy. For example, in the book *Fruit of the Motherland,* Maria Lepowsky shares how the Vanatinai, a society in New Guinea, value men and women equally when it comes to making decisions, marriage, childcare, and sexual freedom.[6]

In today's modern world, when women are clearly as capable of doing the same work as men, it's time to leave the patriarchy where it belongs: in the past. Given that cooperation has been the key to survival for most of human history, it seems like an egalitarian society—one in which men and women are equally valued and can contribute to work in a meaningful way—might be in everyone's best interests.

Patriarchy persists in most modern-day societies because men have maintained their dominance at work through established systems of inequality made up of policies, programs, practices, and personal beliefs. This keeps the status quo intact. Men are better able to preserve their political and economic power because organizations were designed to support them to advance, lead, and maintain power. This creates a cycle of male privilege, which is evident in the expectations we hold for how women and men should behave, known as "gender stereotyping." In society, it is generally expected that men will conform to the masculine ideal of being a provider—someone who is powerful, strong, assertive, competitive, and dominant. Women need to adopt the feminine ideal of being a good homemaker—someone who is beautiful, submissive, meek, caring, and self-sacrificing. Evidence of gender stereotyping is everywhere, and it affects the design of the modern-day workplace.

I know it's hard to believe with all of the supposed advances we've made in diversity and inclusion, but gender stereotyping is alive and well. In 2018, the Pew Research Center surveyed more than forty-five hundred Americans to understand what traits society values for men and women. The findings reveal that respondents are much more likely to use the word *powerful* in a positive way to describe men. The word *provider* is exclusively used to refer to men and traits such as *strength, leadership,* and *ambition* are valued more highly for men than for women. For women, respondents valued qualities that included *beauty, compassion, kindness,* and *responsibility*.[7] The standards we hold for the ideal man and woman form our expectations for how people should behave. We want men and women to align their behavior to meet this standard at home and at work.

This is a lot to live up to—for both men and women. And it also comes at a cost. Women who are not compassionate are likely to be perceived negatively because they are violating the shared expectations and beliefs society holds for women. If women take on self-promoting "masculine" behaviors—like telling people what they are good at, asking for a promotion, owning their ambition, and highlighting their achievements at work—they tend to be viewed as less likable, less socially attractive, and subsequently less hirable than men who self-promote in this same way.[8]

It's not just women who are penalized for going against gender expectations. If men behave in a way that is seen as "feminine"—by showing their emotions, demonstrating compassion to colleagues, or being modest about their achievements—they are likely to be seen as less leader-like, because this isn't the type of behavior we associate with masculinity and power.[9]

Gender stereotypes are more than just biases, they are handcuffs. They limit how men and women can behave. When it comes to gender stereotypes in workplaces today, we all face the same challenge: fit in or forget it.

Meet Don Draper: The Ideal Standard for Men and Women at Work

During my time in HR, I used to manage the performance-appraisal process for a large multinational company, which was very similar to the promotion process undertaken for Sarah. Every year I would meet with the senior leadership team—all of whom were white males—and we would debate which employees had performed the best. Those that did well would get a high-performance rating and hefty bonus. The process was often painful and lacked substance. Leaders would rely on weak arguments or clichés to make their case, saying things like "He did a good job and he is a nice guy to work with," or "They have shown leadership potential this year," or "People really like him." Unqualified statements like these would be thrown out there in the hope something sticks. If left unquestioned, these statements would result in the low-performing employees getting high performance scores.

During one particularly long meeting, I couldn't take the lame justifications any longer. I raised my hand to speak, and said, "I think it would really help if we could maybe agree on what 'good' looks like. I know we have promotion criteria but what is the real standard for success. Who in this organization is the kind of leader that people should aim to be like?" One name was thrown out that everyone agreed with. Let's call him Mike Smith. Mike was smart, extremely hardworking, politically skilled, decisive, dedicated, ambitious, outspoken, and married with two children. It didn't hurt that Mike was tall, good-looking, and played football. I didn't know Mike, so as people were describing him, one image kept popping into my mind: Don Draper, the successful ad man from the hit TV show *Mad Men,* which reveals the experiences of men and women working in the American advertising industry in the 1960s. This was the moment I realized the standard for success in workplaces today is still a 1960s man. And this stands to hurt men as much as it does women.

So, who is this ideal worker, this Don Draper? He is a shared mental image of what success looks like at work. And he's stereotypically masculine. Research published in 2014 by the global management consulting firm Bain & Company found that most organizations surveyed acknowledge a deeply ingrained worker prototype, and 60 percent of respondents described this ideal as someone who is willing to maintain a high profile, work long hours, and put the organization's needs ahead of family requirements.[10] In short, Don Draper. I was so fascinated by this finding I decided to test it by surveying a total of 735 men and women in a professional-services firm to find out what they thought the ideal worker standard was in their organization. Overwhelmingly, 70 percent of all the respondents stated that this was someone who is typically white, male, and heterosexual, but importantly, who is willing to

✔ commit most of their time to the organization
✔ promote their own achievements
✔ take action and tell others what to do

✔ work hard and make work the number one priority
✔ be extroverted and dominant in social situations
✔ assert themselves, speak up, and ask for what they want
✔ be decisive, even if this means going it alone.

It's no surprise that women have a hard time living up to this standard, given that they have to conform to gender roles and continue to manage most of the domestic and childcare responsibilities. In fact, women do up to three times as much unpaid care work as men, which works out to about fifty minutes more a day.[11] Household chores are still considered "women's work," and this is evident in Bain's research, which found that 58 percent of women and 47 percent of men believe managing both work and family commitments slows or disrupts women's careers.[12]

The ideal worker standard we have today is built on the unconscious belief that men are best suited to the world of work. Patriarchy is alive and well in workplaces today, and the Don Draper success prototype is evidence of this. To live up to the image, we must engage in stereotypically masculine behaviors. This means being tough, assertive, aggressive, dominant, unemotional, and commanding. It also means being free from dependent-care responsibilities and being able to commit all your time, energy, and focus to your workplace. The ideal leader is willing to set the direction and ensure employees follow. Work environments—which are made up of individual behaviors, norms, cultures, systems, policies, processes, and structures—function to enable this ideal worker to succeed.

The Don Draper success prototype hinders minorities and women from advancing in organizations because they can never fully fit this ideal. In fact, women are penalized for even trying to act like Don, even though most of the career advice they get tells them to do just that. Women leaders are often told that the key to succeeding at work is to be more confident—like men—because, in part, confidence is associated with influential leaders. But displaying confidence results in different outcomes for men and women. A study found that when men display self-confidence they are perceived to be higher performers, more leader-like, and more influential.[13] But women need to conform to the feminine gender stereotype. If they display self-confidence they must also be nurturing and supportive of colleagues, in order to gain the same influence as their co-workers. Women have a very narrow range of acceptable behaviors they can engage in at work to advance. If women don't adhere to these expectations, they don't benefit from self-confidence in the same way as men.

This example demonstrates the extra challenges women face in the corporate world and the pitfalls with typical career advice. Acting like men is not the answer. Worse, acting like men in order to lead only reinforces gender stereotypes, the idea that masculinity is the only standard for what effective leadership looks like. This, in turn, reinforces the idea in society that men are more valuable.

The Success Prototype Costs All of Us

"What should I tell my boss?" my husband asked me one recent morning, as he was getting ready to take Rex, our son, to the doctor. I had a meeting that morning, so I was not able to do it. "I don't understand. What do you mean?" I asked as I was making my way out the front door. I looked up to see the flash of panic rush across his face. "Well, I can't tell him that I'm taking Rex to the doctor, I need a real reason for being late. What should I say?"

I put my bag down and took a deep breath. Now I was going to be late, but luckily my employer, UN Women, would understand the importance of this conversation. I told him he had no choice but to tell his boss and colleagues the truth—even if it costs him. My husband didn't want to tell his boss the real reason why he was late because he was worried his boss might question his dedication to work, or his career. He too was a victim of gender stereotyping, and he worried about not living up to the Don Draper image if his boss knew he missed work to take care of his child. Living up to success prototypes is one thing; hiding your life from your colleagues is quite another.

Yet there seems to be an unwritten code in offices that you're supposed to check your personal life at the door. But why? Once again, to understand where this idea—that we need to hide our identities at work—came from, we need to look at the history of organizations.

In 1913, Ford Motor Company became one of the first organizations to adopt an assembly-line process for the mass production of cars.[14] Instead of having one individual perform all of the tasks to build a car, the assembly line assigned different tasks to different workers. The assembly line was all about efficiency—getting more done in less time. It was rooted in one of the first management theories, known as Taylorism, developed in 1911 by Fredrick Winslow Taylor, whose primary goal was to make workplaces more effective.[15]

To achieve this, Taylor recommended workplaces use hierarchical structures to separate people into employees and managers and then organize people using standard rules and impersonal relationships between managers and workers. Routines become standard for all jobs. Maximum efficiency, he theorized, can only be achieved by turning people into the ideal worker. When Henry Ford implemented the assembly line in 1913, he didn't need people, he needed workers who functioned like machines. And managers who would keep everything moving to a constant rhythm. In this workplace, success is defined as the ability to maintain the status quo. People stand in one spot repeating the same task again and again, perfecting one move for eight hours a day. By working to a constant routine, employees were slowly stripped of their identity, creativity, and thought. Wake up, clock in, clock out, go home, go to sleep. Repeat. The person becomes the worker, whose value is determined by how much they produce.

For a corporation, this is the ideal: workers who function like machines and produce. However, creating the ideal worker is not as easy as it sounds. Workplaces need employees to separate their work life from their home life to live up to the ideal standard. As Ford found out, this is a big ask. Employees are not willing to lose their humanity without a fight. In the first year of introducing the assembly line, the annual turnover rate for Ford Motor Company was 400 percent.[16] But rather than improve working conditions to support employee's needs, Ford implemented the ultimate "fix the worker" solution. He tried to manage people's home lives to make them better workers.

In 1914, Ford Motor Company introduced the five-dollar day, where employees who worked an eight-hour day and were deemed worthy would get a share in the company profits that amounted to about five dollars a day.[17] The catch was the company determined who was "worthy." To evaluate their employees' worth, they created a Sociological Department. Going door to door, this department would check if men were sober and clean, and if women had dependents and were really deserving of the profit sharing.

It's ironic that Ford's attempts to increase productivity by stripping people of their identities led him to create an organization that closely managed and evaluated his employees' lives. The fact is, you cannot separate work life from home life, no matter how hard you try. Individuals bring their biases, racism, privilege, class, misogyny, capabilities, personalities, and difficulties from their home life into the office. When you hire a worker to do a job, what you are getting is the whole person—like a man who has to take his sick child to the doctor once in a while.

So, while the Don Draper prototype may create a common standard of performance and compliance, it's a hugely problematic one. For one, it only benefits corporations, not employees. Gender stereotypes ensure that only men can live up to this ideal standard if they have someone at home willing to manage all the domestic and childcare activities. Don Draper isn't encumbered, expected, or given the opportunity to manage caretaking responsibilities.

You don't have to look hard to find this ideal standard in workplaces today. You can even see Ford's model in the design and management of fast-food outlets, factories, schools, offices, and hospitals today. We expect leaders to value productivity over people, to put in long workdays, and to separate their home life from work. This standard makes it much easier for corporations to manage their employees. There is one version of success, one career path, and one playing field. Everyone is treated the same, because, the belief is, we are all the same.

The trouble is, we aren't all the same. Yet this meritocracy myth—the idea that the harder you work, the more you will succeed—is used to motivate employees, who are promised equal rewards and advancement in exchange for living up to the ideal standard.

Meritocracy Is a Myth

If everyone looked, thought, and acted like Don Draper, then the idea of meritocracy might actually make more sense. The harder you worked, the more you would succeed. You wouldn't be passed up for a promotion year after year just because you looked or acted differently from other senior leaders.

But each of us is different or unique in some way. The illusion of meritocracy is harmful to both men and women. When we buy into the idea that everyone is the same, we assume everyone experiences work in the same way. We ignore our differences. We become blind to our individual identities related to gender, age, ethnicity, marital status, race, religion, mental and physical ability, and sexual orientation, to name a few. Organizations promote one type of worker, which means the more ways you differ from Don Draper, the more challenges you are likely to encounter trying to advance at work. The one-size-fits-all standard for career success is hugely detrimental, particularly for women.

When we think about career advancement, we often have one idea of what this looks like—a ladder. This tends to be how men view careers because for men achievement is intrinsically linked to where they sit on the organization's hierarchy. But women have a much broader definition of success, as shown in research undertaken in 1999 by Jane Sturges from the Department of Organizational Psychology, Birkbeck College, University of London.[18] Women want their careers to be intrinsically rewarding. Specifically, they want an opportunity to engage in meaningful work, manage competing priorities, and develop professional expertise. This study found that women won't sacrifice a job they enjoy simply to advance up the chain of command. Women care about hierarchy if it helps them engage in more interesting work or increases their influence.

Women define careers differently because women are different. Achieving at work is not enough; women want to feel fulfilled in all aspects of their lives. Interestingly, in Sturges's study, men mentioned wanting all these things as well (and more, like better work-life balance), but they felt climbing the corporate ladder *should* still be their number-one priority. This is what often results in men hiding their true identities, feeling pressure to fit the success prototype, suppressing the challenges they experience at work and at home, and keeping a lot of these difficulties to themselves.

Current approaches to career development, which include treating workplaces like meritocracies or climbing the corporate "ladder," are built for the ideal worker, just like the offices we work in. Ironically, women enable this. Men can only advance in a system that requires the separation of work life and home life, which means women must be willing to manage domestic and childcare responsibilities. Women only stand to lose in this system when, for instance, they must forgo work to take their child to the doctor so their husband doesn't have to.

Being Peggy Olson in a World Designed for Don Draper

While completing my master's in psychology, one of my part-time jobs was to conduct personality tests for a recruitment firm. Every year in New Zealand a large law firm would run a graduate recruitment program. My job was to administer and interpret the personality assessments. This firm used these tools to determine how closely individuals matched the personality they felt would best fit within the firm. I was asked to find lawyers that were slightly introverted but very confident, ambitious, self-focused, unemotional, and with a strong attention to detail. This was considered the ideal standard for lawyers, because this reflected the traits the existing leaders had. Those that didn't match this standard rarely stood a chance. This law firm did the same thing when it came to selecting partners. Leaders who closely matched these traits were more likely to be promoted. Ironically, for legal reasons, it was never explicitly stated that this was a job requirement, but we all knew it.

Here I was, implementing a standard I could never live up to. I was nothing like the personality I had to recruit. I could never make it in this workplace, even if I tried. Imagine the stress and mental energy you would experience trying to fit in every day and become someone else in meetings or daily interactions. Your qualifications and achievements would never be enough because underneath it all there would always be that feeling that somehow you were an imposter. Eventually, you would realize it is impossible to work this way. You'd be forced to quit. And this happened. People who didn't fit in, quit. After all, that's what the firm wanted—nothing but like-minded individuals who do well because they meet the collective standard for success.

Twenty years later, I have come to accept that the joke is on me. My experience of the law firm really describes my experience of organizational life, except the dominant personality standard is Don Draper. The success prototype affects how leaders, teams, and organizations function. We hold gendered expectations for how women and men are meant to behave at work based on this prototype. When leaders behave in a way that matches our expectations, they are perceived to be effective. Therefore, leaders who closely match the success prototype are considered better leaders.

Mad Men is as much a story about Peggy Olson, a secretary who became a copy writer under Don's management, as it is about Don Draper. Peggy had to learn how to succeed in a male world, navigating unwanted male attention, isolation, discrimination, and trying to live up to the male-success protoype. The challenge for women like Peggy is that the success prototype creates standards for leadership behavior that do not match gendered expectations for how women should behave. Dr. Virginia E. Schein, professor emerita of management and psychology at Gettysburg College, has researched this topic extensively since the 1970s and uncovered just how ingrained this expectation is. Schein found that both men and women middle managers believe that men are more likely than women to possess the characteristics associated with managerial success, like being objective, assertive, and forceful. She called this the *Think Manager–Think Male* phenomenon.[19] Schein went on to replicate this research globally in 2001, showing how little has changed when it comes to this gender bias despite thirty years of potential progress.[20] Women are simply not recognized as leaders because their style of leadership does not align with the masculine prototype.[21] Training women to adopt masculine leadership behaviors is unlikely to help: women must conform to their gender stereotypes. Workplaces place a premium on men. Simply by looking, sounding, and acting like Don, you will be viewed as more leader-like.

Take a moment to consider all the ways people could differ from the success prototype. Sure, Don Draper makes it harder for white women like Peggy to advance, but what about all the other areas of difference? What about race, ethnicity, sexual orientation, physical or mental ability, age, physical appearance, or religion? In 2018, the *Harvard Business Review* published findings from a study titled "Interviews with 59 Black Female Executives Explore Intersectional Invisibility and Strategies to Overcome It."[22] The study found that black women executives in the United States often feel overlooked, disregarded, or forgotten. They felt invisible. Because of their race and gender differences, women of color are less likely to fit the leadership prototype, making them more likely to be perceived negatively when they try to live up to the prototype. Worse, when black women make mistakes in organizations, they are more harshly penalized, and the mistake is unfairly used to highlight how much they do not fit the leadership prototype.[23] The less you conform to the success prototype, the harder it is to advance.

If we're going to design workplaces that support everyone to succeed, we need to start by recognizing the privilege that the success prototype affords certain individuals. When we evaluate someone's performance, promotability, or potential at work, we are really evaluating them against the prototype. Workplaces are hardwired to support Don's success. The building blocks of most organizations—the systems, policies, processes, structure, leadership, and culture—were designed to reinforce and support this prototype. One of the reasons organizations look the same is because they too are all prototypes, and this creates a range of barriers for anyone other than Don.

We generally take the social and structural aspects of work for granted by assuming that it is too difficult to change things. But when we accept the status quo, we unknowingly buy into the core beliefs that keep it intact. Take, for example, the idea that employees need to be in a physical office to work. The logic behind this is that time spent in an office equates with productivity. To be a good employee, you need to put in the hours, which means you need to physically be in the office. The idea of working in an office is widely accepted as the best (or only) way to structure work. But think about how different offices might be if they had been designed to support the needs and interests of all employees outside of work. Parental leave wouldn't be up for discussion, nor would it be considered a benefit. In fact, dependent-care leave, childcare, breastfeeding accommodations, return to work programs, paternity leave, and flexible and remote work infrastructure would all be the bare minimum. Yet these are all classified as benefits, because they were added into organizations as an afterthought—a lot like women were.

If our workplaces were truly supportive of women (in the way that they claim to be), they would focus on what mothers—and fathers—need in order to succeed. They would design career-development paths that support both maternity and paternity leave arrangements. They would understand the value of parenthood, and how it can help both women and men in developing new skills. They would recognize the value that mothers, and fathers, add to their corporations, and double down their retention efforts. But our jobs weren't designed with women—or difference—in mind.

Think about it: If you could create your ideal work environment, what would it look like? Ask the women you work with the same question. Chances are you will get some pretty "out there" ideas. I know, because I ask this question all the time. I have received responses like "Well, it would be great to hold meetings outside while I walk my baby in the stroller," or "It would be great to be able to breastfeed in meetings," or "I want a senior job that is designed in relation to outputs. That way I don't have to be in the office. If I deliver, I will get rewarded."

The "ideal worker" image of the man in a suit in the office from at least nine to five is so embedded in our minds that it's hard to deviate from. That's why adding a flexible work policy to improve work-life balance (something that's generally seen as a "women's issue"), often does very little to change an underlying nine-to-five culture. How many senior leaders within your organization job share or work on a part-time or flexible work schedule? How much do you buy into the nine-to-five idea? Do you think you could lead a major company or department in your organization remotely, or on a compressed or reduced work schedule? For most people, the answer is no, because the standard for a good worker is someone who spends a solid eight hours—or more—in the office each day.

Imagine how much working mothers and fathers could achieve if organizations were structured to support their needs instead of forcing employees to fit the one-size-fits-all standard of work. A large multinational organization I worked for took active steps to do just this. Mothers and fathers were given significant parental leave, between six and twelve months. Before mothers went on leave, they developed an entire plan to accommodate the transition out and back into the organization, which included things like reduced work schedules and an ongoing development plan. Parents were also afforded paid time off to go to doctors' appointments or care for children as well as paid days for mothers to visit the office and keep in touch during leave. Employees were assigned a coach to support them through the transition and to manage their dual roles. In addition, the workplace had childcare facilities, changing stations, and breastfeeding rooms.

These flexible workplace practices and job-sharing options were available to all employees, and mothers were valued for their contributions instead of overlooked for their differences. They were afforded opportunities to lead and take on stretch assignments with reduced, compressed, and remote work schedules. What made all these programs feasible was the way leaders supported them. Employees were encouraged to share the challenges they faced, and leaders worked with them to identify solutions. Individual needs were accommodated. There was no one way to work or one prototypical way to succeed in this organization.

The impact of this program was astounding. Not only was it great for recruitment, but the annual employee survey found that employee satisfaction was consistently high. Employees want to work for organizations that value them.

Birds of a Feather

It is not just the structural elements of an organization that are hardwired to enable the masculine ideal to succeed, the social aspects of work also present challenges for women. Jeffrey Pfeffer, the author of *Power* and a well-known expert on influence and authority in organizations, argues that the more powerful your job is, the more likely people are going to want it, which is why one of the most important questions a leader can ask themselves is "Who can I trust?"[24] Research shows that we all naturally favor and trust people who are like us. The extent to which you share the same gender, age, race, sexual orientation, interests, values, and beliefs really determines how much you will like someone—this is known as the "affinity bias." For example, candidates in a recruitment process who look like or share the same outside work interests as the hiring manager can use this similarity to build rapport and enhance their likability.

This means that employees who are most like their leaders will have an unfair advantage, as they can establish trust and relationships with powerful people more easily. Male leaders tend to hire, groom, accommodate, and promote those who look like them, often unconsciously. This is why a lot of leaders look the same. It is also how the success prototype ensures that straight white men stay in leadership positions, which serves to reaffirm that this is what power looks like in workplaces.

Since men were the first to enter corporate America, they were able to set the standard for leadership. They created ways of cooperating with one another that maintained their dominance, like office politics, which is using power, influence, and relationships to get things done at work, or male solidarity groups, which include social networks like men's-only soccer or golfing teams. These informal social systems enable men to band together and advance their individual and collective power. By hiring and forming relationships with like-minded people, male leaders ensure their employees will toe the line, remain loyal, and support them with maintaining their dominant position. Male employees benefit from this arrangement, as it ensures their own job security and career advancement. Power is maintained by a few when everyone plays by the same rules. This type of privilege is often to the detriment of women, who don't have access to the same solidarity groups, networks, power, or influence as men because they don't fit the prototype.

A More Equal Workplace Is Better for Everyone

To create offices that work for women, we need today's leaders (the majority of whom are white men) to want to change the unfair work culture. But why should men do this if the current system fulfills their power ambitions? That's simple . . . men are also more likely to advance in organizations that work for women because we are no longer advancing a small number of people who fit the success prototype. Everyone has an opportunity to make it. A more equal workplace is a better workplace for everyone.

If there is one message that I hope I convey loud and clear, it's that gender equality is not about raising women up at the expense of men. It is not about making men feel bad or listing all the ways that men need to change. Quite the contrary. It is about creating a workplace that values men *and* women equally and gives everyone the freedom to be themselves. Equality is freedom.

Creating a workplace that practices equality starts with changing the way we think. It is about enabling everyone, especially men, to step outside of rigid gender stereotypes, which are almost always misaligned with our true identity, core values, desires, and ambitions. In fact, as chapter eight, "Breaking Up with Don" details, men face a wide range of challenges at work, which are all created by the pressure to conform to gender stereotypes. A recent study by the Canadian Men's Health Foundation found that 81 percent of men find their day-to-day work to be stressful, and 60 percent of men struggle to get a proper night's sleep because of stress. Men also feel pressure to live up to the ideal worker standard: 60 percent of men surveyed go to work when they are sick and 46 percent work extended hours. These long workdays add to men's already high stress levels and prevent them from having any sort of work-life balance. This is no way to work or live.[25]

A major part of the problem is that men are encouraged to keep their worries and challenges to themselves, which comes at a cost. Research finds that men in powerful positions may also feel disenfranchised by masculine workplace cultures, but they are compelled to hide their feelings for fear of being ostracized by their peers.[26] Women are more likely to speak up about the negative impact of inequality, which just reinforces the idea it is a "women's issue." Both men and women reported disliking cultures with a lack of work-life balance, in which employees are under pressure to conform to stereotypical masculine behaviors. But these challenges were harder for women, who felt that their organizations did not value diversity or appreciate their individual needs and experiences. Cultures of inequality reward "masculine men"—like Don—and marginalize women and men who engage in a wider range of behaviors. That includes anyone who speaks up and shares these challenges.

The Femininity Stigma

Ford's assembly line set the standard for most of the workplace practices we have today, including the hours we spend (or are expected to spend) in the office. It's assumed that work hours equate to productivity, commitment, and ambition. Working excessively is a sign of strength, determination, stamina, endurance, and resilience. Men often display their masculinity by out-working everyone else, by being the first one in the office in the morning and the last one out at night.

Even if companies have flexible work policies for employees to use, if success is measured by the number of hours spent in the office, then this is what employees will live up to. This model of working long hours doesn't allow men or women to pursue a life outside of work, whether they have dependents or not. It's also very hard for men to deviate from normal working hours because when they do they are actually deviating from the masculine ideal. A 2016 research study found that organizational culture plays a key role in men's use of flexible workplace practices as men are informally discouraged to reduce their hours in the office—by other men.[27] There's a lot of self-policing among men to ensure they are spending an acceptable amount of time in the office, like trying not to take sick days, staying late, working weekends, and only leaving the office when everyone else does. Men who chose to adopt flexible workplace practices were considered "ground breakers," and seen as separate from other men.

Masculinity doesn't just set the standard for working hours, it also determines which nonmasculine behaviors men need to avoid at all costs. Largely, men are encouraged to reject anything typically associated with being feminine. This "femininity stigma" coupled with the need to work long hours make work-life balance, and fatherhood particularly, difficult to manage. When men embrace their identity as fathers at work, they are penalized for taking on the feminine caretaker role. A 2013 study, published in the *Journal of Social Issues*, found men who requested family leave were not seen as contributing to the organization, and consequently they didn't receive the same rewards as colleagues.[28] This was even more challenging for black men who were also subject to racial stereotypes and seen as lazy or hostile for making the request.

While the femininity stigma may be an issue for all men, it disproportionately affects working fathers. Between 1965 and 2003, American men have more than doubled the time they spend on housework and childcare. Based on these figures, you might assume that work-life balance has gotten easier for both men and women. But while lifestyles may have changed, the success prototype hasn't. Workplaces continue to believe the ideal worker is someone who has no outside interests or dependent care responsibilities and is fully committed to their job.

A 2012 study found that male employees still feel pressure to ensure they don't appear too committed to their families.[29] The only way men can reconcile these two parts of their lives is to keep their identities separate, by hiding their needs and interests outside of work (think back to my husband's reluctance to confess that he'd have to miss work to care for our son). If men don't, they are penalized. Research estimates that men who choose to reduce their work hours for family reasons receive a wage penalty of 26.4 percent, compared to women who face a 23.2 percent reduction, after controlling for the usual factors that affect wages.[30]

Men are expected to provide for their families, and working long hours is one way to do this. Not surprisingly, fathers tend to work longer hours than childless men; however, men who don't support gender equality at home (and share the burden of domestic work) tend to work significantly longer hours than men who do. Men who take extended leave or reduce their working hours to care for their children will likely earn less and have limited access to work opportunities. Flexible workplace policies and programs do very little to address the fact that parental leave and flexible or reduced work schedules are generally things we associate with women, who are expected to take up the role as primary caregiver (and part-time work comes with its own financial penalty, as discussed more in chapter six).

Women are penalized for the femininity stigma too. Research surveying MBA graduates found that 73 percent of men and 85 percent of women believe the number-one barrier to women's advancement is that they prioritize having a family over work, despite the fact that men and women often have similar career goals.[31] Women are stigmatized once they have children, and so, like men, if they take up flexible work opportunities, they will be overlooked for high-profile opportunities and promotions. Women exit organizations not because they don't want to advance, but because they do. Women are looking for an organization that will accommodate their dual roles rather than forcing them to choose one.

In masculine workplace cultures, men must prove their masculinity by concealing their anxiety and self-doubt. Men are told, in so many words, to "man up." Working fathers are encouraged to deny the pressure and exhaustion they experience managing their dual roles. This leaves men with one solution: keep their personal lives out of the office. You see this playing out whenever men make an excuse for taking their child to the doctor or manufacture work justifications for reducing their office hours so they can spend more time at home. These workarounds are stressful since they force men to hide who they are. This also does nothing to solve the underlying problem. If workplaces don't work for all men, even though they were designed with them in mind, just imagine how challenging these environments are for women.

The Bottom Line

By examining the origins of inequality, it becomes clear that workplaces value men more than women because our patriarchal societies do. By valuing people differently, we value success differently. Success does in fact discriminate because people who conform to the Don Draper ideal are the ones who tend to advance. Those who don't—whether they are women or men who opt for flex time or don't exhibit traditional masculine behaviors—aren't given the same promotions and career opportunities. Over time, this encourages employees, teams, and leaders to all think, look, talk, and act like the success prototype. This is how inequality becomes part of working life—and it's costing all of us.

> *Success does in fact discriminate because people who conform to the Don Draper ideal are the ones who tend to advance.*

The bottom line is this: if the culture you work in doesn't value difference, and you are different, then it doesn't value you. This is a hard pill to swallow, which is why, more often than not, we deny this fact and instead applaud diversity and inclusion efforts aimed at fixing women. Hiding behind the smokescreen of such initiatives sets us all back and winds up being counterintuitive and counterproductive. Our denial encourages us to believe that workplaces are meritocracies, and that by fitting the ideal worker standard anyone can advance. But fitting the standard means denying our differences and our challenges. In short, we are in denial about the inequality in our workplaces—and in the next chapter we will uncover how this denial feeds inequality and keeps it alive at work.

2.

Gender Denial

In the process of selling this book, I spoke to several editors at major publishing houses. One editor revealed that she was thankful her workplace was "not gendered in any way." In that moment, I realized how much we all take inequality for granted at work. This made me determined to find a way to explain how systemic this issue is and how most workplaces don't work for men and women in the same way—even industries that aren't seemingly male dominated.

In fact, the publishing industry is a great example of this. While women make up a large proportion of employees in the industry, men maintain a hold on positions of power. In 2018, the Government Equalities Office (GEO) in the United Kingdom reported that while women make up almost two-thirds of the workforce in publishing, men are paid more on average. For one publisher, Hachette (United Kingdom), the mean gender pay gap was 29.69 percent.[1] Reasons cited for this included the higher number of men in senior roles; the higher proportion of women in lower pay brackets; and the higher number of women with flexible work arrangements.

These figures may be specific to Hachette, but the issues are universal at the same time (other big UK publishers like Penguin Random House and HarperCollins also had significant gender pay gap statistics); they could describe just about any industry because nearly all workplaces are gendered—they were built by men, for men. But it's not always obvious how this negatively impacts women at work from day to day.

Gendered workplaces create both visible and invisible barriers for all women, which limits their advancement. The visible barriers that hold women back at work include any policies, programs, or processes that exclude or discriminate against women because they reflect the values, needs, and preferences of men, such as a lack of parental leave policies, or the subtle pressure and expectation that employees will work long hours and weekends or attend work-related social events after hours. All of these expectations are built on the assumption that workers are either child free or have someone at home to take care of the kids. That someone tends to be a woman—even if she works.

These obstacles prevent women from advancing, but as I realized in that phone call with the editor, telling people about the gendered nature of organizations is pointless. It only starts to make sense when employees see it for themselves. Are there visible barriers in your own office or corporation? Consider these questions:

✔ Who makes the hiring decisions? Are women equally represented as decision makers?

✔ When you're filling an open position, do you see as many female candidates as male?

✔ Do women equally contribute and actively participate in meetings and are these contributions respected and valued?

✔ Are flexible work arrangements used equally by men and women in your organization?

✔ Is there a maternity and paternity leave policy and do both men and women use it? Do leaders use it?

✔ Does your organization reward and promote individuals who demonstrate inclusive behaviors, like people who collaborate and include others, work well with colleagues from a wide range of backgrounds, and actively work to speak up and tackle inequality?

✔ Does your organization ensure that both men and women are equally represented in teams, projects, or group initiatives?

✔ Does your organization train senior management and members of your board to foster gender equality from the top down?

✔ Has your company made a public mention or commitment to helping women advance at all levels, including the board level?

If you answered no to some or all of these questions, then it's likely you have experienced or witnessed examples of the *visible barriers* in your organization. However, if you answered yes to most of these questions but your company still lacks women in leadership positions, you are not alone.

Like most organizations, your office has a range of *invisible barriers* that prevents women from advancing. Often unknowingly, companies can operate in a way that marginalizes, excludes, or devalues women at work. Take, for example, the expectation that leaders need to be assertive; when women act in a more collaborative way, their contribution as leaders is not valued in the same way as men who engage in more aggressive behaviors. By not seeing how behaviors, norms, and workplace cultures create different challenges for women and men, it is easy to deny women's experiences of inequality.

It is this denial that makes us blind to the inequality in our own workplaces. It's why this editor didn't believe that her workplace was gendered in any way, despite the widespread evidence of inequality within her industry. Gender denial is also why companies keep implementing the same old tired solutions but fail to make any progress. We are not seeing the challenges for what they are. As discussed in chapter one, inequality is everywhere. It is in our values, behaviors, and norms—the fabric and very makeup of our workplaces. This pervasiveness makes inequality very hard to see, but easy to deny.

Modern Sexism: Practicing Gender Denial at Work

We all know how to spot *overt sexism*—it happens whenever people openly discriminate against women with blatantly sexist comments, harassment, or discriminatory behaviors. However, in recent years, overt sexism has fallen out of favor. It's just no longer socially acceptable to engage in these practices, even if you believe women are not as competent or valuable as men.

Today you are much more likely to see people engage in *modern sexism*, which includes any beliefs that indirectly condone the unequal treatment of women and men.[2] This includes the certainty that inequality is a thing of the past and workplaces function like a meritocracy. Modern sexism is a lot harder to see because people often deny having these beliefs or engaging in these behaviors. This makes it particularly difficult to tackle. Modern sexism, then, is fueled by denial, which keeps inequality intact in workplaces today.

Given that gender denial makes modern sexism hard to spot, it's worth taking a moment to consider how these views shape your workplace. Examples include:

✘ Employees generally do not engage in overt forms of discrimination like publicly stating sexist beliefs or attitudes and engaging in sexist behaviors. But they are willing to engage in subtle behaviors that exclude women from formal or informal social groups at work, like Friday drinks or sporting activities outside of work.

✗ Employees display an insensitivity to behaviors that discriminate against minorities at work as well as a tendency to explain away these situations as simply joking or harmless banter.

✗ Employees are not aware of how their individual behavior contributes to creating cultures of inequality. Consequently, they do not understand how to support marginalized groups at work and create cultures of equality.

✗ Minority groups are not comfortable with sharing their identities or differences at work and try to fit in by hiding aspects of themselves.

✗ Leaders are not aware that men and women have vastly different experiences at work. They believe that gender equality has been achieved or simply will be with the passing of time.

✗ Individuals often overestimate the advancement and number of women in senior leadership positions as well as the success of existing diversity and inclusion efforts.

✗ The standard for success is the Don Draper prototype, and employees try to conform to this by engaging in informal social practices that exclude minority groups at work whether consciously or not. This can include things like not inviting everyone to office drinks or meetings, leaving people off email chains, or excluding people from team lunches. Or simply ignoring people in meetings.

✗ Employees believe that gender inequality is a result of biological differences. They harbor discriminatory beliefs like the notion that because of motherhood women are simply not cut out for corporate life.

✗ Leaders tend to rely on women-focused solutions to solve gender inequality rather than focusing on the behavioral change needed to create cultures of equality.

✗ Employees lack awareness and deny the career barriers minority groups experience at work.

The belief that gender inequality issues have been resolved is kept alive thanks to the meritocracy myth, along with the barrage of corporate initiatives for "diversity and inclusion." Take, for instance, how exceptional women who have managed to obtain leadership roles are often referenced as examples of how gender equality has been achieved. I am reminded of an advertisement I saw the other day that said companies need more women in leadership roles because women serve as a "beacon of light and hope to all minorities." This uninspiring message completely misses the point and does nothing to advance women or equality. Companies shouldn't hire women leaders because they are a "beacon of hope." They should hire women leaders because they are *exceptional*. Corporations need to shift their rhetoric from wanting women represented in leadership positions so they can be more diverse, to hiring and promoting women because they want strong and capable leaders.

I also believe that these corporate initiatives, which companies publicize to prove that they have cured the gender-inequality problem, are in themselves a form of denial. They encourage employees to believe gender equality has been achieved, when in fact it hasn't. For example, a Gallup poll conducted in 2005 revealed that 53 percent of Americans believe that men and women have reached equality when it comes to job opportunities at work.[3] This makes sense given that research finds that 63 percent of men think their company is doing what it takes to address gender inequality.[4] This is because the mainstream approach to solving this issue—which includes diversity and inclusion initiatives like diversity training, diversity recruitment targets, and women-focused development programs—depersonalizes the entire problem. These initiatives make it *appear* like companies are addressing the issue when really the problems remain untouched.

This approach only fuels denial and lets employees off the hook since they think the company is handling it. This is despite the fact that according to a 2017 Pew Research report, 42 percent of women in the United States say they have faced discrimination at work because of their gender. This included being treated as less competent, receiving less support from leaders, enduring social isolation, or being denied opportunities to advance.[5] Inequality happens every day, but denial prevents us from doing anything about it.

When discrimination shows up at work, employees may acknowledge it, but they believe these are just one-off events that women need to overcome on their own. This makes it easy to believe that women are the problem, not workplaces. For example, many leaders believe that the reason there are so few women in leadership positions is because women choose to have children and become mothers—in fact, this is a common response to the question of why women don't advance. This makes it easy for leaders to avoid changing the way organizations work to better accommodate working mothers and fathers by doing things like implementing parental leave, creating job-sharing roles for leaders, accommodating flexible workplace practices, and developing different career paths for people on reduced work schedules. Consequently, women are left on their own to manage all the ways motherhood and working life are incompatible. When women struggle to do this, they are believed to be less competent. This is more modern sexism.

The study "Gender Gap in the Executive Suite: CEOs and Female Executives Report on Breaking the Glass Ceiling," published in 1998 in the *Academy of Management Perspectives*, examines the challenges women face in leadership positions.[6] This widespread survey of women leaders, with more than a thousand participants, revealed that women believe an inhospitable work environment is the main reason for the lack of women in leadership. This includes workplaces that promote stereotypes, foster a negative corporate culture, and exclude women from networking.

Women in this study likened working in an inhospitable work environment to hearing "white noise." This negativity is like a constant, inescapable, distracting humming sound in the background. Male leaders, however, don't pick up on the noise, since they're the ones humming. As the humming persists and women's experiences are denied, women start to wonder why no one else hears it. Managers might even claim women are making it up or—worse still—that women are the ones humming. Women go to work and struggle to advance because of inhospitable work environments, but their experiences are continually denied by the corporate culture, their bosses, and their companies at large. This is gaslighting, and it causes women to continue to look inward to figure out what it is that they're doing wrong, and the fix-the-woman solutions persist.

Male CEOs are ultimately accountable for the work environment women experience, yet they are usually the ones asking women to stop humming. Research finds that men and women attribute the lack of gender diversity in leadership to different things, and they prescribe different solutions to the problem. Male CEOs tend to prefer solutions that focus on "fixing women"; women leaders prefer solutions that focus on fixing the negative work environment.[7] Fixing women denies and invalidates women's experience of inequality at work while still putting the onus on women to solve it.

Practicing Denial: How Current Solutions Make the Problem Worse

If we don't understand how the current diversity and inclusion approaches are failing women, we are doomed to keep repeating the same mistakes. We will also continue to believe that our efforts are solving the problem.

Take the word *diversity*, for instance. The term was initially used in corporations to refer to demographic diversity; however, over time, its use has shifted to refer to cognitive diversity.[8] Companies now push to have greater "diversity of thought," which means hiring people of more diverse backgrounds, experiences, and contributions. As related in the 2018 *Harvard Business Review* article "Research: When Boards Broaden Their Definition of Diversity, Women and People of Color Lose Out," researchers investigated diversity on corporate boards for nearly two decades and found that during this time boards slowly shifted their focus from increasing the representation of individuals with demographic diversity to increasing the number of individuals with functional and industry diversity. The broader definition of diversity has unsurprisingly coincided with fewer women and minorities represented in board positions. Boards can now report higher rates of diversity without having to be demographically diverse.[9] This is not equality.

Existing approaches to diversity and inclusion can reinforce modern sexist views. These approaches include either women-focused solutions such as mentoring, networking, sponsorship, training, and individual coaching. Or structural changes such as diversity targets, women-focused development initiatives, and hiring programs, which aim to fast track women into leadership positions. Both approaches encourage women to fit the leadership prototype without questioning why this is the only standard for what "good" looks like. Moreover, these initiatives are used as examples of the "special treatment" minority groups receive at work. This encourages the belief that women are not as capable as men. It also fosters resentment from men, as women are perceived to be getting special treatment.

In 2018, I ran a survey for a large financial services organization to understand men and women's perceptions of the barriers to career advancement. I received more than seven hundred responses, from men and women across all levels of the organization, roughly equally divided between genders. Overwhelmingly, when asked what the number-one barrier was to their success, men blamed gender and diversity initiatives. You read that right: men believed that bringing women up was bringing them down, limiting their access to key positions and opportunities. Men resented the organization's focus on promoting women, which they believed was only driven by the organization's need to improve their diversity targets. For men, advancing the interests of women meant they had to give up their seats at the leadership table. This left men feeling both threatened and attacked. Not surprisingly, they pushed back on existing diversity and inclusion efforts and resented joining these initiatives.

Despite this push back, it's interesting to note that male respondents were conflicted. On the one hand, they resented the belief women were receiving a "free ride," and on the other hand, they had to acknowledge that there were only a handful of women leaders in their organizations. In fact, the exact number at the time of the survey was 8 percent. Overwhelmingly, most of the leaders were white, straight, married, middle-aged, able-bodied men. This dichotomy exists because solutions to date have focused on fixing women, to the exclusion of men. Organizations continually announce their commitment to increasing the number of women and publicize program after program to develop them. All the while they continue to deny and ignore the social and cultural elements that create and maintain inequality at work. This makes it *look like* women are advancing, even if the numbers tell a different story. This window dressing approach to diversity and inclusion in organizations today is a result of effective branding and communication activities that serve to keep the status quo intact.

I saw this happen again and again when I worked in HR. Take our friend Sarah, whom I introduced in the introduction to this book. I finally did get her a promotion, except it wasn't as sweet an accomplishment after all was said and done. After we made the case for Sarah's promotion, I kept looking around the room waiting for someone to say something, especially when the COO commented yet again on those "glasses and hair clip." Everyone avoided my gaze and stayed silent as one of their own openly discriminated against their friend and colleague.

So, I advocated. I asked why. "Why do you think Sarah's appearance has anything to do with her promotability or leadership capability? Is it because she doesn't look like any of you?" The senior leader laughed nervously. That one question called out the inequality moment and prompted other leaders to speak up. They agreed the senior leader was being ridiculous. So he made light of it, and laughingly said he would promote Sarah because of his "commitment to diversity." Sarah got promoted but it was a hollow victory, because now she belonged to a leadership team that would view her as a token, when she more than deserved her seat at the table.

Why We Should Ditch Diversity Targets

In my study, male respondents saw diversity and inclusion initiatives as favoring women, who were described as having "every advantage." Consequently, women leaders were seen as "tokens," having advanced because of their gender rather than their capability, just as the senior leader insinuated when he gave into the pressure of promoting Sarah. These attributions reinforced a wide range of negative gender stereotypes, like the belief that women are not capable leaders or should be solely responsible for raising children.

Look at your leadership team. Does everyone look and behave the same way? If so, then your organization has a dominant standard for leaders, which represents an underlying culture of inequality. Often companies try to solve this problem by simply adding more women or minorities to existing leadership teams; in fact, many make a public commitment to doing so by setting ambitious diversity targets or recruitment quotas. These are just quick fixes that simply lead to short-term gains and long-term pain—and more denial.

As a gender equality practitioner, I have worked with many organizations over the years, and the issue of targets has always come up. Why am I so averse to mandating the makeup of leadership teams? After all, setting targets for a 30 percent representation of women across all levels of the organization seems, at face value, like a good way to address the Don Draper problem. If the makeup of leadership teams begins to look different, doesn't that mean the organization values difference? It's incredibly common to see business leaders make external corporate commitments like this, which are often not hard quotas but rather "aspirational targets." The aim is to achieve a trickle-down effect by hiring other female leaders; the hope is they will work to increase the representation of women, thereby magically transforming the culture. What could possibly go wrong?

Male leaders who achieve these targets are often rewarded, so, naturally, they begin to earmark certain roles for women. Some leaders do this overtly, which in and of itself is a form of discrimination, while others do this covertly, by actively filtering out male candidates. As part of my research, I discovered a range of negative outcomes associated with this. For example, women who were hired into roles earmarked for diverse candidates were seen as token hires; they weren't perceived to be the most qualified or experienced pick for the role. Male employees at these organizations saw this as a form of discrimination and marginalization, which increased their resistance to diversity efforts. It also further reinforced their belief that women are not as competent as men, because women need special treatment to get ahead. Women also questioned the legitimacy of their female colleagues, and, in turn, themselves, which increased pressure to perform at an even higher standard than they already were. Naturally, women in the study were frustrated that being appointed to a leadership role was one more hurdle they had to overcome. Sadly, women leaders felt insecure and isolated and they began to question their legitimacy.

While the number of women represented increased, this success was short lived. As these women leaders left, they were often replaced with men. None of these efforts solved the issue of inequality. In fact, it often made things worse, because these targets and diversity appointments gave employees and companies a false sense that equality had been achieved. Despite advancing, women on the receiving end of these "aspirational targets" reported feeling excluded, marginalized, and lacking the support needed to lead.

The truth is that you can't put a number on equality because it is something employees experience and practice; it is not an outcome to be achieved. Reaching an arbitrary target does nothing to ensure women and men will be valued in the same way. Believing it does is just another form of denial. You can have a company with a seemingly healthy 36 percent representation of any minority groups, and yet still have a workplace that marginalizes and discriminates against people. So long as inequality like racism and sexism exist in the world, it will continue to exist at work.

Leaders who advocate for targets are driven by the need to measure their progress. Often this is expressed with statements like "What gets measured, gets done." But who gets to decide what the ideal demographic mix of an organization should be? What is the acceptable number of women, men, LGBTQ, black, Hispanic, Asian, Latina, and Native American employees? And why is this the measure of equality? If we are going to measure anything it should be the cultures of equality that employees experience every day. This is where inequality happens.

Creating a corporation that supports equality is an ongoing job that belongs to everyone in an organization, because everyone has a hand in creating the culture. To start, organizations should ditch their quotas and targets—which are the scoreboard, not the game. An equal representation of men and women in leadership roles is a natural outcome of an organizational culture that supports equality.

> *To start, organizations should ditch their quotas and targets—which are the scoreboard, not the game.*

To create a more equal workplace we need to design, build, and foster a culture that is designed for the needs, experiences, and differences of all employees, rather than a select few. All women will be more equally represented when workplaces champion their interests. This approach is a lot more sustainable, as having the right culture in place positively impacts both the recruitment and retention of women. This also eliminates the issue of tokenism, because the focus isn't on minority groups at work, it's on inequality.

The End of the Line

As diversity and inclusion efforts increased over the last decade, discrimination went undercover. The same beliefs are there, they just look and sound different. Women are still perceived as being less competent than men, which is why they need all these special programs. Having these initiatives theoretically levels the playing field, so the thinking goes that if women are not advancing into senior leadership roles, then it really must be their problem, so they keep trying to fix themselves.

Unfortunately, for the most part, women-focused solutions and structural changes are as far as workplaces are willing to go. Any attempts to change employee behavior, team norms, and workplace culture are resisted because it seems like these efforts are not needed—gender denial case and point.

WAL-MART: *The Largest Case of Sexism at Work*

The largest class action gender discrimination lawsuit in the history of the United States was *Dukes v. Wal-Mart* in 2011. In this case, 1.5 million female employees accused Wal-Mart of discrimination when it came to pay, promotions, and job assignments.[10] A 2016 *Huffington Post* report states that while the Supreme Court dismissed the class action lawsuit in 2011 on the basis that "Even if every single one of these accounts is true, that would not demonstrate that the entire company operates under a general policy of discrimination," many of the plaintiffs are still in the process of filing smaller suits against Wal-Mart.

Lawsuits aside, solving this issue starts with understanding these women's experiences of inequality. According to *Huffpost*, based on the new case-intervention filing, "A 1998 survey of Wal-

Mart managers revealed that there was a 'good ol' boy philosophy' at Wal-Mart, that many managers were 'close minded' about the diversity in the workplace, and that some District Managers 'don't seem personally comfortable with women in leadership roles.'" These leaders are not comfortable with difference because they have only known one version of success: people who look like them. To truly accommodate difference, they would need to change their behaviors, team norms, and possibly even their beliefs.

Instead, they denied the existence of inequality and made it a problem for women to solve. For example, Huffpost reports that the Wal-Mart survey findings reveal that managers believe women don't get promoted because they are not aggressive enough, too focused on family commitments, and not attractive enough, as women were advised to "doll up." When leaders refuse to take accountability for the inequality women experience at work, they are practicing sexism and ensure gender inequality remains a "women's issue."

Consequently, we are left with the same tired solutions. For example, the 2017 Wal-Mart "Road to Inclusion" report states that the company's vision is to create an environment where "everyone feels included," which is supported by various commitments to increase the number of women in leadership positions.[11] Solutions include setting targets, minimizing unconscious bias, and providing women with access to sponsors and mentors. But which one of these initiatives requires male leaders to transform their approach? How do any of these initiatives dismantle the masculine leadership prototype embedded in the company's culture? How does any of this address the 1.5 million women's daily experiences of inequality?

Gender Denial Is a Leadership Issue

"What are the barriers to women's advancement at work? I mean why are there so few women leaders?" I asked, for the thirtieth time, as I conducted hour-long interviews for my PhD study. I was only halfway through collecting the data from two large multinational organizations—one from the energy and resource sector, the other from the financial services sector—and I honestly didn't know if there was any point in continuing. The more I asked this question, the more the responses frustrated me. In nearly every interview with senior male leaders, I received the same answer, "There are no barriers, I can't think of any except for women choosing to have children. Motherhood is the reason there are so few women leaders. We can't change that. I mean it is a woman's 'natural role' in life." These responses were shocking and worrying. How were we ever going to solve inequality at work if the people in positions of power didn't believe that it existed?

Even when I encouraged leaders to think more carefully about their own organizations, which had a dismal number of women in senior leadership roles, most of them couldn't name one barrier. Those that could always cited motherhood. These leaders saw motherhood as a decision by women to put their home life ahead of their working life. The two identities could never coexist. This belief was reinforced by the fact that most of the senior women leaders in the study didn't have children. The results remained the same for most of the interviews. I continued to feel deflated because none of these leaders had any insights about why there are so few women leaders in their organizations.

I shared the findings with a fellow PhD student hoping to make sense of the data. After thinking it over she asked, "Well, what is the greatest barrier women face at work?" Without thinking, I replied, "This, the denial of our individual differences and the inequality that creates at work." There was silence as she waited for me to realize what I had just said. "Oh, of course," I said. "You can't tackle all the barriers if people don't think they exist." Leaders create organizational cultures that don't support women but are unaware of how they do this and the specific challenges this creates for women.

The truth is that not everyone experiences workplaces in the same way. We live in a society that values men and masculinity more than women and femininity. That is why when it comes to power and leadership, men are the standard for what "good" looks like. Leaders model behaviors associated with the success prototype, which encourages employees to follow suit. Over time these behaviors become the standard for how employees engage—especially if they want to lead, as outlined in the "How Gender Inequality Works at Work" illustration on page 63.

The denial of difference is the denial of inequality.

Behaviors associated with the success prototype become the standard for the way "work gets done" and how organizations function. That means performance standards, policies, procedures, structures, leadership norms, and workplace cultures are all built with this ideal worker image in mind. Organizational cultures reinforce the male, white, middle-class, heterosexual, able-bodied standard for success, making it harder for anyone who differs on one or more of these elements to succeed. This is what creates inequality at work, but this is only half the story because the one thing that keeps it intact is the denial that it exists. Modern sexism is difficult to tackle because leaders are in denial. They don't realize that minorities have additional barriers to overcome. The denial of difference is the denial of inequality.

HOW GENDER INEQUALITY WORKS AT WORK

The success prototype for leaders and employees is a white, middle class, able-bodied, heterosexual male that displays attributes associated with stereotypical masculinity.

The success prototype sets the standard for leadership

Leaders work to fit the prototype and in doing so set
the standard for employee behaviors

Employee behavior becomes normalized over time, creating
a workplace culture that reflects the prototype

All of this happens in workplaces that claim to be meritocracies, which function for everyone in the same way, while in reality they enable one prototype to succeed. Consequently, difference is denied and so is the experience of inequality, making it impossible to solve the issue.

Gender denial enables modern sexism to maintain its hold on organizations. Sure, workplaces may not be as overtly sexist as displayed in *Mad Men*, but the success prototype still creates the standard for success and leadership. We are still all expected to conform to this same outdated ideal. Research finds that when individuals hold modern sexist views, they also display negative attitudes toward feminists, insensitivity toward sexist language, and unfavorable attitudes toward Affirmative Action initiatives.[12] Modern sexism is underpinned by the belief that biological differences are responsible for gender segregation at work rather than discrimination. It's something that leaders use, much like a "get out of jail free card," to avoid taking accountability for their role in creating a culture of inequality. By denying people's experience of inequality, they deny the need to change.

What makes these beliefs particularly damaging is that they get rewarded. Research finds that holding modern sexist views helps with career advancement.[13] That's because we tend to turn to people with similar views for work-related advice. We inherently trust people who have values and beliefs similar to our own. Maintaining these beliefs becomes a way to bond with powerful individuals and build advantageous relationships. If people with modern sexist views are in leadership positions, this means that it is more likely people who also hold modern sexist views will be advanced. By maintaining these beliefs, people demonstrate that they are willing to fit the dominant prototype and culture. Those who fit in get rewarded.

Not surprisingly, there are many negative outcomes associated with this. For example, women who hold modern sexist views may not be willing to advance other women or support equality efforts. And men who support women who hold similar modern sexist views are perpetuating inequality. When leaders believe that workplaces are meritocracies and they deny the barriers faced by women and minorities, it makes it impossible to solve these challenges. We can't tackle inequality if we are in denial that it even exists.

Modern sexism is further compounded by race. For example, research finds that people who discriminate against black people at work are more likely to act on their discrimination when a leader endorses this behavior and provides a justification for engaging in it.[14] Leaders perpetuate modern sexism and racism by supporting and rewarding people who hold these beliefs. Importantly, racism is also denied. Research has found that one of the key features of modern racism is denial. Examples of this can be seen everytime someone says "I don't see color" or "I have nothing against black people but." Like modern sexism, these statements justify or hide racist beliefs, ideas, and biases. When white men and women are confronted about the impact that these statements have, they deny that there was any negative intent or impact. This provides the opportunity for white people to take offense at being told their words, ideas, and beliefs are racist. This makes being confronted about racism and sexism more offensive than the racist and sexist behavior, which encourages all minority groups at work to remain silent about the everyday discrimination and marginalization they encounter.[15] Combined, this creates an entire workplace culture that fosters inequality that has extremely negative outcomes for women of color.

Disrupting Your Own Denial

How do you know if you are practicing gender denial at work? It's hard to believe something exists if you can't see, understand, or experience it. Disrupting denial starts with understanding differences at work. Ask yourself the following questions:

- ✔ What kind of leaders do you think succeed? Can you describe their attributes? Are they associated with the success prototype?
- ✔ Do you think women should change their behavior or do things differently to advance and ultimately lead?
- ✔ Do you think men and women experience the workplace differently?

✔ Why do you think there are so few women in leadership positions?

✔ What barriers do you think all women face in their careers and as they advance into leadership positions?

✔ How do you think these challenges differ for individuals based on demographic differences like race, ethnicity, sexual orientation, and physical or mental ability?

✔ Aside from existing diversity and inclusion initiatives, what else can the organization do to create an environment that supports all women to lead?

✔ How do leaders and employees practice equality every day through their actions, behavior, and routines?

Asking these open-ended questions will reveal whether leaders understand men and women's experiences of inequality. As part of my research, participants found having this conversation a valuable starting point for disrupting their denial, which is the most important thing we can do outside of educating employees about the barriers all women face at work.

Why Is Culture the Key to Solving Inequality?

In August 2017, Google fired software engineer James Damore for writing a memo titled "Google's Ideological Echo Chamber," which essentially suggests that men and women have biological gender differences that results in the gender imbalance in technology. For example, Damore argued that women have a stronger interest in people than things, which means they are more social and prone to neuroticism making them less suitable to working technical fields.[16]

While this memo was widely criticized, it is clear from my research that Damore isn't alone with his opinions. He is merely espousing modern sexist views. The core of Damore's argument is that innate biological differences explain the lack of women in leadership roles. This sounds very similar to the responses from men in my research study. They believed that motherhood, not discrimination, is the reason why there are so few women in leadership positions. Ignoring the inherent sexism in these arguments, the main issue with this way of thinking is that it ignores the role environments play in determining individual success.

Employees like Damore who hold modern sexist views are merely reflecting the cultures of inequality in workplaces today. White men dominate leadership positions across nearly every industry, despite a significant investment in corporate initiatives to advance women and other minority groups. Work environments support men to succeed, which disadvantages everyone else. This is privilege and yet we deny it. To enact true change, however, we need to address the fact that organizations do not equally value and support all employees and that some are simply more privileged than others.

3.

Privilege at Work
How Denial Feeds and Breeds Inequality

am privileged. Because I grew up in South Africa, this was always obvious to me. I remember the day black children were finally able to attend my school. I was in a local primary school in South Africa when Monica, a black girl, walked into my class. All we were told was that a new student was joining our class. We were completely unaware of the magnitude of the situation. Monica was the first black girl that we had ever seen in our school, let alone class. No matter how much she tried to fit in, all we could see was how different she was.

Monica was neatly dressed and well behaved, but she kept largely to herself. As a white person, I was blind to all the reasons why she might want to keep her head down. I had no sense of how she might have been feeling. To be the only black girl in an all-white school in South Africa as the system of apartheid was being dismantled must have been terrifying.

My experience in South Africa was not uncommon. I grew up during the apartheid era, where an all-white government enforced racial segregation through targeted policies and legislation. My family immigrated to New Zealand when I was sixteen, with the hope it would be a safe place to live with better job opportunities, the standard reasons most people immigrate. Looking back on this move, it is almost comical how different these two countries were. New Zealand was the first country to give women the right to vote, as early as 1893, whereas a hundred years later South Africa was still grappling with apartheid. Despite their obvious differences, both countries taught me about the power of privilege. I come from a middle-class family. I don't have connections, money, or social status. I have never had a mentor or sponsor. I paid for my education and applied for every job, like just about everyone else. But I am exceptionally privileged because I am white. Being born white comes with benefits.

Education and employment were a certainty for me. As was freedom. Moreover I knew people would value me and I could expect them to—regardless of my socioeconomic background. This is white privilege. This is not something that only South Africans experience, but it is a lot harder for us to deny, given that apartheid only began to unravel in the nineties and its impact can still be seen today. Regardless of where you live, if your value is derived from your race, gender, class, sexual orientation, and physical or mental ability then you are privileged. You receive better treatment and benefits derived from racism, sexism, homophobia, classism, or ableism.

It took me a long time to understand that ignoring or denying my privilege perpetuated other people's experiences of inequality. I would rationalize that it was difficult enough for me to advance at work as a woman, so how could I possibly take on the burdens that all other minorities face? These were also not my challenges or my battles to fight. But then I realized that I had heard this same tired argument many times before—from male leaders dismissing the need for another gender diversity initiative. They viewed the challenges women face as "women's issues," without realizing they had a hand in creating them.

I too have accepted inequality by simply turning a blind eye to it. For me this is particularly ironic given that I have spent years advocating for gender equality, only to realize I was part of the problem. Being unaware of people's experiences of inequality, like racism or sexism, often inadvertently and unwillingly leads to behaviors that are racist and sexist. We are simply blind to inequality. Being able to learn about inequality, without ever having to experience it, is really the ultimate privilege.

But just like inequality, when we deny our privilege we are blinded by it. Privilege makes it easy to deny other people's experiences of inequality and keeps us from seeing the workplace in the way others see it. Denial is what keeps inequality alive in workplaces today. When leaders and employees see how being a part of the dominant group gives them access to power and privilege, they will also become aware of the unique position they are in to dismantle the very inequality they benefit from. Some of us will never know what it is like to be a woman of color, or a person with a disability, or a member of the LGBTQI community. Men may never know what it is like to be the only woman on a leadership team. But we can try. We can educate ourselves about the benefits our privilege affords us and in turn the challenges this creates for others.

This is just the start, because it's what we do with this knowledge that counts. As activist, educator, and writer Brittany Packnett, in an article for the online publication *The Cut*,[1] encouraged white people to spend their privilege because after all they never earned it. This extends to all areas of difference. Spending one's privilege makes gender equality everyone's problem to solve. Your fight becomes my fight.

Privilege and the Boys Club

When I raise the topic of privilege and how it works in organizations during my corporate work, I often get push back. But this is how we come to understand inequality. No one is denying that men work hard, but so does everyone else. The difference is that not everyone benefits from their effort in the same way. Success does discriminate.

> *The difference is that not everyone benefits from their effort in the same way. Success does discriminate.*

Male privilege at work is the ability to fit into your work environment by default. Men (especially straight white men) never have to consider how their identity might differ from the dominant group and limit them. Take a moment to consider some of the daily challenges women encounter, just because they aren't men:

✘ Ensuring people perceive you as a leader but also as a woman, because the two don't go hand in hand.

✘ Managing interruptions when speaking up and ensuring your perspective is heard, as women are more likely to be talked over or ignored.

✘ Being perceived as pushy, despite displaying the same assertive behaviors as men.

✘ Finding ways to work long hours to get ahead, despite the fact that you are likely shouldering most of the burden of dependent care and household chores.

✘ Worrying about being paid less than male colleagues but not being afforded the opportunity to address this. When women ask for a raise, they are penalized for asserting themselves.

✗ Dressing just right to ensure you won't be sexually harassed but will still be considered feminine, which is a prerequisite for being liked.

✗ Being taken seriously. As women don't fit the prototype, they must work harder to be viewed as competent, capable, and legitimate leaders.

✗ Managing any risks of being sexually harassed or assaulted when socializing with male colleagues to build relationships that could enhance your career.

✗ Accessing networks and mentors who can support your career. Men are less willing to provide this support to women, and even if women can access this social support, they are less likely to benefit from it in the same way as men.

✗ Worrying you don't fit in at work and constantly evaluating any difficulties you encounter to determine if they are a result of your race, age, disability, sexual orientation, appearance, or gender—or some combination of your demographic characteristics.

These are just some of the very many challenges women face at work—issues that are rarely, if ever, recognized by employees who fit the Don Draper prototype. This list could go on and on but the examples provided highlight why this privileged status makes it easier for men to assume powerful positions, and how the cycle of inequality continues.

Dominant groups set the standards for behavior in organizations, which we are all encouraged to adopt. As humans, we're hardwired to try to fit in, and we take our cue from our environment, in the same way children learn how to behave in masculine and feminine ways. According to social identity theory, we come to understand what it means to belong to a team, group, and organization by watching and learning from others.[2]

We observe how our colleagues behave, talk, dress, speak, and think. We learn to fit in through an ongoing process of observing and interacting with people at work, something known as socialization.

But what are we trying to fit in to? The success prototype. This ideal standard has a far-reaching impact because it sets the tone for individual behaviors, group norms, and organizational culture. Conforming to the standard determines how easy it is for you to fit in. To be an effective leader you need to be as similar to Don as possible. Fitting in makes people think you are a better leader than you necessarily are, which impacts how confident you feel about taking on a leadership role.

The longer we work in corporate life, the harder it is to challenge our own beliefs of the "ideal worker." Women in leadership roles experience this disproportionately more; the longer they work in an organization, the less likely they are to feel as though they fit in. This also happens to be one of the invisible barriers women leaders face when they enter the third phase of their career, as discussed at length in chapter seven. Research undertaken in 2014 by the global management consulting firm Bain & Company found a 39 percent decline in how new versus experienced women felt they fit in with their organization, nearly double the 23 percent decline for men.[3] This decline led to a more than 60 percent drop in women's aspirational levels for senior leadership roles. In contrast, men's aspirational levels remained the same.

Only 30 percent of women in middle management roles believed that they had an equal opportunity to be promoted on the same timeline as men.[4] Imagine year after year not getting promoted and not understanding why. Despite trying to fit in, lead, and get promoted, eventually you must accept that this may never happen. What disrupts this process? The privileged do. Everyday men and women in dominant positions get to decide how much they will include, respect, and value minorities at work.

Men can choose to enable women to have a seat at the table. More important, they also decide how much legitimacy that role will have. What a powerful position to be in.

The Fault in Feminism

The only way to use your privilege to dismantle oppressive work cultures is to champion equality. In today's organizations, promoting equality might cost individuals time, effort, and status, but this is the tax we need to pay for living in a world of privilege. While men may be in powerful positions because of inequality, gender is just one form of privilege. Race and class are other forms of privilege that keep inequality in place. This concept is all too familiar in the feminist movement.

There has been a fundamental flaw in the feminist movement from the beginning, when white women liberationists devalued, marginalized, and excluded women of color from fighting alongside them. Feminism was stolen a long time ago, and white women need to acknowledge this fact or else we stand to perpetuate the very inequality we are advocating against. In the book *Ain't I a Woman?*, feminist scholar Bell Hooks[5] shares how the women's movement prioritized the interests of middle- and upper-class college-educated white women. These "feminists" wanted social equality with middle- and upper-class white men—not for all women, but for all middle- and upper-class white women. White women activists focused on expanding employment opportunities primarily for white women workers, who did not identify with black women. Fix-the-women solutions were created to help women work in a man's world, but they never advanced equality for all women, just primarily white women who were better able to fit into the white-male-dominated culture.

Feminism was stolen a long time ago, and white women need to acknowledge this fact or else we stand to perpetuate the very inequality we are advocating against.

The more people differ from the ideal standard, the more barriers they will face trying to advance at work. For example, while white women face many barriers at work because of sexism, they have their whiteness in common with most of the male leaders. This is a form of privilege. In contrast, black women need to battle both sexism and racism. The same holds true for nearly every area of difference. The more barriers minorities face, the less likely they are to have access to the power and privilege needed to change the culture from within. Conversely, people who most closely resemble the success prototype are in a powerful position to affect change.

When it comes to gender inequality at work, there is one golden rule all feminists need to own: what white women want from men in organizations, they need to be prepared to give to women of color and every minority group. To understand how women's careers differ from this standard we have to unpack the very different needs *all* women have. There is a tendency when looking at career advancement to consider women's experiences with a unified view. The problem with this is that it tends to reflect the experience of white women because they make up the dominant group of women leaders in corporations today. In 2017, white women comprised 21.8 percent of senior executive positions; however, Asian women made up just 1.8 percent, black women 1.3 percent, and Latina women 1.2 percent.[6] Adding different identities into the mix—like those associated with gender, race, ethnicity, age, religion, ability, and sexual orientation—often carries with it the burden of different forms of discrimination and marginalization because of variation from the success prototype. There isn't one experience of inequality; it shows up differently for everyone at work.

The barriers women of color face are significantly more complex than those of white women. In the 2010 journal article "Women and Women of Color in Leadership," authors Janis Sanchez-Hucles and Donald Davis[7] argue that women of color face the compounded effect of "gendered racism." They cannot separate the multiple aspects of their identity. This means that women of color carry a heavier load because they experience both sexism and racism—as well as the interplay between these forms of inequality. Their research finds that African-American women experience greater negative stereotypes because of the combined impact of racism and sexism. As such, African-American women are more likely to experience discrimination, prejudice, and unfair treatment when it comes to promotions, training, advancement, and support. This compounded disadvantage is associated with increased stress and lower self-esteem.

The more people differ from the ideal standard, the more barriers they will face trying to advance at work.

Women of color are not a uniform group, there are a variety of ethnic and racial backgrounds that individual women may identify with. This is further differentiated when you factor in age, sexual orientation, religion, and physical or mental ability. The more identities a person has and the more these differ from the ideal worker standard, the more likely it is that they will experience the compounded effects of inequality.

Without this understanding, it's very easy to assume that any attempts to level the playing field at work are really efforts to "help" those who are just not as capable. This creates a sense of unfairness, which in turn creates resistance to equality efforts. This is why we can no longer afford to hide people's identities and experiences at work. The movie *Hid-*

den Figures is a great example of how the experiences of women of color are often erased at work, along with their contributions. The film tells the story of three talented African-American women who worked at NASA Langley in 1961 and had to confront institutional racism and sexism as part and parcel of doing their job.

In 2018, I interviewed Dr. Christyl Johnson, NASA's deputy director for technology and research investments, about the movie and her experience working in the organization.[8] Johnson joined NASA in the summer of 1985 and is often described as a "modern figure," a reference to the main characters in the film, Katherine Johnson, Dorothy Vaughan, and Mary Jackson. "Although things have significantly improved at NASA since the times represented in *Hidden Figures*, I too have experienced similar struggles with racism and sexism. I resonate with the women in the movie, because I see them as strong African-American women who were determined to succeed despite their circumstances," says Johnson. It becomes obvious after watching the movie why there were and still are so few women, and particularly women of color, in male-dominated fields.

We can replicate this awareness in our own workplaces by unpacking the challenges all women experience. Recognizing different experiences of inequality is an ongoing process because it is impossible to account for all the ways discrimination might show up. However, every woman can make it a daily practice to educate themselves about the barriers all women face at work, by reading about and researching these challenges. This includes inviting all women to share how they experience the barriers in different ways within your workplace and being open to understanding how you might contribute to this. Only by doing this can we form a unified view of what it is we are trying to fix, and then get to work.

Office Politics: How Power and Privilege Show Up at Work

When I began my career in human resources more than eighteen years ago, I started to notice that some people were better equipped to manage the political aspects of work. At the time, part of my job was supporting senior leaders with managing their teams. As the years passed, I started to notice the same individuals getting promoted or rewarded over their peers, peers who were often far more qualified and experienced.

I was surprised by this, so I voluntarily interviewed thirty-two senior leaders to better understand why these individuals were so successful. I always got the same answer. These frequently promoted people all have one thing in common: they are masters at getting the support they need for an idea, promotion, pay rise, project, or opportunity. In other words, they know how to "play the game." They have political skill. To navigate workplace politics, you need to be able to build relationships, network, collaborate, and persuade others. If you do this in just the right way then you can significantly improve your performance ratings, promotion opportunities, reputation, and career progression.

Ryan, one of my male colleagues, is a master at office politics. He knows how to get anything approved or supported at work. One day I asked him how he managed to get people on his side. He told me that the key to his success was spending time with leaders or decision makers. He would take every opportunity to have drinks, get lunch, or even go on bike rides with key leaders. This was how he developed enough goodwill that when it came time to ask for a favor or approval, there was a good chance he would get it.

While Ryan was charming, persuasive, and good at his job, he had one thing that women in similar positions did not: access. Ryan could go for drinks, lunches, and bike rides because he was invited. He was similar to his leaders—this is male privilege in action. Ryan would always be accepted by these leaders because he looks, speaks, and dresses like most of them. This makes it easier for Ryan to bond with men who are in positions of power. Men engage in politics by including, favoring, being loyal, trading favors, and protecting each other.[9] For men, engaging in politics is simply about following the rules of the game, and it's something they do frequently within companies to get ahead. While being politically skilled might help people advance at work, there is one major problem with this: it doesn't work for everyone in the same way.

Women don't have the same privilege of engaging in office politics that men do. This makes it harder for women to build relationships, alliances, and supportive informal networks. It is no surprise that women often rely more on formal systems and career development processes to advance than office politics. Because of this, experts might conclude that women just don't understand office politics or value it the same way men do. The book *Political Skill at Work: Impact on Work Effectiveness* argues that women deny the value of corporate politics, which makes them "politically naïve."[10] As such, it is recommended that women undergo training and mentoring programs to fix their lack of political engagement.

Of course, it's not that simple. Research finds that engaging in office politics is something we associate with men.[11] The behaviors people use to gain access to powerful individuals, important information, or opportunities are more masculine. This would happen all the time with Ryan. He found it easier to bond with male leaders, not only because he had access to them, but he could joke and talk with them about sports in a way that was harder for women on the team. Even if we fix women by teaching them to joke in masculine ways and become one of the guys, women still won't be accepted because they are violating the standards society holds for how women are meant to behave.

When it comes to office politics, all women face a catch-22. They can't engage in office politics like men do because they risk being seen as masculine, so they lack access. Women also can't engage their political skills in more feminine ways, because that's not how you play the game. Balancing this requires significant mental energy from women and racial minorities, who must learn to play office politics in just the right way. Women who engage in political behaviors often find it to be draining, stressful, and tiring. They're being asked to adopt behaviors that are not their own. It's unfair to assume that this is even possible or will result in the same benefits that white men receive.

Not only does office politics feel inauthentic to women, but women find office politics to be irrational, aggressive, competitive, and important for advancing individual goals but not for wider organizational success (which is more important to women).[12] In fact, in one study, women's descriptions of barriers to their career advancement actually described office politics, which included things like being excluded or not having access to networks. Some studies have even found that women may turn down management roles because of their distaste for office politics. This really matters. The way organizations are structured requires that you engage in masculine political behaviors to advance your career. But if the only ones playing the political game are white men, we need a new game.

How to "Spend" Your Privilege at Work

Mike Gamson, the former senior vice president for LinkedIn Global Solutions, was like most white, male leaders I have worked with. He was well intentioned and believed he was doing all he could to support minority groups at work. But then one day something changed and Gamson began to use his position of power and privilege to solve gender inequality within his team once and for all. In 2017, I interviewed Gamson to find out what sparked his motivation and how he was transforming his organization's approach to advancing women.[13] "If you stopped me five years ago and said, 'Mike do you think you are doing everything you can to help the company be more successful?' I would have told you unequivocally, 'Yes I am doing everything I can.' I was blind to what I was not yet doing. I became one of those guys who unconsciously hired people who looked and spoke and sounded and acted a lot like me," he said.

To better understand some of the challenges faced by women in his organization, Gamson engaged employees in discussions to identify instances where they experience the organization's culture differently. For example, observing how men and women interact in team meetings, as women may be overlooked or interrupted, which limits their ability to contribute and be heard. These conversations made him realize his own privilege. "I used to think that the world is fair. That it was a meritocracy. I no longer believe that. I think people who think it is an even playing field are probably like me—they have had it easy their whole life. They are probably a guy, they may be white, and they have likely been in the majority their whole life and they assume that it is like that for everyone else," he says. These conversations encouraged other leaders to convene broader conversations with their own teams, and employees began to share their own firsthand accounts and admissions of error.

Gamson's team then used these experiences to identify ways to make diversity and inclusion a part of everyday life for employees—something they referred to as demonstrating "acts of inclusion," which really are simple actions everyone can take to spend their privilege. This is something that each of us can do by investing our time, effort, and social status to support the inclusion, development, and advancement of minority groups at work. This also means being willing to give up some of your reputation, acceptance, and standing at work to advocate for others. Each of us can make an intentional, consistent effort to do this at work. Here's how:

✔ Make it a priority to get to know the barriers women and minorities face at work, by reading books like this, researching these topics, and asking minority employees about their experiences.

✔ Ask minority colleagues you know well to share their stories or examples of marginalization and discrimination at work. And be open to learning about how you or your privilege may contribute to these experiences.

✔ Identify how workplaces don't work for individuals who are different from the success prototype and then raise awareness in your organization about these challenges by sharing or speaking up when you see this happen at work.

✔ Work to identify solutions to these challenges that you can support or champion, including changes to your own behaviors.

✔ Be an ally to individuals who share their stories of discrimination or their ideas for how this might be solved. If needed, amplify their message and start an allyship program.

✔ Join an employee resource group (a group of employees who join together based on shared characteristics like being a veteran or a member of the LGBTQ community, with the aim of providing support and career development to one another) to which you have no demographic affiliation, to better understand the challenges that different employees have.

✔ Encourage your colleagues to understand how inequality is experienced at work. You could start an employee resource group, which focuses on understanding inequality in your workplace.

Spending your privilege is an intentional practice that aims to disrupt the status quo. This is not something you do once; it is an ongoing commitment to put equality into practice every day at work.

Change the Conversation, Change the Culture

One of the most well-known quotes from Don Draper in *Mad Men* is "If you don't like what's being said, change the conversation."[14] In the case of gender equality, it's time for a new conversation—one that is devoid of denial and filled with acknowledgment and acceptance of privileged roles some of us occupy. We need to start talking about the role that power and privilege play in the marginalization and discrimination of minority groups in workplaces today. We need to openly discuss how privilege creates invisible barriers that women face throughout their careers.

The inequality you experience at work doesn't exist because of you. It exists because of the culture in your workplace. The only way to solve this is to stop denial and learn about the different ways people experience inequality at work. This is how to start dismantling the patriarchy, including gender stereotypes, success prototypes, white privilege, male privilege, and gendered organizations, which all create the numerous barriers to women's career advancement detailed in the following chapters of this book. Only by making the invisible visible can we begin to chart a new way forward, together. The next chapter sheds light on how we begin this journey.

4.

It's a Path, Not a Ladder
Becoming Aware of Your Workplace

Until the age of twenty-eight, I had never owned a pair of hiking boots nor heard of leech-proof socks. In fact, I had never really hiked. So, when my (now) husband suggested we go on a rainforest walk while on a vacation, I naively thought it would be a good idea. He likes extreme sports and we were dating at the time, so I wanted to impress him.

This two-day trek required socks that leeches couldn't eat their way through—this fact alone should have been enough to put me off, but I really liked him, so I bought the socks. I hated the entire experience. The sun burned my skin, there were flies swarming around my face, and my backpack started cutting into my shoulders. Covered in what I kept hoping was mud, the hike seemed to go on forever. But every time I wanted to complain, I looked over at our local guide and felt guilty. He wore nothing but a T-shirt, shorts, and flip-flops. Holding a machete half his height, he tore through the bushes in our way in what seemed like a never-ending fight. He carried our bedding, water, and food in a backpack that must have weighed as much as he did. We hiked and hiked.

Our guide didn't appear to be bothered by the mosquitoes, heat, and humidity. Never slipping once, he would scramble over boulders in our path and pull us up along the way. Eventually, to help me climb more easily, he took my backpack and carried that too. Each time we stopped at a water station, he would fill up more drinking containers to ensure we had enough water for the entire journey—this only added to his load. His backpack got heavier as the hike progressed and his journey got harder.

As we continued through the rainforest, he moved bigger obstacles out of the way. He climbed over more and more boulders, pulling us up each time, while carrying all the gear. This was strength I didn't know humans had. He walked in front of us to create a path around potholes in the ground and at times missed a few—falling and injuring himself, but never once complaining. When we finally reached the end of the hike, I looked over at him and realized in that moment that while we might have ended up in the same place, we had walked an entirely different journey.

If you believe we all have an equal chance to advance at work, you also accept the idea that we are all the same and experience workplaces in the same way. When you enter a workplace you leave your identity, race, gender, sexual orientation, disability, personality, and home life at the door. You become the worker. Our different experiences of working life can be extremely difficult to see because organizations keep telling us that all employees are essentially the same and are treated in the same way. We're told they are meritocracies. This is how workplaces deny differences: they believe there is only one conventional experience of working life that everyone is expected to have. The truth is women and men have different experiences and challenges advancing at work because they are different and organizations were not designed to accommodate this. This is true whether workplaces accept this fact or not.

Just like that hike, we might all work for the same organization, but our experiences of it differ tremendously. Companies still largely approach career progression based on the belief that employees are climbing the corporate ladder with the aim of making it to the top. Men and women, therefore, have an equal chance of progressing at each rung on the career ladder. But what if there is no ladder? What if there are different career paths each of us choose to walk down, with different challenges unfolding along the way because our needs, identities, family responsibilities, interests, career aspirations, and ambitions all differ?

There is a widespread belief that men and women start out on the same career track, but women eventually drop out, choosing instead to step onto the mommy track. In her now-famous *New York Times Magazine* article of 2003, "The Opt-Out Revolution," Lisa Belkin makes the argument that women don't rise to the top of corporate life because they choose to leave and care for their children.[1] What makes this argument compelling is that a lot of women do feel the strain of working and managing a household. But not all women have a choice; a lot of women need to work. According to a 2015 Pew Research Center report, dual income families are the norm; they represent 46 percent of married or cohabiting couples with at least one child under the age of eighteen.[2] Families where fathers work full-time and mothers work part-time represent 17 percent, and households where fathers are the only breadwinner represent 26 percent. Families with two full-time working parents are the norm because families need this income.

While women make up nearly half the labor force, representing 46.9 percent in 2018, according to the nonprofit firm Catalyst, they do not progress at the same rate as men.[3] Women and men start out at similar levels, representing around 44.7 percent of employees in S&P 500 companies, but women seem to get stuck at the management level, representing 51.5 percent of all management, professional, and related occupations. After that, women's participation declines to 26 percent of executive, senior leadership positions and only 5 percent of CEOs.

Based on this data, it's easy to assume women don't make it to the top because they are in fact "opting out," which places responsibility for the lack of women solely back on women. This is not the case at all. Women and men leave corporations at similar rates and for similar reasons. A comprehensive study conducted in 2000 and published in the *Journal of Management*, examined turnover rates and found that not only do men and women leave their employers at the same rate, but women are more likely than men to remain in the workforce as they age.[4] So why do employees leave? The study found men and women actually have the same reason: a lack of promotion opportunities. However, when women are promoted, they are less likely to leave their organizations compared to men. The problem is women are not promoted at the same rate as men. The 2015 study by LeanIn.Org and McKinsey & Company found that women are 15 percent less likely than men to get promoted, and at this rate the researchers say it will take more than a century to achieve gender parity in the C-suite.[5] It doesn't matter if you are a man or a woman, if you are not progressing it's more likely that you will leave your employer.

> *At this rate the researchers say it will take more than a century to achieve gender parity in the C-suite.*

So, why are women not progressing? Because they are not valued, treated, respected, and rewarded in the same way as men. "Climbing the corporate ladder: Do female and male executives follow the same route?"—a research study published in the *Journal of Applied Psychology*—investigated the career experiences of sixty-nine men and women and found that throughout their careers women reported greater barriers to career advancement, including, but not limited to, a lack of career opportunities, exclusion from informal networks, gender stereotypes, and failure of senior leaders to support women's advancement.[6]

Sure, women continue to shoulder most of the responsibility for managing childcare and domestic life, and some women might leave their careers because of this, but only those that can afford to, which represents a small number of single-income households. Most women want the same opportunities as their male counterparts to progress, but gender inequality at work prevents this from happening. When we deny the barriers women face when trying to advance, we deny inequality.

Knowing Your Workplace Matters: Gaslighting and Women's Experiences of Inequality

Ariel Letterman landed a job as a freelance associate producer in a large television news network in New York straight out of journalism school. I met Ariel a few years prior at UN Women, where she interned while completing her degree. We became friends, often sharing stories about the different challenges women face at work.

Excited to have her first full-time job, Ariel worked really hard to prove herself by putting in long hours and working most weekends. Ariel had received much praise for her work from her colleagues and her boss, Mitch, after just a few months in the role. With all this praise, Ariel hoped she might be able to ditch her freelance status and secure a permanent full-time employment contract with the company.

Then a few weeks later Mitch called Ariel into a meeting. "So, you know I'm looking for someone to permanently hire into your spot, right?" Ariel nodded, hoping this was the good news she had been waiting for.

"Well, I am not sure you are the right fit for this role. Your performance is outstanding—I mean you are the best producer we have ever had—but you don't make 'small talk,' so it's hard for me to get to know you or see you as my friend. We don't have to be friends but obviously whoever I hire I would like to be friends with," Mitch said.

Ariel was confused and tried to hold back the tears of righteous indignation—she didn't want to live up to the emotional woman label women are often stereotyped with. She was trying to understand how Mitch's reasoning was in any way related to the job itself. She felt her character was being attacked and wanted some examples to understand how she could improve. Elaborating, Mitch told Ariel that by not spending time chatting with him or going to the regular social gatherings on Fridays, Ariel was coming across as "difficult," and if she wanted the job she needed to "work on her personality." Ariel was stunned into silence. Mitch ended the meeting by letting Ariel know that he was doing her a favor by telling her this and she should be grateful.

Ariel didn't get the job. Steve, the less-qualified, less-experienced, and by far less-capable producer got the job. When Mitch explained the decision to Ariel, he said even though Steve wasn't the better candidate he was easier to work with because Steve laughed at his jokes. Ariel was devastated and she called me to share what had happened, hoping to make sense of it. After listening to her experience, I nodded and said, "Well, the good news is—it's not you, it's your workplace."

Ariel's experience with Mitch is a classic case of the *Conformity Bind* at play (which you'll read about more in chapter five). Mitch wanted Ariel to fit in and become more like the prototype. More like Mitch. No matter how hard Ariel worked, she would never be good enough. At the time,

Ariel was blindsided by this feedback and didn't realize this was an actual barrier. If I hadn't explained it to her, Ariel might have believed that she has a personality flaw that would forever prevent her from advancing—even though she was the best producer the company had ever had.

The more organizations deny women's different experiences of work (as addressed in chapter two), the harder it is for all of us to see the barriers women face. What's even worse is that when women do encounter a blatant gender-inequality issue, they assume it is a one-off event, which they alone are responsible for managing. This is really a form of gaslighting, as workplaces try to convince women that their experiences don't match reality. This is how women end up doubting their capability and fixing themselves.

Navigating the invisible barriers is difficult, and as women struggle to advance, they start to believe that they are not good enough. Over time, their unique identity and differences become something to hide, work around, or overcome. When organizations, leaders, and employees deny the existence of the barriers, they are essentially devaluing women's experiences at work. This comes at a great cost to women's self-esteem and confidence.

BBC journalist and coauthor of *The Confidence Code*, Katty Kay, says that when it comes to women's personal lives, they have the same confidence as men, but as soon as women enter the workforce, their professional confidence drops off. To support this, Kay references a 2011 report titled "Ambition and Gender at Work" by the Institute of Leadership and Management in Britain, which found that men are much more confident than women across all age groups, and about 70 percent of male managers have high levels of self-confidence, compared to 50 percent of women. Importantly, women with low confidence have much lower expectations of reaching leadership roles in the organization.[7]

It makes complete sense that men would feel more confident at work and have a stronger belief that they can make it—the workplace supports them in this effort. Men are also not gaslighted into believing that their experiences of inequality don't exist and that the reason they are not progressing is because they are not good enough. It's time to start seeing women's careers for what they really are—a minefield of invisible barriers, rooted in inequality, patriarchy, and privilege.

> *It's time to start seeing women's careers for what they really are—a minefield of invisible barriers, rooted in inequality, patriarchy, and privilege.*

Arm Yourself with Awareness

Not seeing inequality is what keeps it in place. Becoming aware—like Ariel was able to—disrupts our denial and makes it easier to navigate the challenges we experience because we can see them for what they are. Even if you accept that men and women might have different career experiences or challenges along the way, it is still easy to assume that by and large they are treated as equals. This assumption underpins how we approach women's advancement at work, as it is widely assumed women and men share the same experience until women hit one key barrier—also known as the "glass ceiling." This is misleading: there isn't one barrier women need to overcome at one specific point in their careers.

The idea of the glass ceiling encourages companies to implement quick fixes, like training women to negotiate or network rather than dealing with the more complex issue of creating work environments, cultures, and leaders who help women advance. The reason the glass ceiling seems to make sense is because when women start out in corporate life, they are roughly equally represented in entry-level positions. However, throughout the organizational hierarchy, women's representation systematically declines. With the lowest numbers of women represented in leadership positions, it is easy to assume that this is where women must face the greatest challenges to advancement.

While this argument is commonplace, it isn't the reality of working life. Women and men are in fact on the same career path, they just experience very different journeys. Instead of a glass ceiling, you could say we're working in glass offices. Janeen Baxter and Erik Olin Wright researched the experience of women at work in the United States, Sweden, and Australia and found that across all levels of an organization women experience gender bias and the challenges associated with it.[8] Interestingly, female participants in this study said they faced tougher challenges at lower levels of the organization. Like the challenges Ariel encountered in her first job, women are faced with numerous barriers from the moment they enter the workforce, which accumulate over time, creating the gender gap in leadership positions we have today.

> *Instead of a glass ceiling, you could say we're working in glass offices.*

Only by understanding what the barriers are and how they are likely to show up in your career can you begin to navigate them. After Ariel shared her story with me, I started to explain some of the barriers she was experiencing. This immediately helped Ariel because she could see how the invisible barriers, specifically the conformity bind and negative gender norms (as discussed in chapters five and six), were affecting her career and confidence. Her newfound awareness helped her push back against the idea that she was "difficult," which had the potential to destroy her self-confidence early in her career. Such awareness is the greatest way to prepare women for the various ways they are likely to experience the invisible barriers throughout their careers. It's also the essential first step that leaders need to take if they want to remove these challenges altogether.

Seeing Your Career in a Whole New Light: The Three Career Phases

Several researchers have investigated women's career life cycles to try and understand how they differ from those of men. In an attempt to illustrate how career patterns for women differ from the traditional career ladder, researchers have come up with various analogies, like a labyrinth and a kaleidoscope. These comparisons are used to illustrate how men tend to progress their careers in a predictable way, advancing from one position to the next up a hierarchy—even if they change jobs every five years. However, women often work around career barriers as they navigate the integration of their personal and professional lives—much like a labyrinth.

> *Women often work around career barriers as they navigate the integration of their personal and professional lives—much like a labyrinth.*

While men's careers tend to follow a linear path, women's can be grouped into distinct phases that coincide with the changes in their personal lives. In the 2005 research paper "Women's Career Development Phases," authors Deborah O'Neil and Diana Bilimoria interviewed sixty women with an age range from twenty-four to sixty years. Their findings reveal that women experience three phases in their careers, which can be divided, for simplicity purposes, by age.[9] These include the following:

✔ **The Idealistic Achievement Phase**, which includes women aged twenty-four to thirty-five
✔ **The Pragmatic Endurance Phase**, which includes women aged thirty-six to forty-five
✔ **The Reinventive Contribution Phase**, which includes women aged forty-six to sixty and above

Descriptions alone of these three phases should be enough to put women off working in most organizations—even without layering the invisible barriers on top. For example, imagine you are applying for a job and the advert reads: "In this job, you will start off 'idealistic' about what working life will be like, believing it is possible to achieve your dreams. But then very early on you will have to endure the reality of inequality, experiencing discrimination and sexual harassment, which forces you to become dissatisfied and disenfranchised with your job. As if that isn't enough, you will face the impossible task of managing the incompatible demands associated with working long hours, managing a household, and caring for children. Given you are likely to fail at this, your self-worth will take a hit, negatively impacting your mental and emotional health. But if you can survive this phase, then you might get to engage in meaningful work, but only if you contribute over and above the basic elements of the role. If you really want to make a difference—in a world that never valued or treated you in the same way as the men you work with—then you need to prove just how capable you are—again and again."

No one would ever apply for this job.

But yet, for women, this description is the best-case scenario, as this advert doesn't include all the invisible barriers women face. This is why women need to be aware of what their careers actually look like, as opposed to how they are expecting them to look, thanks to the meritocracy myth. To gain a full understanding of women's experiences of work, it is important to identify the invisible barriers women face throughout their careers so that we can disrupt denial and remove these obstacles. That's why, in Part II, for simplicity I have renamed the phases and identified the invisible barriers women are most likely to experience within these phases, as follows:

Phase I: The Achievement Phase: Six Invisible Barriers from Graduate to Manager

Women in this career phase are generally between the ages of twenty-four and thirty-five and are idealistic, as they want to realize their dreams and make a difference—and they believe they have what it takes to do this. During this phase women are mainly concerned with "doing it all and having it all." Even though roughly 91 percent of the women in this phase did not have children, they were becoming increasingly aware of how work and home life don't integrate. While women may be confronted with gender inequality at work, they are largely in denial about the impact it might have, believing that they alone can overcome these challenges.

Examples of the barriers women face in this phase include things like *Conditioned Expectations*, as women are conditioned to expect school life to mirror working life. Like Ariel, the gender inequality they experience early on can come as a bit of a shock. This negatively impacts their confidence and self-esteem. Women progressing in this phase also face challenges like the *Conformity Bind*, as they have to live up to Don Draper if they want to get ahead, which as we know is an impossible thing to do.

Throughout this phase women also have to perform at a higher standard than men, something known as the *Performance Tax,* and it limits women's pay and promotion opportunities. These are just a few of the impediments women are likely to face early on in their careers, which prepares them well for the challenges that lie ahead.

Phase II: The Endurance Phase: Balancing Management and Motherhood

The second phase is really a perfect storm for women because it's when motherhood, sexism, discrimination, and inequality combine to create a difficult experience of working life. The endurance phase affects mostly women aged thirty-six to forty-five. At this point in their careers, women have spent enough time in the organization to realize that no matter how motivated they are, their career advancement is dependent on other people—like their boss, colleagues, husband, or children. The focus for many women is to "do what it takes" to manage the incompatibility of work and home life. Regardless of whether women have children or not, in this phase women are likely to feel as though working life limits their personal happiness and fulfillment. This makes sense given that a lot of women encounter sexism, discrimination, masculine work cultures, office politics, harassment, and poor managerial practices. The result is women feel disengaged and dissatisfied with their careers.

This experience makes sense when we examine the barriers women are likely to face in this phase, which includes things like *Negative Gender Norms*, which is a form of modern sexism that includes sexist behaviors that marginalize women at work, which I'll explain more in chapter six. Or barriers like *Role Conflict*, which is the difficulty women encounter managing the incompatible roles of worker, wife, and mother—also outlined in chapter six. Not only that, but this is when women who have children are likely to face the *Motherhood Tax*, where despite performing at a higher standard, they are likely to face a per-child drop in their wages of 5 percent, simply for being mothers. These are just some of the challenges women face, which makes them question whether they have what it takes to endure their working life, go the distance, and lead.

Phase III: The Contribution Phase: The Six Invisible Barriers Women Leaders Face

Toward the end of their careers, women aged forty-six to sixty plus years enter the third phase, which is where women want to undertake work that can make a difference to their communities, families, and workplaces. At this point, women have remained committed to their careers despite going through the painful process of reevaluating life, work, and relationships. Despite having to overcome many challenges throughout their careers, women in this phase want to make it easier for the next generation of women leaders, and they are seeking opportunities to make a difference.

Given the age range of this phase, it includes women in leadership positions or senior levels within their organizations. I've included common barriers that women leaders face in this phase, like the *Identity Conflict* women experience, trying to lead in workplaces where only Don Draper management styles are recognized and rewarded. Women also have to navigate *Stereotypical Typecasting*, which happens when they are labeled with negative gender stereotypes like "bitch" or "queen bee," which limits how people see, value, and respond to them as a leader. Women also have to overcome isolation created by the in-group, such as male *Favoritism*, whereby male leaders engage by socializing and supporting other men to the exclusion of women.

While these barriers have been mapped onto the main career phases women experience at work, it is important to note that this is simply to illustrate when these challenges are likely to show up. But this will be different for every woman. Not all women have children, or at the same time in their lives and careers. Not all women advance to leadership positions in their later years. Your experience of inequality is unique to you. This book, and specifically the chapters that follow, are a road map to guide you through how, when, and where inequality is likely to show up in your career.

It is also important to note that these barriers are not experienced sequentially, or as isolated events. Instead, I would argue, they are cumulative. For example, navigating the *Conformity Bind*—an invisible barrier discussed in chapter five, which requires that women live up to the Don Draper ideal if they want to succeed at work, is an issue for all women who want to progress. The invisible barriers often show up for women at different points in their career, often repeating or adding to several other barriers women may be experiencing. For example, while women encounter the *Conformity Bind*, they might also endure *Role Conflict* while trying to integrate their work and home lives.

The compound effect of multiple barriers is what makes gender inequality particularly difficult to bear. For example, when men and women enter the workforce they hold similar leadership aspirations and they are equally confident about their ability to achieve this.[10] However, after just two years of work experience, the number of women aspiring to senior leadership positions falls from 43 percent to 16 percent. In contrast, the number of men aspiring to senior positions falls by only 3 percent. Moreover, as women gain more experience, their confidence falls by half, whereas men's stay the same. This drop off isn't affected by motherhood, rather the more time women spend in organizations, the less confident they are in their ability to advance at the same rate as men. Given the numerous challenges and compounded difficulties of having to overcome several barriers at the same time, it is not surprising that women start to question whether they have what it takes to endure workplaces.

It's far too easy to consider the barriers in isolation, but when we look at the entire picture it becomes clear that women may be on the same path as men, but they experience different challenges and carry a much heavier load. A bit like my guide in the wilderness, women have to scramble over bigger and bigger boulders, clear obstacles out of their path, and carry an increasingly heavier load in order to reach the same destination. The more barriers women encounter, the more they become aware of inequality and the more they begin to doubt whether they can succeed.

That's why we need to speed up the awareness process. Imagine if we could arm every woman and man entering corporate America today with twenty years' worth of knowledge about the invisible barriers women will face before they even start work. This includes an education on gender denial and the many ways women's experiences of inequality create challenges for men. Women would never question themselves. Men could never question women. Both would know how unfair organizations are. And every time inequality is experienced at work, men and women would know how to tackle it.

Get to Know the Barriers

Men's and women's work experiences vary greatly, but not acknowledging this is one of the major obstacles to advancing gender equality. Every man and woman who claims to support gender equality at work should be able to name the barriers women are confronted with at each of the three career stages—as outlined in the following chapters of this book—and then practice awareness of them on a daily basis. This is essential, because each of us has a role to play in tackling these challenges.

Throughout each chapter of Part II, I have outlined suggestions for how to address each of the seventeen barriers in dedicated sections called "The Fix." And then in chapter eight, I demonstrate how gender inequality creates challenges for men and give tailored advice for how they can tackle gender inequality at work. Finally, in chapter nine, I present every supervisor, manager, and leader with a series of actions they can take to start addressing these challenges, regardless of whether they lead a small team, department, or entire organization.

But all of this starts with getting to know the barriers. This is extremely important for every manager because they play a critical role in supporting women with their career development. How can leaders provide mentoring, coaching, and career development advice to women if they aren't aware of the barriers their employees will face? If managers are not supporting women with their development and advancement, then they are not managing. Women need managers who are not just aware of the barriers but are committed to changing workplace culture to eliminate these barriers. This awareness is even more important for women because you can't navigate the barriers if you can't see them.

Part II
UNDERSTANDING

"Tackling inequality starts with making the invisible visible by getting to know the barriers women face at work."

5.

The Achievement Phase

Six Invisible Barriers from Graduate to Manager

etween the ages of twenty-four and about thirty-five marks the beginning of the career track for many women. Their main focus is on achievement, but not at the cost of having a satisfying career where they can engage in work they find fulfilling and making a positive contribution in their organization. Women enter the first phase of their careers expecting that their road to success will be a meritocratic one. Women work hard and try to advance—believing they alone are in control of their career success. Like men, women want to do it all and have it all, the only difference is women experience invisible barriers early on that men do not. Women encounter these barriers before they even first set foot into an office, but without awareness it is difficult for women to understand why they are struggling.

Even having access to that first career opportunity is more challenging for women because the standard of what "good" looks like in most recruitment processes—the model that all candidates are measured against—is a male one. The challenges continue to unfold over the course of these years, as women are held to higher performance standards and have less access to promotion opportunities or powerful individuals. All of these challenges begin to add up in the early years, making it harder and harder for women to advance.

But once you are aware of the broken culture that exists in your organization, as laid out in Part I, you will be prepared to see the invisible barriers for what they are: inequality. With that knowledge, you gain power over the barriers and will begin to see how exceptional you really are. This knowledge will help you preserve your mental and emotional energy and go from wondering how to fix yourself to recognizing that the problem is not you, it's your workplace.

Barrier #1: Conditioned Expectations

Several years ago, I was on the beach in Busselton, Australia, about to complete my first half Iron Man triathlon. It was early in the morning and I stood on the beach staring out at the ocean trying to calm my nerves. This was the moment I had trained for. The course included a grueling 1.9-kilometer ocean swim, a 90-kilometer bike ride, and 21.1-kilometer run. I felt ready to dive in. I was prepared because I had read all the books, bought the equipment, completed the training, swam countless hours in a pool, and even completed numerous smaller triathlons. I knew what to expect and was mentally prepared for the journey ahead. I understood the potential dangers of sharks and jelly fish—this was Australia after all—but like everyone else at the race I just didn't believe any of them would be a problem for me. As I waited for the starting bell to ring, I felt my heart racing. To calm my nerves, I kept saying to myself again and again: "You've got this. Just run this race like you practiced."

As I dove into the waves, those words washed away. This was a battle I hadn't prepared for. Most of the male swimmers were scrambling, kicking and pushing to make their way out to the front. I was struggling to breathe through the sea of people. I felt an elbow to my ribs and a sharp kick to my face from swimmers who were also fighting for their spot. This was not only painful, but it disoriented me. For a moment, I couldn't breathe and ended up swallowing a lot of seawater, which made me fall behind. If I was going to finish this race, I would have to give up any hopes of making it to the front. The crowd of swimmers began to dissipate and finally I was able to swim, but something wasn't right. Due to a storm surge the night before, the waves were bigger than anything I had prepared for. Each wave felt like it was lifting me up and then just as quickly dropping me back down. With each stroke, I was fighting against the tide and getting pulled farther and farther off course. This made my journey longer than it needed to be. All I could see beneath me was darkness and with each stroke I felt more and more alone. Occasionally I looked back at the shore for reassurance, but I was farther out than I realized.

When I finally reached the shore, I dragged myself to the beach, on my hands and knees. As I vomited up ocean water, I tried to wipe away my tears, which blended into my wet face. After eventually composing myself, I looked up at the cheering crowd and my heart sank—this was just the start. Now I had to jump on a bike for 90 kilometers and then run a half marathon—for another four or five hours with bruised ribs that made it difficult to even breathe. Although I practiced for months, nothing had prepared me for this. I trained in a pool. There were no kicks to the face or elbows to the body. No storm surges. No darkness. Unprepared and defeated, these obstacles shook my belief that I could finish the race.

In many ways, entering the workforce mirrors starting a race. We step out into the darkness with the belief that our education and training will guide us. For women, this notion creates the expectation that the same rules apply to all employees—that we are playing on a level field. Many individuals graduate from school and enter the workforce thinking they can succeed and achieve at work by putting in the hard work, just as they did with their education. No one warns students about how gender inequality will show up in their workplace. Inequality is missing from university courses, corporate induction programs, and leadership development initiatives. Without this knowledge, women and men are not fully prepared for the world of work. More importantly, leaders are ill equipped to support, guide, and lead women through the various challenges they will encounter over the course of their careers.

This oversight perpetuates the meritocracy myth; everyone expects women to advance at the same rate as men. When they don't, it is assumed that women aren't cut out for corporate life. Sarah Damaske, associate professor of sociology, labor and employment relations, and women's studies at Pennsylvania State University, researched the expectations women hold when they first enter the workforce. She found that women often assume the behaviors that helped them to succeed at school will help them succeed at work.[1] Women expect to mirror experiences like earning high grades, participating in school programs, and receiving positive feedback. Middle-class women are conditioned to succeed at school because this is their path to future work opportunities and career success.

To research how women's expectations of working life are formed early on, Damaske interviewed eighty women from a range of ethnic backgrounds. Her findings reveal that middle-class parents of white, Asian, African-American, and Latina women consistently promote the importance of education for future employment. Consequently, women from middle-class families were raised to achieve excellence in the classroom and at home. As a result, middle-class women had high expectations regarding their workforce participation, with 81 percent expecting to be continually employed and progress in their careers. Similarly, African-American women with working-class backgrounds expect to engage in continual work because this is the norm for most of the women in their households. However, only 50 percent of white and Latina women from working-class backgrounds expect to continually participate in working life. They anticipate breaks in their careers to care for their families based on the expectation set by parents and authority figures. These findings demonstrate the important role that parents and authority figures have in shaping young women's expectations of school and working life.

But women's expectations often don't measure up to the reality of working life. Because men and women are conditioned to have faith in the meritocracy myth, it makes it easy to deny gender inequality from the moment employees enter an organization. This is evidenced by a 2006 survey of more than three thousand undergraduate students in the United States, which found that almost 90 percent of students do not believe that their gender will affect their opportunities for advancement, networking, and mentoring.[2] Moreover, 75 percent of students do not believe women will face pay disparity, and 60 percent do not believe that gender is an obstacle to women's advancement at work. Given the increased media attention and mainstream focus on gender inequality in the workplace, it may be hard to believe that these findings are still true today. Yet more recent findings from a 2013 study show similar results as students continue to believe that gender inequality would not impact them personally and deny the influence it will have on their careers.[3] Students believed that they were entering a gender-neutral workplace—the same race.

What these findings highlight is the personal exemption rule. This is the belief that gender inequality happens to some people, but not you. This is something a lot of women believe when they first start out in their careers. For example, the 2006 study found that only 45 percent of female students believe women will experience gender bias at work. More astonishingly, only 13 percent of female students think they will experience gender bias. Researchers found women born after 1977 in particular tend to hold the belief that gender equality has been achieved and that organizations are meritocratic.[4] But they aren't, and women are likely to encounter this from the moment they apply for their first job. Research finds that while women earn more bachelor's degrees than men, and have for decades, they are less likely to be hired into entry-level jobs.[5] This issue is worse for women with disabilities, who face double discrimination stemming from the combination of sexism and ableism. This negatively impacts their access to job opportunities, as roughly 75 percent of women with disabilities are unemployed according to a United Nations report.[6] Given the numerous barriers women face at work, these beliefs about gender inequality are a sign of a lack of awareness or denial, which makes these challenges harder to overcome.

IT'S NOT YOU:
How to See Things for What They Are

Yomi Adegoke and Elizabeth Uviebinené are British coauthors of the book Slay in Your Lane: The Black Girl Bible, *which they wrote after struggling to find a career self-help book that spoke to black women. I interviewed Adegoke and Uviebinené in 2019 to better understand the challenges black women encounter at work.[7] Uviebinené says the aim of their book was to help young black women become aware of the challenges they will encounter working in a predominantly white space, something she has experienced firsthand working in very corporate, white, male, middle-class environments: "It was important for us to kind of be open and talk about the experiences that we feel with things like microaggres-*

sions and stereotypes of how black women should be and how this can be a barrier to . . . thriving in places not set up for you to essentially excel." Uviebinené says that challenges for black women are different, and recognizing this is important. Take for example the "angry black woman" stereotype, which unfairly characterizes black women as irrational, difficult, and hostile; this is something that Uviebinené is constantly aware of and works hard to overcome. This even extends to things like emails, as Uviebinené says she will read her emails several times to make sure there is no negative tone, or if she is having a disagreement over email that it doesn't somehow reinforce the negative stereotype.

This constant self-monitoring can be exhausting, which is why Adegoke says that it is critical for black women to realize that the problem doesn't lie with them. "It lies with white supremacy and sexism," she says. To deal with these challenges every day, Adegoke says, we must acknowledge that they exist. Adegoke recommends regularly reminding yourself that the challenges you face are not because of you. These are simply barriers that your workplace created and needs to remove.

While it is easy to admit that women as a collective group face gender inequality at work, it is a lot harder to acknowledge the personal impact. Marginalized employees are reluctant to confront the individual discrimination they face because it hurts (and it's not always easy to spot). When we own the problem, we also must come to terms with the fact that our colleagues think less of us, which is why they treat us unfairly.

The conditioned expectations that women and men have of working life also shapes their beliefs about what the ideal worker looks like. Graduate school socializes women to be the *ideal student,* and this establishes a pattern of behaviors that women carry into working life. Alison Mountz, a researcher from Balsillie School of International Affairs at Wilfrid Laurier University in Canada, found that during graduate school women learn to push themselves beyond their own limits, by studying and working long hours, often leaving little time for family and self-care.[8] Women in this study believed the *ideal worker* was someone willing to work long hours, compete, and give up aspects of their personal lives for their jobs. These expectations are reinforced as soon as women enter workplaces, where the dominant success prototype is Don Draper.

Only through continued exposure to discrimination and marginalization does it become clear that living up to this prototype doesn't serve the interests, ambitions, or aims of women. The more time women spend at work, the more they become aware of inequality, even if they do not experience every barrier. Just by spending time in organizations employees will be exposed to discrimination by observing the inherent inequality in hiring, promotion, development, and pay decision-making processes.[9] This discrimination happens in day-to-day moments—inequality moments. These moments can include small things like only ever asking women to do the "office housework" by making coffee, scheduling meetings, or taking notes. Or these moments can be bigger, like managers promoting a less-qualified male employee over a higher-performing female employee simply because he is "one of the guys." It's assumed his similarity makes him more likable or easier to work with.

Compared with graduate school women, experienced professionals tend to be more aware of the impact gender inequality will have on their careers. For example, a survey of 1,684 experienced medical professionals published in 2012 in the journal *Social Science & Medicine* found that 75 percent of women identified gender discrimination as the first or second most important challenge women face in their careers out of eleven factors that included things like work-life balance and access to mentors and suitable role models.[10] Conditioned expectations coupled with a lack of education on the barriers women are likely to face at work encourages graduate women to believe the *personal exemption rule*: inequality exists but they do not believe they will experience it. When they do, they believe they alone can overcome it. Consequently, when women struggle to navigate the barriers at work, they blame themselves, not gender inequality, for their failure to thrive at work in the way they'd anticipated. Only by recognizing gender inequality can we dismantle it, instead of leaving it up to women to discover the hidden barriers for themselves and work around them.

THE FIX: Know the Barriers to Name Them

One major takeaway of this book is that men and women are unaware of the challenges that difference creates at work. While women become aware of inequality over the course of their careers, it's not particularly helpful to have this knowledge after the fact. Knowing the challenges you are likely to face throughout your career is essential to effectively navigating them.

For example, respondents from the survey of experienced medical professionals said they felt they weren't prepared to deal with gender discrimination, even though this was a significant challenge for them. Like a lot of women, these participants felt set up to fail. Not knowing what the barriers are makes it harder to overcome them, because women are encouraged to believe they are the problem. This can negatively impact your confidence early on. By learning about the barriers *before* you experience them, you can better manage this. And only by educating men about the barriers women face at work can we begin to remove them. In practice, for women, this means:

1. Get to know the barriers in this book. While reading about the barriers is a good starting point, the next step is to understand the different ways you have experienced or witnessed inequality throughout your career. Think about your experiences—how have you encountered the barriers at work?

2. Reflect on your career to identify the barriers you have encountered and write them down. This can include mapping out your career path and noting difficult moments or experiences you have encountered along the way. Then match these moments to a specific barrier outlined in this book. Recognizing how the barriers show up for you is the first step in disrupting your own denial and realizing it's not you.

3. Consider what barriers you anticipate experiencing in the career phases you are yet to encounter. This will make it easier for you to name the barriers when they happen and manage these experiences because you understand what is happening.

Workplaces have an important role to play in educating men, in particular, about inequality. Every corporate induction, learning, and development program can include a focus on inequality and the barriers women face at work. This is how organizations disrupt men's denial and raise awareness of inequality. In chapter nine, I detail additional actions leaders can take.

Barrier #2: Matching Women to the Male Standard of Success

After studying the barriers women face at work, it never occurred to me to label any of them "men." I had never thought of it in this way, perhaps because, like most women, I know better than to say aloud that men present a challenge to my career advancement. This would, after all, alienate the men I work for and with. But the reality is that male dominance at work does hold women back. This shows up the moment women try to enter the workforce because of the expectations we hold for how men and women should behave (gender stereotypes) and the standard for what success looks like at work (success prototypes).

When hiring managers assume female candidates are too soft, emotional, bad with numbers, or lack expertise in technical aspects of a role, they are making a hiring decision based on gender stereotypes. This type of discrimination can be hard to spot, but it is possible to manage it with tactics like having objective hiring criteria (such as education, qualifications, and years of experience), using several selection methods, and ensuring diverse selection panels.

Prescriptive gender discrimination is a lot harder to spot. This happens when leaders set the standard for hiring decisions (that match the success prototype) and then penalize women for not living up to it, or change the criteria to match their preferred candidate. For example, research finds men are preferred for traditional masculine roles like police chief and women for traditional feminine roles like teacher.[11] To ensure men are selected for these roles, hiring managers in this research changed the hiring criteria to match the preferred male candidate. In the case of the police chief role, when male candidates were described as educated and family-oriented, hiring managers would overemphasize how import-

ant these attributes were. However, when male candidates lacked these
attributes, hiring managers would downplay how important they were to
be successful in the role. Female applicants did not receive this benefit.

Even when qualified women—like Sarah from Part I, who didn't
get promoted because the hiring manager didn't like her hair clip and
glasses—are considered for the job, leaders will apply subjective criteria
to justify hiring someone who fits the Don Draper standard instead.
This is how leaders unknowingly favor men over minority candidates.
Research finds this tends to happen when hiring managers overstate
the importance of men's qualifications and understate their weaknesses
in relation to the job requirements.[12] In contrast, for female applicants,
hiring managers often downplay their expertise and education and overemphasize their weaknesses. The more subjective or ambiguous the hiring criteria is, the easier it is for managers to justify this bias. Therefore,
this tends to be an issue associated with white-collar roles and leadership
positions, where candidates often have the same education, experience,
and training.

This is, of course, not just a gender issue. White hiring managers consider information differently about black and white candidates in order
to justify or rationalize racial bias. This is known as *aversive racism*, and it
happens when white people believe they are not prejudiced but continue
to discriminate against racial and ethnic minorities in subtle ways. In one
study, when black applicants had an average résumé, which included a mix
of strong and weak credentials, they were less likely to be recommended
than white applicants who had the exact same credentials and résumé.[13]
Hiring criteria plays a critical role in discrimination because it creates the
opportunity for leaders to discriminate while upholding the belief that
they are being impartial.

IT'S NOT YOU:
Naming and Shaming Inequality at Work

Yassmin Abdel-Magied is a Sudanese-Australian social advocate, engineer, and author. Throughout her life she has had to overcome stereotypes. As a young, black, visibly Muslim woman, Abdel-Magied says she always felt as though people saw her as the "other." Her 2014 TED Talk, "What Does My Head Scarf Mean to You?," received more than two million views, and it challenges us to think differently about the beliefs we hold.

I interviewed Abdel-Magied in 2019 to discuss how our brains are hardwired to take shortcuts and process information unconsciously, which biases the decisions we make.[14] While this cognitive bias shows up everywhere, Abdel-Magied maintains it's particularly damaging when it comes to hiring decisions. "The way [cognitive bias] shows up in things like employment is, well, you could show someone this exact same résumé with a male name and a female name and the female name will be deemed less competent, be offered the job fewer times, and be offered a lower salary—if they are offered a salary," she says.

This bias is even more of a challenge for racial or ethnic minorities to overcome. "In Australia, if you've got a Middle Eastern or Chinese last name, you have to send over 60 percent more résumés in order to get the same number of callbacks as exactly the same résumé as someone with an Anglo-Saxon last name," says Abdel-Magied.

Overcoming these challenges starts with becoming aware of them. "Having the knowledge that it's not you, that you are part of and a reflection of structural inequality is really empowering. It's not that they don't like me, it's that this is the way the world is."

By being aware of the challenges, Abdel-Magied says men and women can begin to take action. For example, Abdel-Magied

*says there are certain situations where she feels comfortable to call
out the biases before they even happen. Like being in an interview and letting the hiring managers know the challenges a Muslim woman is likely to encounter—applying for an engineering role
in a male-dominated organization—by saying things like "I know
I don't look like your typical engineer but I am more than qualified
to do this job." How men and women call out the barriers will differ
depending on what they feel comfortable with, but doing this is how
we make people aware of the invisible barriers women face at work.*

When we hire people, we are evaluating them against the ideal standard for employees, which tends to be white and male. Given that most
leaders today are white men, the success prototype they are hiring is in
fact a version of themselves. This has been happening almost as long as
organizations have been around. For example, Chester Barnard, author
of the 1938 book *The Functions of the Executive,* essentially argues that to
maintain an organization, leaders need to ensure people fit in.[15] Barnard
encourages leaders to carefully consider an individual's education, experience, age, sex, personal distinctions, prestige, race, nationality, faith, politics, as well as physical appearance when making hiring decisions. Nearly
eighty years ago, a leader's job was to hire people like them and maintain
the status quo. Today, it seems leaders are still living up to this ideal every
time they hire people who look, speak, act, and lead like them.

THE FIX: Name the Barriers to Navigate Them

Women encounter barriers even before they enter workplaces,
which is why it's so important for them to know what the barriers

are. This frees women from the burden of constantly having to fix themselves, by taking up one women's initiative after another. By knowing what the barriers are when women join an organization, they can think about their career goals and development and decide if any of the actions they are taking support their advancement or are really just more women fixing. For example, when your boss tells you that you need to be more assertive and aggressive to get ahead, before signing up for the next assertiveness course, you might consider whether this is really just the *Conformity Bind*, an invisible barrier detailed in this chapter, at play. Likewise, if you are being asked to do more than your male colleagues in order to be deemed worthy for that next promotion—even though you have met every requirement—you might want to consider whether you are experiencing the *Performance Tax*, also outlined later in this chapter, before working any harder than you already do.

Knowing what the barriers are helps you to decide if what you are being asked to do supports your development and career goals, or if in fact it's just more of the "fixing women" epidemic in corporations today. A quick way to check if the advice, feedback, or development you are being told to undertake is actually helpful is to consider the following questions:

- ✔ What is the ideal standard for employees in your workplace, and is this the Don Draper ideal? If so, do you think this is what "good" looks like?
- ✔ Are you being asked to change who you are to live up to the

Don Draper ideal standard? If so, can you identify which invisible barrier you might be encountering?

✔ Are you being asked to internalize this barrier by changing aspects of yourself, or is there a clear link between the feedback, advice, and development you are being given and how this advances your career goals?

✔ Is this something that men in a similar position would be asked to do?

Barrier #3: The Conformity Bind: Fit In or Forget It

When we start a job, it takes a few months to learn what the acceptable behaviors, team norms, and routine practices the organization values. This process is called socialization and it continues throughout a person's career, but it is especially important for newcomers who are trying to learn the ropes. Given that workplace cultures tend to be masculine, it's a lot easier for men to assimilate into them. Women, on the other hand, must negotiate around masculine workplace norms, which often exclude them.

As a part of my PhD research, I conducted seventy-two interviews at two large multinational organizations, one from the energy and resource sector, the other from the professional services industry. In every interview, I would ask participants to describe the ideal employee. Men and women consistently said this was someone who works long hours, makes the organization a top priority, has no dependent-care responsibilities, asks for what they want, competes to get ahead, and is generally extroverted. Most of these descriptions are the same because employees learn what looks good from the social interactions they engage in at work and by observing leadership behaviors.

When new hires join an organization, they actively seek out clues for how to fit in. What does it take to succeed? Who gets rewarded and for what? Who gets promoted? How do leaders behave? What do employees need to do to fit in? Employees get a lot of the answers to these questions by watching leaders. Leaders don't just manage the organization; in many respects, they are the organization. Leaders represent the behaviors, norms, and standards employees are expected to mirror if they want to be included. Behaviors that comply with these standards get promoted, developed, and rewarded. The standard for leadership is the success prototype. Therefore, individuals who fit the prototype are more likely to be accepted, included, and advanced into leadership positions, which further reinforces the one-size-fits-all standard of success.

What does conformity ultimately get you? Social capital—in other words, being included and accepted at work. Social capital gives employees access to social groups, networks, mentors, sponsors, and powerful people—all of which are important to career success. For example, networks are critical for women, especially early on in their careers, because they provide access to inside information and advice that aids career advancement. People in positions of power, like executive leaders or board members, are generally connected through similar social ties, like education, wealth, or personal interests. They also tend to look and behave in similar ways. Powerful people are an informal network because only new connections who share similar backgrounds (to the network) are accepted. This limits the ability of racial or gender minorities who lack this similarity and therefore have a harder time gaining acceptance. Given the value that networks provide, it could be argued that these relationships are even more important for minorities at work, who could use additional support to overcome the numerous barriers to their career advancement.

Accessing this social capital can be very difficult for women because they don't fit the prototype. To succeed, women are encouraged to adopt the male standard of leadership by engaging in masculine behaviors, but this just makes it harder for them to be accepted. To thrive at work, men and women need to fit in to access social capital. However, informal networks are a lot harder for women to break in to. Telling women to network more ignores the exclusionary practices men engage in. Men bond and support other men at work. When Steven, a male colleague of mine, went for a job interview, he was asked a handful of questions by the hiring manager about his experience for the leadership role. The rest of the conversation was a discussion about his years playing college soccer. The male interviewer even let slip that once Steven joined his team, he could join the work soccer team. Steven got the job, and even he was amazed at the lack of rigor in the process. Steven joined the soccer team and quickly became one of the guys, getting invitations to Friday drinks, lunches, and golf days. As men make up the dominant group at work, they determine the makeup and membership to most informal groups, but this often includes some degree of affinity bias, as outlined in chapter one.

Informal social groups at work often exclude women and racial minorities, as men decide who gets to join in, and more often than not, this only includes people who look, think, and act like them. This is supported by a 1995 survey, conducted by the Center for Creative Leadership, which finds that 72 percent of participants agree the number-one barrier to career advancement for women and racial minorities is white males limiting their access to networks.[16] Even if women break into informal groups at work, it is unlikely they will be accepted in the same way men are.

A great example of this is mentoring. Mentoring programs are a go-to solution for advancing women in the workplace because they help socialize employees into an organization. While men and women do not differ in their reported levels of mentoring or networking, white men tend to benefit a lot more from this behavior.

The 2018 *Harvard Business Review* article, "Research: Women Ask for Raises as Often as Men but Are Less Likely to Get Them" randomly examined forty-six hundred employees across eight hundred organizations and found that women are mentored as much as men, and in some cases more, but the type of mentoring men and women received differed. Men were more likely to be sponsored by senior executives who would use their influence to help advance their mentees' careers.[17] Men are more likely to be accepted into the inner circle, which means they receive greater organizational awareness and understanding from mentoring relationships. Men support men who conform, by giving them access to information that can help them navigate their workplaces. That's why women are willing to do what it takes to fit in at work—even if it means denying aspects of their identity.

While accessing social support presents a significant barrier for white women, it's even more difficult for women of color. They don't share gender or racial similarities with white men. Both sexism and racism limit opportunities for women of color to access informal networks and mentors, which can become a significant source of stress.[18] According to Sanchez-Hucles and Davis, while white male leaders often exclude white women, they are still more likely to accept white women than women of color. If it is challenging for white women to fit in to male-dominated environments, then it is next to impossible for women of color. What makes this particularly difficult to address is that it's often hard to spot. Men who engage in these behaviors are often unaware of what they are doing or they deny the impact it creates. This is how male leaders can believe they support diversity and inclusion while continuing to hire, promote, and reward employees who look like them.

If women want to be accepted and liked, they need to behave in a way that conforms to gender roles by acting in a more stereotypical "feminine" way, but then they won't be considered leadership material because they don't fit the prototype. Women have a very narrow range of behaviors they can engage in at work if they want to be accepted and succeed. It is not enough for women to be good at their job. Women need to display their competence and leadership capability in a way that conforms to gender stereotypes. This means doing your job well, while ensuring you are coming across as warm, friendly, kind, modest, sympathetic, and pleasant. If women don't do this, they will be perceived as competent but not likable.

Women cannot take on male behaviors and be dominant, outspoken, opinioned, and assertive. But to lead they need to. So, women navigate a very narrow path by being assertive but pleasant, outspoken but warm, and successful but not self-promoting. While this Goldilocks standard is an impossible task for anyone to live up to, it becomes even harder when you layer on other areas of difference, like race or ethnicity. These identities carry with them additional stereotypes, expectations, and constraints for how people are expected to behave at work. This process of getting women to conform to an impossible standard is how organizations slowly filter out difference, because employees need to work around, manage, or hide their differences to fit in.

Hiding your womanhood to live up to the masculine ideal is how women start to lose themselves. I saw an example of this early on in my career when I worked for a professional services firm and I was one of only three women on a team of twenty people. The rest of my colleagues were men. When the women on this team wore perfume to work, the men would verbally harass them, mocking them and implying that they were doing this so that the men in the office would want to sleep with them. The women began to feel unsafe, and so they started to use men's deodorant to blend in and stop the harassment. Notice that the solution was changing *themselves and their behaviors*—taking on a more masculine scent in this instance—in order to fit in and feel safe at work. No one asked or demanded that the men stop harassing women in the office. This is just one example, but research shows again and again that instances like this are all too common. Women are encouraged to power dress, speak louder, and act more assertively—in other words, act like men to fit in at work. Women also face tremendous pressure to tolerate sexist jokes, inappropriate behavior, harassment, discriminatory comments, and office banter for fear of being perceived as difficult or, worse, excluded altogether.

The need to fit in and belong is powerful. When you fit in at work you feel a sense of belonging and physiological safety. This makes being different dangerous and we see this play out every time a woman says "I don't want to be known as a 'woman engineer,' I just want to be an engineer." Or "I don't want to be described as a woman leader; I want to be a leader." Women who succeed in workplaces today often are required to deny their gender because of all the ways it makes them different. As psychologist Paula Nicolson has found through her research, which she shares in her book *Gender, Power, and Organizations,* the ideal successful professional woman is single-minded, tough, autonomous, and willing to distance herself from traditional femininity and domestic duties.[19] When women deny aspects of their identity, they also deny experiences of inequality, which makes it impossible to tackle them.

I know how powerful the need to fit in can be. Having worked in male dominated industries, like the dairy industry, oil and gas, and financial services, I was often aware that I was the only woman in a meeting or on a team. I also observed many women trying to bridge their gender divide with male colleagues. One of my friends Emma Campbell also worked in the energy and resource sector as an engineer. She was one of a handful of women working alongside hundreds of men on a mine site. This environment was so male dominated that there were no restrooms designated for women—only men had restrooms. Women had to share a portable toilet instead.

When Emma started out, she was desperate to fit in and be treated like an equal to the men on her team. So she began to act like "one of the guys" by laughing at sexist jokes, making derogatory comments, and even mocking herself for being a woman working in a man's world. Within a year Emma had transformed. She talked, acted, and even dressed like the men she worked with. But none of this worked. Emma would always be treated differently—because she *was* different. Only her work environment had made her believe that this difference was a bad thing. By trying to fit in to survive at work Emma had lost her identity.

Trying to pretend to be someone else is an exhausting and demoralizing process. So eventually Emma gave up and decided to be herself—regardless of the consequences, like being excluded, mocked, or isolated. This made it easier for Emma to notice all the ways the mine site was unwelcoming to *all* women—a culture she had participated in creating. This made her want to change things. So, when male colleagues tried to engage her in sexist banter, she told them to stop—not caring if this isolated her even more. Emma was liberated. She could finally be herself. Some of the men she worked with saw her new behaviors as the permission they needed to speak up and push back on some of the sexist banter that made them uncomfortable, though they hadn't said anything. Soon Emma realized that she wasn't alone. The negative comments and derogatory behavior toward women were something that only a small handful of men initiated and supported.

When Emma denied her differences, it didn't make them disappear. Just by being one of a handful of women on a mine site, Emma will stick out. In fact, when any employee group makes up between 1 and 35 percent of the relevant employee population, they have a minority status at work.[20] This can create added stress for women because their status makes them more visible and so they are scrutinized in a way that men are not. The term for this is hypervisibility. It feels a lot like working under a magnifying glass, where every move and mistake is examined. This added scrutiny places women under tremendous pressure to perform and prove their worth because they are trying to bridge their difference.

These challenges are significantly more pronounced for women of color, who, because of race and gender differences, face a more extreme version of hypervisibility and must also be on guard to deal with discrimination, insults, or bias at work.[21] For example, a study undertaken by the nonprofit firm Catalyst in 2019 examined the experiences of 649 black employees and included roughly even numbers of men and women. What they found was that hypervisibility is a major issue for black men and women, who felt they constantly needed to be "on guard" at work. This included constantly being prepared to manage negative comments, insults, and exclusionary behavior as well as having to continually demonstrate their credibility. Over time, this negatively impacted participants' emotional, mental, and physical health and well-being as 45 percent of black employees reported sleep problems and 54 percent felt on edge.

How do black colleagues respond to this challenge? Researchers Isis Settles, NiCole Buchanan, and Kristie Dotson find that they generally use three strategies. These include disengaging from parts of the organization where discrimination occurs, performing to a higher standard to overcome racist stereotypes, or simply leaving the department or organization.[22] These strategies clearly demonstrate that if an employee's race and gender are different from Don's, the most they can hope for is to survive their workplace.

THE FIX: Solve the Problems You Create

If men present a barrier to women being accepted at work, men can also remove the barrier. I have seen men do this in organizations I worked for. At one company, male leaders had installed a PlayStation in the lunchroom for employees to use during their breaks. This was meant to be a way for all employees to relax and socialize. However, American football seemed to be the only video game that was ever played. Consequently, this social activity was overrun with men who would regularly engage and bond with other senior men in the organization. They also excluded women from playing.

Frustrated, women raised the issue with the most senior male leader, arguing the PlayStation had become an informal network that excluded women from an opportunity to engage and build relationships with leaders. Instead of dismissing these complaints, the senior male leader decided to take it upon himself to solve the issue.

He took three specific actions that all men can do to disrupt homosocial practices at work. First, he spent time with the women in his office to analyze the issue. He wanted to educate himself and understand how this informal social practice excluded women. Second, he raised the issue with the men in the office— despite facing significant push back in the process. At first, male leaders didn't understand why this was even a problem, but the senior leader took time to share women's accounts of how this social practice excluded them and the impact this was having. He even invited women to share their experiences and supported them when they did. This built men's awareness and ownership of the problem. Men were then engaged to identify solutions to the inequality they had created, which was the final step.

The aim was never to remove the PlayStation or the game, but to provide women with an opportunity to play. For women who don't like PlayStation, the aim was to give them access to the same informal social opportunities the men had and used to develop relationships with senior leaders. As such, male leaders committed to spending one-on-one time with each of the women in their teams, which included regular coffees, lunches, or breakfasts. In addition, leaders identified an activity the whole team could undertake to ensure everyone interacted more. These leaders doubled down on their investment to level the playing field by spending time and effort to engage the women on their teams. This is something all men can do.

Barrier #4: The Confidence/Competence Catch-22

What do you have to do to advance at work? Despite popular beliefs, formal processes don't play a major role in determining promotion decisions. Rather, individuals need to be well known in the organization and make an impact through their work.[23] This often involves having exposure to high-profile opportunities like special assignments or important projects. Accessing these opportunities requires confidence. People who get promoted are confident—they engage in behaviors to demonstrate their ambition, assertiveness, and self-assuredness. This matters because how confident people think you are affects their perceptions of your competence—not your actual levels of competence or confidence but rather how much of these traits people think you have.

Women are often encouraged to be more confident, proactive, and assertive at work. This is often offered as a solution to the belief that women lack ambition. Displaying these traits will demonstrate their ambitiousness. However, research finds that men and women (at similar levels in an organization) have the same career aspirations.[24] Women don't lack ambition; they just can't demonstrate it in the same way men do for good reason. When it comes to ambition, women face a trade-off: if they demonstrate dominant, assertive, confident behaviors they will be less likable. Yet these are the very behaviors they need to demonstrate to get ahead. To solve this, women are often encouraged to put up with not being liked. But this isn't a true solution because likability is important.

Research finds that when women demonstrate ambition it decreases the likelihood they will be hired (because they are less likable); in contrast, it has no impact on men's hirability.[25] When women demonstrate confidence and ambition, they are ignoring the standards people hold for how women should behave. As a result, employers think they lack required so-cial skills and are less willing to employ them. When women are viewed as less confident, they are also seen as less competent—limiting their access to high profile projects, assignments, and development opportunities—negatively impacting their promotability.

This lose-lose situation is even more difficult for African-American, Asian, and Latina women. Research finds that they are more likely than white women to face the triple burden of racism, sexism, and classism. In practice, this means women of color must display leadership behav-iors that do not reinforce any of the various stereotypes related to their minority status. Specifically, women of color are required to be confident and assertive in a way that doesn't disrupt gender norms and reinforce racist stereotypes. Something as simple as speaking up carries with it the burden of triggering gendered racist stereotypes. For example, a survey of 259 black women found that 90 percent had experienced microaggres-sions related to the "angry black woman" stereotype.[26] This experience of everyday discrimination through microaggressions had a negative impact on black women's psychological health. Attempts to live up to the ideal leader standard comes at a detrimental cost to all women, but in different ways and amounts.

IT'S NOT YOU:
Amy Cuddy on How Competence Shapes Perceptions of Confidence

In 2018, I interviewed Amy Cuddy, body language expert and former professor and researcher at Harvard Business School, on the topic of con-fidence.[27] In the interview, Cuddy and I discussed how confidence can impact people's perceptions of women's competence at work. Cuddy says research clearly demonstrates that perceptions of confidence and compe-

tence are extremely highly correlated. "If women are seen as less confident, people attribute that [lack of expressed confidence] to a lack of competence. But really this is about what women think they are allowed to do. Women are simply trying to conform to the [gender] stereotype of their group," she says.

Living up to these stereotypes is something Cuddy says women are socialized early on in life to do by the adults in their lives. "Little kids don't differ. Boys and girls behave similarly. In middle school, at around age eleven you really start to see the change in how girls carry themselves. They start to make themselves smaller. They worry about weight and actually want to be smaller," says Cuddy.

This isn't about asking boys to take up less room, rather it is about giving girls the freedom to take up more space early on. "Girls still feel that looking strong is risky. We can make it safe by encouraging it. Then we won't be dealing with questions when people are in their forties about how to get women to speak up in the boardroom," says Cuddy.

It seems there is no right way to be a woman at work. To advance, women need to be assertive and warm if they want to avoid backlash. To be seen as competent, women need to be ambitious but not dominant. Living up to these impossible standards is a tall order for anyone. In my PhD research, women participants shared how trying to maintain this delicate balance resulted in stress, mental exhaustion, and self-doubt. Women felt they could never live up to this impossible standard, which ironically knocked their self-confidence.

When it comes to the behaviors needed to get ahead at work, women walk a fine line that slowly chips away at their self-belief, which is something that men never experience. This is supported by 2016 research findings which highlight the global gender gap in confidence, with men from forty-eight countries consistently reporting higher levels of confidence than women.[28] Perceptions of confidence matter. They determine how competent people think women are and this can determine the opportunities women are given to advance. It isn't surprising that research finds women are less likely to be given opportunities that provide high visibility and potential for recognition.[29] Navigating the confidence/competence catch-22 not only negatively impacts women's mental and emotional health, but ultimately it costs women in terms of their career advancement. To combat this, organizations need to remove the barriers women face accessing opportunities, by investing in women's career development.

THE FIX: Invest in Women's Diverse Work Experiences

What does it take to succeed at work? A 2001 research study, published in *Gender, Work & Organization*, examining this issue found that men and women believe access to the right opportunities is the key to progression. To progress, employees need to be able to demonstrate their competence by undertaking high-profile assignments, projects, and job opportunities. But accessing these opportunities requires confidence, which is demonstrated by engaging in Don Draper behaviors. However, doing so only serves to penalize women because of invisible barriers like the confidence/competence catch-22. Is the Don Draper ideal the standard of success in your organization? Consider the following questions:

✔ Are employees rewarded for being ambitious, competitive, and self-promotional rather than for their ability to work with colleagues to achieve outcomes?

✔ Do leaders care about achieving results, regardless of how they are achieved and the impact this has on employees?

✔ Do leaders favor employees based on personal preferences and exclude employees who are dissimilar to themselves?

✔ Do employees feel comfortable being themselves at work? And do leaders try to support the needs of employees outside of work?

✔ Does your job reward people who commit all or most of their time and energy to the organization? Are you expected to work long hours and even weekends to advance?

Living up to the Don Draper standard costs all of us, but particularly women, as it limits their access to career development opportunities. This is why it's so important to know if the standard for success you are being asked to live up to is in fact costing you.

To remove this barrier, men and women in managerial roles must support young women early on with accessing opportunities to demonstrate their competence. This includes encouraging, nominating, and supporting young women in their organizations to access a diverse range of development experiences—like leading a high-profile project or undertaking an international job assignment. This support will ensure women have access to opportunities to demonstrate their capabilities, which will enhance their long-term career success.

Barrier #5: Performance and Pay Inequality— aka, the Performance Tax

Before embarking on my MBA in 2008, I sat down with a male mentor to discuss my career ambitions. I already had a master's degree and two undergraduate degrees along with nearly eight years of international work experience. I thought my mentor wanted to have this conversation because he supported my development. Instead he opened our meeting by telling me how he nearly enrolled in an MBA program, but soon realized that he could easily become a leader without one. Shaking his head, he looked up at me and said, "I just don't get it, Michelle, why are you doing this? It seems like a lot of work, why bother? You don't need to prove anything."

My white, male, middle-class, straight mentor assumed that his experience of working life was the same as mine. He thought that if I worked hard, I should be afforded the same career opportunities as him, but he couldn't have been more wrong. Like me, a lot of women constantly work to prove that they are capable, competent, and ready to lead. My boss was a thirty-two-year-old senior manager in a leadership team with absolutely no women. In fact, there were no women leaders my age in his entire company. Women work hard, and often a lot harder than men, by gaining extra qualifications and skills or achieving higher performance standards and taking on extra projects. Women do this not because they necessarily want to, but because they have to.

Women are not perceived to be as competent as men to start with, so they essentially begin their careers with a perceived deficit. To overcome this, they have to pay a *performance tax* at work and consistently exceed expectations to prove they are equal to their male peers. The performance tax is a significant barrier to accessing pay and promotion opportunities.

For example, research finds that, when it comes to evaluating men's and women's ability for a role, women face higher performance standards than white men.[30] Specifically, if women apply for a senior role, like chief of staff, white men will be rated higher on objective criteria for the role, like years of experience or qualifications, even if women have the same abilities. To achieve high-performance standards, all women must outperform their male counterparts to prove that they are just as competent. This performance tax is the price women pay for not being Don Draper. To be considered as capable as men, women need to be exceptional. And they are. Not only do women maintain a higher standard of performance, but they do this while engaging in a very narrow range of behaviors resulting from the mismatch between their gender and the success prototype.

Women are aware of the higher standard of performance they are expected to live up to. In fact, being aware of it presents a challenge for women, often referred to as the *stereotype threat*. When women are aware of the negative stereotypes people hold about them (for instance, the stereotype that women are bad with numbers), and they are put in a stereotype-relevant performance situation (like completing a math problem), then women are likely to feel vulnerable because of the risk involved with potentially living up to these negative stereotypes. Women who work in traditionally male-dominated STEM fields (science, technology, engineering, or math) face increased pressure to perform simply because they are women. In turn, this pressure detrimentally impacts performance. Simply being aware of the negative beliefs about your capability can adversely impact your performance.

This is not just a gender issue. Women also face stereotype threats related to their race. Research finds that black, Hispanic/Latinx, Asian, and Native American female respondents have all reported feeling that their achievements were invisible to their organizations, despite the organization overly scrutinizing their performance.[31] For example, as a double minority, black women are hard-pressed to ensure they don't confirm people's negative stereotypes related to their race or gender. They do this by going above and beyond their role requirements and consistently exceeding expectations. This is even more challenging for black women who are the "first" or "only" to work in a particular environment as they often feel like their performance represents their entire minority group. As such, black women who are the first or only employee in their domain feel tremendous pressure to perform at a high standard. However, the performance tax ensures that even if black women outperform their peers, they are likely to receive limited recognition and praise, making them feel self-conscious, invisible, and devalued.

Men and women are also held to different standards when it comes to taking risks and making mistakes. Any error made by women only serves to reinforce the idea that they are not as competent as men. While women pay a *performance tax,* men are given a *performance bonus.* When men make mistakes at work, it doesn't confirm people's view of them as less competent. Instead, they are seen as trying to develop.

This plays out in women's careers in meaningful ways. For instance, it's often said that women hold themselves back by only applying for roles for which they meet all of the job requirements. This idea became widespread following the publication of the popular book *Lean In: Women, Work, and the Will to Lead,* where author Sheryl Sandberg references an internal report at the technology company Hewlett-Packard. The report revealed that women only apply for open jobs if they think they meet 100 percent of the job criteria, while men apply for open jobs if they meet 60 percent of the requirements. Sandberg writes, "This difference has a huge ripple effect. Women need to shift from thinking 'I'm not ready to do that' to thinking 'I want to do that—and I'll learn by doing it.'"[32]

But women aren't shortchanging themselves; the patriarchy is. Men have the luxury of being able to take career risks, try new roles, and make mistakes at work without being penalized for it. Men can afford to work in a role they are not qualified for or take on a stretch assignment because failing is simply equated with learning. When women fail, they confirm the gender stereotype and are deemed incompetent.

The performance tax is evidence that we devalue the work, contribution, and performance of women. This creates a ripple effect, limiting women's career opportunities and earnings. When it comes to promotions, women are likely to receive less favorable ratings if they engage in behaviors that differ from the success prototype. For example, research finds women receive lower performance evaluations and fewer promotions if they are perceived as less dominant.[33] Fitting the success prototype pays, because we value masculinity more than femininity. A 2008 research study published in the *Journal of Applied Psychology* finds that people have a tendency to value "male" jobs like a teacher in industrial art or editor of an automotive magazine more highly than "female" jobs like a teacher in elementary school or editor of a food magazine. Even when jobs do not differ on any factors that contribute to pay, this study found that salaries will be higher for jobs that are considered more "male"— the average salary for "male" jobs is $39,651.71, for "female" jobs it's $36,527.31.[34] A job is simply seen as less valuable if it's associated with femininity. For example, the study found that an automotive magazine editor salary (male job) was $47,471 and the food magazine editor salary (female job) was $42,934, even though the job requirements were exactly the same.

The performance tax has a ripple effect, which limits women's pay and promotion opportunities. Women across the board earn less than men after controlling for job experience, education, and other factors that could impact pay. The unexplained share of the gap is attributed to discrimination and this tends to be greater for women of color. The 2016 research report *Workplace Justice: The Wage Gap: The Who, How, Why, and What to Do*, published by the National Women's Law Center, states that for every dollar earned by a white man, an African-American woman earns 60 cents, a Latina woman earns 55 cents, for Asian American women it is 84 cents, for Native Hawaiian and Pacific Islander women it is 62 cents, and for Native American women it is 59 cents. Lesbian women make less than men for undertaking the same work regardless of men's sexual orientation. For transgender women, the average earnings fall by nearly one-third after transition. Women with disabilities who are employed fulltime will be paid just 65 cents to every dollar that men without disabilities are paid and 72 cents to every dollar men with disabilities are paid.[35]

While we like to think that the pay gap is only an issue for women later in their careers, new research finds that this is something that impacts all women from the moment they enter the workforce. In a 2018 report published by the consulting firm Accenture, "Getting to Equal 2018—Spotlight on Young Leaders," 2,907 young professionals working in corporations were surveyed; the findings showed that within the first five years of working life, professional women on average earn 6 percent less than professional men, across a range of sectors.[36] Women earn less because they receive fewer pay increases; the report relates that within the first three years of working life 67 percent of professional men reported receiving pay raises compared to 56 percent of professional women. The pay gap not only highlights the inequality women and men experience when it comes to earnings, but it also represents the different way we value and treat men and women at work, which makes the performance tax and associated pay inequality a culture issue.

For example, one of the common misconceptions about the pay gap between men and women is that women earn less because they don't ask for a salary increase as often as men. Consequently, women are encouraged to develop their ability to negotiate, speak up, and ask for what they want. In reality, studies show that women ask for a pay raise just as often as men, but they are 25 percent less likely to be given one.[37] Asking women to close the pay gap may in some cases lead to a pay increase, but it will cost women in other ways. When women assert themselves and ask for what they deserve they are perceived as difficult, pushy, and aggressive because they are violating standards society holds for how women are meant to behave, as outlined in chapter one. These standards exist because fundamentally workplaces devalue women and their contributions, which is why the pay gap exists in the first place.

THE FIX: Be Transparent About Pay and Promotion Decisions

The way to close the performance and pay gap is to create a culture of equality at work. For example, research conducted by Accenture in 2018 reveals that in cultures of equality women are likely to earn up to 51 percent more. In these companies, women trust that the organization adheres to "equal pay for equal work."[38]

One way to create trust is to be transparent about pay and promotion decisions. In 2018, Verve, a technology firm based in the United Kingdom, decided to practice pay transparency. They gave all employees access to the salary information of their coworkers, managers, and even the chief executive officer.[39] According to the company's website, a key motivation for this was closing the pay gap. When organizations track, report, and share salary information, they have to own any gender discrepancies. Making salary information available to all employees is a clear sign an organization is committed to pay parity.

In Verve's case, the benefits have been far-reaching. Since they released the first salary report in July 2018, their quarterly workforce survey found that employees feel they are paid more fairly and there is greater transparency and clarity when it comes to negotiating pay. Employees also reported feeling more engaged overall.[40]

Even if your company doesn't support transparency when it comes to pay, this is something each of us can practice. Managers can be more open when it comes to sharing the reasons behind their decisions related to how work gets allocated, why certain capabilities are promoted, and what the standard for success looks like. Every supervisor can evaluate what "good" looks like in their teams and determine if this is being applied unfairly with their direct reports. This can include regular discussions to unpack questions like the following:

- ✔ Are the reasons behind reward and promotion decisions clearly understood?
- ✔ Are the performance and reward processes transparent?
- ✔ Do women and men have a clear understanding of what they need to do to get ahead?
- ✔ Do women feel like they are required to do more than men to advance?

✔ What subjective criteria are important for roles and do these criteria favor men?

✔ Are women given an opportunity to learn and make mistakes in the same way as men?

✔ Is there a gender pay gap and are employees aware of this? Does the pay gap exist across the organization and its various levels or is it more noticeable in certain parts of the organization, and how is it being addressed?

It's important for employees to play a role in this. The only way managers can know if trust is being created is to ask the men and women who work for them. Employees can share their questions or concerns and ask for more information about decisions made in the organization. They can also point out when that transparency is lacking.

Workplaces need to take extra steps to demonstrate transparency and build trust in order to make strides toward gender equity. This starts with leaders, because they are best placed to create the right environment for open and honest conversations. Chapter nine provides five actionable steps leaders can take to create environments where women can thrive.

Barrier #6: The Invisible Load

If you have ever been to a women's conference or professional development program, you will most likely at some point hear women say that they don't feel good enough. This is the toll that the invisible barriers take on women. After several years in the workforce, women are often more aware of inequality. The barriers outlined in this chapter show up at different and multiple points in these first few years. These barriers can be hard, if not impossible, to navigate alone. When women fail to work around the invisible barriers, they often start to believe they are not cut out for working life or not good enough, which makes solutions aimed at "fixing women" so popular.

This is something that impacts women every day. Like my friend Claire, who after five years in her role as a consultant for a professional service firm finally got promoted. But straight after telling me the news she said, "What if I'm not good enough? What if they took so long to promote me because I don't have what it takes? What if they only put me here to shut me up? Do you think I just got lucky?" When, like Claire, we come up with explanations for why things are the way they are, we are making attributions. Generally, there are two types of attributions people make: internal attributions, such as linking men's success to their natural leadership capability; or external attributions, like putting men's failures down to bad luck.

The environments we work in not only influence the attributions we make about our own performance, but they determine the attributions we make about other people. When women and minorities are successful, companies are more likely to attribute that success to things like luck. Women who engage in behaviors associated with the success prototype will still be disadvantaged by the attributions people form regarding their success or failure.[41] Female employees who are more assertive, dominant, and outspoken consistently receive more blame for their company's failure compared with women employees who are more communal and nurturing. Also, when women make mistakes at work, they are seen as "lacking ability," while men are often viewed as "having a bad day." Attribution is something that both men and women do, and it happens because we are holding on to the belief that women are not as capable as men.

The longer women remain in organizations, the more likely they will be exposed to marginalization, which negatively impacts their sense of belonging and self-esteem. Environments play a critical role in the attributions we make about men and women at work. Research finds that when women work in "unwelcoming environments"—whereby they are treated negatively or in stereotypical ways and underrepresented in leadership positions—they are more likely to discount their own success and internalize their failures.[42] Consequently, women worry whether people's judgments of their competence will be influenced by gender stereotypes. In fact, just witnessing the negative treatment of other women increases women's own attribution bias and makes them feel less confident.

These challenges are further compounded by race. A 2018 survey by Lean In and McKinsey finds 48 percent of women of color aspire to top executive positions compared with 37 percent of white women. Despite their ambitions, women of color face more hurdles in getting to the top, as they have to deal with less support from senior leaders, less recognition, and less access to promotion opportunities. Black women in particular have to work harder than white women to prove themselves, as they are more likely to have their expertise or judgment questioned.[43] Even when women succeed in negative work environments, their achievements are attributed to anything but their individual capability. This invisible barrier slowly chips away at women's confidence, self-esteem, and sense of fit with their organization. This is an invisible load all women carry to varying degrees.

THE FIX: Support Your Sisters: Use What You Know to Lighten the Load

When women encounter invisible barriers at work, which negatively impact their confidence, self-esteem, and ambition, they can disrupt this cycle by calling out the barriers and sharing what they know with other women. This might be as simple as naming these challenges when they show up for women in your workplace—like I did with Ariel. As soon as Ariel recognized the barrier, she stopped internalizing it. But it took me calling it out and explaining it to make her aware.

This is a small but powerful way women can come together and support one another. Developing a deep understanding of what the barriers are that all women face and sharing this information with the women in your workplace can change the way they see themselves, as women no longer have to question their capability. This is also how we free each other from the invisible load inequality forces us to carry. This practice can dissolve the mental and emotional strain that comes with internalizing the invisible barriers we encounter every day and the belief that our differences are weaknesses. Calling the barriers out is how we educate our colleagues and remind all women of an important truth: *It's not you, it's your workplace.*

Shining a light on the first six barriers helps men and women see the many ways women are set up to fail. This awareness is the antidote to our own denial. When women can recognize their personal experience within the barriers and see the way these challenges exist in their organizations, it makes the invisible barriers easier to navigate because it becomes obvious that these challenges exist not because of women, but because of the way workplaces function. This is the starting point for changing how we see ourselves and each other.

6.

The Endurance Phase
Balancing Management and Motherhood

Even if women advance early in their careers and make it to a managerial level, there is no escaping inequality. Most women experience the second career phase between thirty-six and forty-five years of age, and often this is the most difficult time in their professional lives. The midpoint in women's careers is when the gloves come off and organizations must decide who best fits the leadership prototype—this tends to be white men.

For example, the "Women in the Workplace 2018" study, conducted by McKinsey in partnership with LeanIn.Org, surveyed more than sixty-four thousand employees and finds that women enter corporations at roughly similar rates to men, at 48 percent and 52 percent, respectively.[1] However, by the time they reach a managerial level women's representation has dropped to 39 percent and men's has increased to 61 percent. This is when the effects of inequality start to take hold and become evident in the unequal representation of men and women in leadership positions.

Attrition does not explain this difference, but gender inequality does.

Men and women leave organizations at similar rates and have similar intentions to remain in the organization. Very few women and men report any intention to leave work for family reasons. The main difference between men and women is that women are less likely to be hired and promoted into managerial roles. These challenges exist whether women have children or not. The inequality women face at work is intensified for mothers who must overcome additional invisible barriers created from the incompatibility of motherhood and working life.

The second phase in women's careers is all about enduring inequality. While women have new challenges to overcome, the barriers from the first phase can still show up. There is no expiration date on discrimination. The only difference between women in the first phase and women in the second is that now women are likely to feel dissatisfied and disenfranchised with their employers. Having been in the workforce for ten years or slightly more, women's advancement starts to stall, and the day-to-day sexism, exclusion, male favoritism, and marginalization are starting to weigh them down.

> *There is no expiration date on discrimination.*

Women want to work for better organizations. They want meaningful work. They want achievement, recognition, opportunities, and satisfaction from their hard work. Instead, in this important second phase of their careers, when women should be coming into their own in the workplace, women are offered a whole new set of invisible barriers to contend with. As if motherhood wasn't hard enough, workplaces have some additional difficulties in store for all women who care for dependents, including children or elderly parents. The mere fact that women survive this phase, and for working mothers in particular, is ironically what makes every woman valuable to organizations. We don't just do our jobs. We achieve the impossible.

We don't just do our jobs. We achieve the impossible.

Barrier #7: Negative Gender Norms

I can still remember how I felt the day I became a supervisor for a large multinational organization. I had finally made it. I was now a leader. My hard work and effort had finally paid off. I felt determined to do everything I could to succeed. But there was a catch: I didn't know the rules had changed.

I was confronted with this reality on my first day when I walked into the office kitchen where some of my direct reports and my boss, who had hired me, were hanging out. They were all men. My boss looked up at me and smirking said, "Hey, Michelle, there are dishes in the sink, and you are a woman, so, you know, wash them." Everyone laughed, as I stood there in disbelief. Was I in a scene from *Mad Men*? While his remarks were blatantly sexist, they were also unexpected. The person meant to lead, support, and champion me was openly mocking me because I was a woman. The men I was newly appointed to manage were laughing at me. This was only day one.

In that moment, no one could look me in the eye. Except my boss, who was staring right at me with a smile on his face as if to say "gotcha." And he had, in many ways, gotten me. If I complained, it would mean that I couldn't take a "joke." If I laughed and played along, I would be mocking my gender—a pretty core part of who I am—and undercutting my own authority to manage and lead. Welcome to the thin line women walk in gendered workplaces. The only way out of this exchange is if someone steps in and calls my manager out on his sexism, which no one was willing to do.

Caught between these two bad options, I chose to stand up for myself. "You have two hands, why don't you wash the dishes yourself. Unless you don't know how?" I said as I walked out of the room. The response that followed was almost predictable: "I was just kidding! Why can't you take a joke?"

Later that day, my boss tried again. In our one-on-one catch-up he mentioned the kitchen incident and said, "This is why I hate working with women—they can't take a joke." I was the only woman on the team. Instead of supporting me and helping me tackle the challenges I would face as a woman leader in a male-dominated environment, my boss chose to openly mock my minority status. It became clear to me in that moment: *I might have had the title of manager, but he was never going to treat me like one.*

Gender and power work together to marginalize women at work. Biological sex—whether you are male or female—is not the same as gender. From a young age, we are socialized to understand what it means to live up to prescribed gender roles, which depend on the environment we are in and the people we interact with. Gender is more than just a way of classifying people; it is a frame of reference we use for interacting with the world around us and includes the shared beliefs we hold for how men and women are meant to behave. Not everyone fits into these socially constructed, prescriptive, binary choices, which is why people often identify with a range of sexual and gender identities. However, overwhelmingly, men and women are largely encouraged and even required to live up to the binary, traditional gender roles. When we identify with these roles, they serve as anchors to our own behavior by continually pulling our actions in line with the shared expectations society holds for men and women.

Not all gendered behaviors are negative. But when gendered behaviors result in the discrimination and harassment of women, and become normalized over time, like those outlined in the chart "Examples of Negative Gender Norms at Work," they create cultures of inequality. This includes any efforts to dismiss, undermine, bully, humiliate (verbally or physically), harass, assault, or overpower women. It also includes any behaviors that result in men gaining preferential treatment. For most women, these behaviors show up in day-to-day encounters and exchanges with men—what I call *inequality moments*. This happens every time men try to maintain their powerful position by belittling women and making women aware of their less valued status. My boss's behavior in the opening story is a perfect example of this. His "joke" made it very clear that because he was a man, he didn't need to burden himself with domestic duties like doing dishes, and, by extension, that because I was a woman, my true place was in the kitchen, not in the workplace.

Negative gender norms are compounded by other areas of difference as research finds that roughly 64 percent of all women encounter negative gender norms, like microaggressions associated with having to provide more evidence of competence and having judgement questioned.[2] However, black women are more likely than other women to have their competence and capability questioned. Similarly, lesbian women, bisexual woman, and women with disabilities are more likely to face increased exposure to discriminatory and demeaning comments related to their minority status.

> *Inequality is created in day-to-day moments.*

Gender inequality still exists in most workplaces, because organizations try to solve the issue with structural initiatives, like targeted policies, programs, or training initiatives. But inequality is created in day-to-day moments and informal social interactions, which vary in their magnitude depending on the context. This makes some *inequality moments* difficult to spot. Like asking women to take notes in meetings, rather than sharing this responsibility equally among attendees. Or making comments about a woman's appearance, which on the surface may seem complimentary but ultimately has sexual undertones. If left unchecked, these interactions become accepted, repeated, and normalized over time—setting the standard

EXAMPLES OF NEGATIVE GENDER NORMS AT WORK

Features of gendered workplace cultures	**How this shows up through our shared standards of behavior at work**
There is a shared acceptance that when it comes to leadership, men and masculinity are valued more than women and femininity.	✔ Employees demonstrate a willingness to engage in behaviors that support and reinforce the masculine leadership ideal. This includes any behavior that demeans, devalues, and dehumanizes women— like asking women to wash the dishes in the sink because, well, this is women's work! ✔ Employees tolerate behaviors that negatively impact minority groups at work. This includes accepting the preferential treatment of men. Speaking up is not encouraged or supported and may even come at an individual cost.
Leadership is displayed by largely following a command-and-control style. Good leadership is seen as setting the direction and having employees unquestioningly follow.	✔ Employees demonstrate a transactional, authoritative working style, which doesn't foster collaboration, innovation, creativity, and diversity of thought.
There is a shared belief that employees experience the organization in the same way. The organization denies individual identities at work by encouraging employees to conform to the success prototype.	✔ Employees do not value difference, and they feel pressure to conform to the ideal worker standard by hiding their different identities. This includes not feeling comfortable sharing individual identities or differences related to gender, physical or mental abilities, sexual orientation, religion, age, ethnicity, or race.

Aggression and dominance are taken for granted as the means to achieve results.	✔ Employees that succeed have a pushy and combative interpersonal style supported by a willingness to exclude others or make them feel uncomfortable. This includes engaging in microaggressions such as speaking over others, dismissing different viewpoints, and excluding minority groups from decision-making processes. ✔ Minority employees feel devalued, excluded, and unimportant. Over time, all employees do not speak up or try to change the status quo.
Competition and performance are valued over people. This is supported by policies and practices that reward what is achieved rather than how it is achieved. At times self-interests are put ahead of the organizations.	✔ Employees tend to focus on achievement at the expense of outside work interests. Work is considered the number-one priority—there is little regard for the impact this creates on individuals. ✔ Employees come to accept that profits are more important than how those results are achieved, in terms of equality and environmental sustainability. But this idea is a masculine norm, as women place more importance on having a positive impact than achieving short-term financial gains. For instance, women are even more willing to accept a 15 percent lower salary if their organization provides an opportunity to make a long-term impact on social issues.[3] ✔ At times employees and leaders support actions and decisions that are not in the best interest of the organization, shareholders, or community.
The workplace accepts and rewards individuals who achieve results by working long days, managing significant workloads, and denying their home life.	✔ Employees demonstrate a competitive workstyle and willingness to do what it takes to succeed— even if this comes at a cost to themselves or their coworkers. ✔ Employees feel pressure to put work ahead of their health, happiness, well-being, and family needs. ✔ Leaders do not prioritize employee work-life balance because they are not aware of how this results in increased employee satisfaction, engagement, productivity, and profits.[4]

for behavior at work. These *negative gender norms* are the building blocks for organizational cultures, which feed gender inequality.

While these behaviors are likely to be experienced throughout a woman's career, they become particularly noticeable when women take on managerial roles. According to research conducted by Deborah O'Neil and Diana Bilimoria in 2005 at the Weatherhead School of Management, Case Western Reserve University, when women start work in their twenties and thirties they have a predominantly internal sense of control over their careers, meaning that women believe being driven and assertive is the way to get ahead.[5] However, as women approach their forties, only a third have an internal sense of control over their careers, as they come to understand that workplaces are not a meritocracy. Part of the reason for this is as women approach managerial positions, the gap between men's and women's career trajectories significantly widens.

Remember Sarah from the introduction, and how she was passed over time and time again for her promotion? Well, this is an example of how the gap between men's and women's careers begins to take hold in the second phase. There was really not much else Sarah could do to advance. Without having people advocating for her and removing the invisible barriers to her advancement, she might never have been promoted. Sarah isn't alone. Women are generally less likely to be hired into manager-level jobs, and they are far less likely to be promoted into them. Women come face to face with inequality, often at the exact moment they are ready to take on leadership roles.

IT'S NOT YOU:
Sallie Krawcheck on Disrupting Gender Bias at Work

Sallie Krawcheck, founder of Ellevest, the digital financial service for women, was one of the most senior women to work on Wall Street. Krawcheck started her own business after being ousted from Merrill

Lynch in 2011. She has firsthand experience battling gender bias and holding her own as one of the few female executive leaders in the industry. At the New Yorker TechFest in 2016, Krawcheck said the reason she was fired from Merrill Lynch was because she was a woman, and board members dismissed her because she didn't follow the typical boys' club mentality, which is pervasive in banking and finance.[6]

In 2017, I interviewed Krawcheck to discuss her experiences with gender bias and to find out what women can do to manage these negative behaviors. "Women don't need to be fixed; they just need to take back their power. The world is really coming our way. The days of command-and-control style are numbered," she says. While women are making progress, the day-to-day challenges associated with managing gender bias, like navigating the invisible barriers women face at work, can be exhausting. Krawcheck says her number-one piece of advice for women is to start talking about gender biases, and if they feel comfortable, to share their experiences.

"Most people are well intentioned. We all have gender biases and that is because of how we were brought up. If I bring it up and talk about it, people will want to learn about it or understand it. Even if they don't agree. My view is if you get smart about it and have the courageous conversation, good people will want to learn about it." This can be as simple as pointing out behavior when it happens. Like in a team meeting when an employee refers to women as darling, sweetheart, or girl, both men and women can call this out, by explaining how this language can limit women's legitimacy at work and cause people to devalue their contributions. If employees don't feel comfortable raising these issues in a team meeting, they can provide the feedback one on one. This is how men and women can support one another and start to push back on everyday experiences of discrimination.

Inequality is particularly challenging for women managers because of the continued acceptance and denial of *negative gender norms* at work, examples of which are outlined in the table on pages 152–53. For example, according to one study, about 82 percent of the 350 male CEOs surveyed agree that the key barrier women face at work is a lack of general or supervisory experience. However, only 47 percent of the 461 female leaders surveyed agree that this is a key barrier.[7] This difference comes down to the widely held belief, established through the patriarchy and outlined in chapter one, that women are simply less capable than men. This shows up when men say things like "She needs more time to round out her experience" or even "She needs more time to prove herself" about women (like Sarah) who are just as experienced as their male colleagues. Experience is not the issue here. Women must overcome the widespread belief that they are just not as competent as men.

Research by Fatima Tresh, Dr. Georgina Randsley de Moura, and Abigail Player from the University of Kent found that male job applicants with a high level of leadership potential are rated as a better employment prospect than a female job applicant with a proven leadership track record. We assume men are capable and have what it takes to do the job, so we don't weigh actual experience as heavily—it's just not as important.[8] This is how inequality is invisible to most of us.

But the day-to-day inequality moments are often hidden through silence. Patriarchal beliefs come to life in the negative behaviors men and women engage in at work. When these behaviors are repeated over time, they become tolerated, adopted, and accepted as the way things get done. The impact becomes hard to see and often conditions employees into silence. Think about that exchange with my boss in the kitchen; no one spoke up. A few of my team members came up to me afterward to express their irritation, but they also said that they didn't feel they could say anything because everyone was laughing and he was their boss too. It is even harder to question behaviors if they are endorsed or perpetuated by leaders.

While this puts women at a distinct disadvantage, it's bad for all of us. Research finds that working in a misogynistic work environment has negative consequences for the well-being of men and women within that environment, even if they are never on the receiving end of harassing behavior.[9] This includes any behavior considered rude or condescending toward women. When employees see female coworkers being marginalized and discriminated against, their mental and physical health deteriorates—particularly if the organization doesn't act to correct this behavior. This makes discrimination, marginalization, and sexual harassment an organizational issue, not an individual one.

THE FIX: How to Fight Back

Nearly all of us have witnessed inequality. It might be the person who makes offensive comments, watches inappropriate content at work, mocks colleagues, constantly hits on women or makes them physically uncomfortable. While we all know this person, how many of us have said something? When we don't speak up, we are legitimizing the behavior, which makes it normal. It also makes it the victim's responsibility to manage.

To push back against the barriers in your workplace, it helps to ask questions. My husband is a perfect example of this. It is important to mention that he is a middle-class white male in a powerful position at a major corporation—and a feminist in training. Over the years, I've explained the concept of the gendered organization to him. As he became more aware of the issue, he started to notice some of the challenges women faced in his organization. He started to call these barriers out by asking why. For example, his manager mentioned in a one-on-one conversation that a woman on his team shouldn't be promoted because she was getting married and might want to have a baby. My husband asked one question, "Why? Why is this even a part of the decision criteria?" By asking that simple question, he pushed back on invisible discrimination as it was happening. She got promoted.

You have the power to advocate for yourself and your colleagues. When decisions are made in your workplace about women or minorities that limits them or their advancement, always ask why. Why is this requirement used for promotion decisions? Why are we not asking the same of men? Why do women need to do more to be considered for a promotion? Why can't mothers lead? Why are there so few women leaders in our organization? If you are ever unsure about whether to ask why—whether the situation is an example of an invisible barrier—consider if the situation is something a man is likely to experience. Would men's promotability be limited if they got married? Is a man's leadership capability questioned when he becomes a father? If the answer is no, then push back. Keep asking why until the real problem surfaces.

Each of us can speak up when colleagues are being marginalized or excluded. Some companies even formalize this through bystander-training programs, which educate men and women on how to anticipate, recognize, and intervene in these situations before they happen. The key is that companies cannot con-done dismissing, mocking, or harassing bystanders when they *do* speak up. Leaders need to maintain zero tolerance when it comes to negative gender norms. By doing so, they will reset the way employees engage with one another, which over time trans-forms the entire culture.

Barrier #8: Role Conflict: Manager or Mommy?

"We can't promote her. She's getting married and won't want to take on a new role. Besides, she is probably on the 'mommy track' and will be having kids soon, so there is no point promoting her." Believe it or not, this is something I have heard male leaders say countless times over the course of my career. During my role in HR, I would take part in the year-end succession planning processes, where leaders would discuss who would get promoted. Time and time again, women would be overlooked or held back by outdated and unsubstantiated comments like this.

Worse still, some hiring managers would ask women applicants in interviews whether they plan to have children—and then use this infor-mation to make the hiring decision. It is often understood that all women want to have children at some point and that this is bad for business. It is believed that mothers won't be able to handle the increased responsibility. Even if hiring managers don't ask candidates this question, many manag-ers make guesstimates about when women might want to have children and then factor this into hiring or promotion decisions. Women can ex-perience barriers associated with motherhood even if they never intend to become mothers themselves. The assumption is that women are always less committed to work because they are preoccupied with either looking for a partner, settling down, getting engaged, having children, or caring for dependents. Of course, men generally also take part in every single one of these experiences, yet somehow these nearly universal life milestones are not used to determine their hirability.

Often around the midpoint of their careers, women are hit with the reality of taking on two conflicting roles, the "ideal worker" and "ideal mother."[10] According to typical gender stereotypes, a man's primary role in life is to go to work and provide for his family, while a woman's primary role is to produce and raise children. The expectation is that women who work will still be the perfect mother, caretaker, and wife—as well as the ideal worker. Men, however, are still largely expected to fulfill their one role as breadwinner. While the number of women in the workforce has steadily increased, workplaces still do the bare minimum to accommodate parents, making it incredibly challenging for women and men to manage both roles. Workplaces still require men to live up to the breadwinner role, and this makes it impossible for men to accommodate fatherhood without it having a detrimental impact on their careers and their well-being—something that is revealed in more detail in chapter eight.

> *While the number of women in the workforce has steadily increased, workplaces still do the bare minimum to accommodate parents, making it incredibly challenging for women and men to manage both roles.*

When I was pregnant with my first child, I thought that my employer was one of the good ones because they had the following "family-friendly" policies:

✔ Paid maternity leave policy of no less than sixteen weeks
✔ A return to work program to support mothers coming back into the workforce
✔ Childcare provisions or subsidies
✔ Return to work bonus schemes, which includes a percentage of parental leave paid out to mothers and fathers who return to work
✔ Maternity coaching
✔ Keeping in touch days, which includes up to ten paid days for parents who want to come back to work for a few days while on parental leave
✔ Flexible workplace policy, offering employees flexible hours, remote work options, or a reduced work schedule. Often this policy is created with working mothers in mind
✔ Breastfeeding facilities

We're encouraged to see these policies and programs as benefits. With all these initiatives in place it is hard to imagine what else a working mother would want. After all, these programs are how companies demonstrate that they value mothers, right?

No, it's not. At first this might sound a little harsh, particularly given that a lot of companies might not be able to afford these initiatives in the first place. But these benefits do not guarantee that leaders and employees will value and support mothers and fathers equally, which is something every organization can do. Although these benefits make it easier for women to manage aspects of motherhood, they don't address how mothers are treated, rewarded, and valued at work.

Women who might have been considered for leadership roles often find that their dedication and capability are called into question as they approach motherhood. Simply being at a point in life where society assumes that women might want to have children can stall their career progression. Motherhood is a clear sign women are betraying the ideal worker standard. When women go on maternity leave, return to work, or take up flexible workplace practices, they face a range of beliefs and behaviors that serve to devalue them and their contribution. This is another invisible barrier women face when trying to endure the impossible task of managing motherhood and working life.

> *Motherhood is a clear sign woman are betraying the ideal worker standard.*

Motherhood changes the way we view women as workers. Research undertaken in 2008 by Eden King of Rice University finds that working mothers are negatively impacted by stereotypes, which limit their income and expected advancement.[11] These stereotypes include:

- ✔ The belief held by managers that mothers are less committed to their work, even though mothers and fathers have similar levels of commitment and in some cases, mothers are even more committed because they wanted to provide for their family.

- ✔ Women cannot manage motherhood and leadership roles. Therefore, when mothers return from maternity leave, leaders may demote them to lower status roles with the belief that they are "helping mothers" manage their dual roles.

- ✔ All women, but particularly mothers, are expected to be more sensitive, emotional, and social than men. Working mothers need to behave in a passive, caring, and nurturing way, which simply doesn't fit the Don Draper prototype or the image of the powerful dominant leader.

✔ The assumption that all women want to have children because it is a "woman's duty" to be a mother. Because leaders assume all women will have children and this will affect their leadership capabilities, they limit their development and advancement opportunities.

✔ Working mothers are believed to be less capable and mentally tough compared to their child-free coworkers because working mothers don't fit the prototypical image of the ideal worker. As a result, leaders often give working mothers fewer challenging assignments or assume they don't have what it takes to lead.

✔ Mothers are not as ambitious as men or child-free women. Managers assume mothers don't want to advance because they are focused on motherhood. Because of this, mothers are overlooked for promotion opportunities and their performance or contributions may go unnoticed. Managers may also decide to withhold high-profile assignments or development opportunities, often without ever consulting the employee.

These beliefs are all forms of the modern sexism discussed in chapter two, and they show up in subtle ways that are widely accepted yet undermine women. Many leaders who hold these beliefs limit their female employees' career opportunities because they think they are being helpful. Engaging in modern sexism sabotages women's careers because it aligns all women with stereotypical gender roles.[12] In turn, women are less likely to be taken seriously, developed, or promoted. Workplaces can no longer afford to ignore a leader's behavior when it comes to supporting a mother's advancement at work. Even with the most family-friendly policies in place, a mother's ability to thrive at work will always depend on the sponsorship and support she receives from her manager.

BEST BUY: The Case for Family-Friendly Leaders

In 2001, American electronics retailer Best Buy began implementing a program that fundamentally changed the way the organization approached working hours. This was known as the Results Only Work Environment (ROWE) and the idea was simple: Employees were free to manage their time as they saw fit so long as they delivered on what was required. Time spent in the office didn't matter, it was all about output. Employees could manage their schedules to fit in with their home life.

Seth Stevenson, author of the 2014 Slate article "Don't Go to Work," writes that a number of studies identify a range of benefits associated with the ROWE approach to work, including increased productivity, reduced turnover, increased employee morale and well-being.[13] Despite these benefits, in 2013 the incoming Best Buy CEO, Hubert Joly, decided to get rid of the entire program.[14] In a 2013 Business Insider online article Joly is quoted as saying that ROWE is "fundamentally flawed from a leadership standpoint" because it required that leaders set objectives and delegate to employees how those objectives are met, which Joly says is not always effective.

Empowering employees to manage their own work schedule is not about simply delegating tasks and walking away. Rather than simply giving orders and having employees blindly follow, leaders need to provide ongoing coaching, advice, feedback, and development to support employees with the delivery of their work.[15] When companies implement programs like ROWE, they are in effect transforming the culture of an organization. This means leaders need to change. The way managers delegate, interact with, and reward employees needs to change. Without concerted effort, it's too easy to revert to the Don Draper success prototype and create 9-to-5 workplaces inspired by Taylorism—outlined in chapter one. If companies don't have the right leaders in place, then programs like this will never last.

To create work environments that work for parents, leaders need to create new norms when it comes to how employee contributions are valued. It's too easy to just go back to what we know, but opting for more of the same is not how we change the composition of workplaces or solve the issue of inequality at work.

Even if workplaces have the best benefits in place, they can be the worst offenders when it comes to devaluing women. The 2014 research paper "Giving Up: How Gendered Organizational Cultures Push Mothers Out," published in *Gender, Work & Organization*, finds that mothers are presented with two options when it comes to their work life. They either have to work long hours and use after-work hours to socialize with work colleagues to demonstrate their commitment to work or reduce their work hours and face being downgraded to a role that doesn't utilize all their capabilities.[16] This is just a waste of talent, which isn't good for businesses or women. Family-friendly policies put a Band-Aid on the real problem. When organizations dismiss home life as distracting and unimportant, it places a lot of stress on individuals who are balancing important roles at home with their work. Reducing work hours or working a flexible schedule can often come at a hidden cost to women, who are stigmatized and believed to be less productive and committed to work.

> *Family-friendly policies put a Band-Aid*
> *on the real problem.*

Gender stereotypes ensure that women must manage the demands of a working life, as well as domestic and childcare responsibilities. Integrating these dual roles takes a lot of planning and structure. This makes working unpredictable hours and spending time socializing outside of core working hours difficult. Unfortunately, this is the real "flexibility" that organizations want because it signals that an employee is truly committed to her work. When mothers can't live up to this ideal, they are perceived as less devoted, which curbs their career advancement.[17]

IT'S NOT YOU:
Arianna Huffington On Stress, Burnout, and Managing Role Conflict at Work

Role conflict is an incredibly difficult barrier for women to manage, but the challenges are compounded by the need for employees to always be available and responsive to work issues. In 2018, I interviewed Arianna Huffington, founder of the Huffington Post and founder and CEO of Thrive Global, to discuss how women can manage the difficulties associated with role conflict.[18] "Workplace cultures have been created by men who believe the illusion that to succeed you need to always be on. Never disconnecting," Huffington says. The pressure to constantly be connected is even more detrimental for women, who continue to manage commitments at home and work, and therefore have a higher chance of experiencing stress and burnout compared to men. "I feel we need to recognize that despite so many efforts to improve the numbers—in terms of how many women are on boards and in executive positions etc.—they have not really budged. We need to recognize that something is wrong with workplace cultures, which is that they are fueled by stress and burnout," she says.

Ultimately Huffington says this is a terrible way to work, as it is stressful, tiring, and impairs employee's decision making. Huffington says the best way to tackle this issue is to start with small things: "Like, do you have a room for mothers to go to pump milk for their babies? This sounds obvious but I have spoken to plenty of professional mothers who are in tears because they have to pump in the bathroom. Or are women expected to bond with their colleagues at drunken parties? We need to give multiple ways for people to bond with their colleagues to help advance their career." Outside of this, every employee can make a commitment to respect their colleagues time outside of work by limiting those early-morning meetings, Sunday emails, and after-hours work phone calls.

Adopting family-friendly policies is pointless unless employees can utilize them without being penalized for doing so. Researcher Heejung Chung, from the Faculty of Social Sciences at the University of Kent, conducted a survey of 2,767 parents and nonparents and found that 32 percent of participants believe flexible work hours lower an employee's chances for promotion.[19] Also, one out of five workers who used flexible work arrangements in the past twelve months experienced a negative consequence at work, like being perceived as lacking commitment and/or ambition or were unfairly penalized with reduced rewards, pay, and promotion opportunities. This is overwhelmingly an issue faced by mothers who are more likely to say they experienced negative career consequences due to their own flexible arrangement.

If we want to create cultures that value the contributions of mothers and fathers, we must tackle the negative attitudes and assumptions leaders hold about working mothers. We need to make sure all policies or programs don't perpetuate gender stereotypes, but instead free men and women to manage their home lives. We need the right kind of managerial behaviors at work to ensure both men and women are not stigmatized for utilizing these programs. Creating an enabling environment for working parents to thrive is about having the right culture in place that supports *all employees* with managing their dual identities.

> *Creating an enabling environment for working parents to thrive is about having the right culture in place that supports* **all** **employees** *with managing their dual identities.*

THE FIX: Practice Family-Friendly Behaviors at Work

Each of us can support our colleagues in managing the integration of work and home life. This starts with understanding the identities, challenges, and interests our co-workers have outside of work and supporting them. For employees, this might be as simple as not calling out or shaming colleagues for leaving early or being transparent about your needs. For men, it may mean being open and honest about taking time off to care for dependents. When men and women start to own their needs it takes the shame out of having a life outside of work. And when men are open about their responsibilities at home, it means this isn't a "woman's" issue, but is instead a human need.

Leaders have a critical role to play in this. Generally, organizations prefer a one-size-fits-all approach to supporting parents or anyone who wants to reduce their working hours for personal reasons. This is why most companies approach this issue in a standardized way, with one flexible working or dependent care leave policy. But if workplaces want to retain parents, they need to start seeing the individual, which includes considering the unique situation of every employee.

In practice, leaders should take the time to understand the needs individual employees have and identify ways to accommodate them. For example, managers could check in once a month with their team members to understand any challenges they face integrating work life and home life and identify what, if any, support is needed from the organization to help manage this. These needs are likely to change over time, so these conversations can't be one-off events. They need to be part of a consistent, ongoing effort by leaders to demonstrate that they value the contribution of men and women equally.

Barrier #9: The Part-Time Penalty

In 2017, I was working away from home, hosting a UN Women event in New York. After managing an entire event with more than three hundred attendees, I was exhausted and ready to head home to my kids in Texas. As I was leaving a female attendee turned to me and said, "Michelle, you work so hard. Who watches your kids when you're away?" I didn't even look up from what I was doing, I just automatically replied, "The other person who helped make them."

This was a programmed response, because like so many working mothers, I am used to getting asked this question. But the world has changed since the Don Draper days. Working mothers are the norm. There is a common misconception that working mothers choose to work rather than care for their children, but a lot of women have to work. According to the U.S. Department of Labor in 2017, around 70 percent of mothers with children under the age of eighteen work. In 40 percent of households, mothers are the primary breadwinners.[20]

Because many mothers need income, part-time employment is often put forward as the solution working mothers have been waiting for. But the truth is many women are forced to take part-time work because it is the only way to stay employed while caring for children or earn a living when full-time employment isn't an option.

In the United States, women make up two-thirds of all part-time employees.[21] Of women who work part-time, some volunteer or choose to do so primarily because they are still considered the primary caretakers at home.[22] For example, a 2019 survey of 546 mothers, by parent resource app Winnie and online talent marketplace The Mom Project, found that for an overwhelming 81 percent of mothers, childcare was a key factor in their decision to work or not. And 53 percent of mothers stated that childcare costs greatly influenced their decisions regarding work.[23] Part-time work is not really a choice. It's a necessity for many women because they are still mainly responsible for housework and childcare. The only way for these mothers to accommodate both roles and manage the associated childcare costs is to work part-time.

However, a lot of women who work part-time really can't afford to. Mothers in the United States at the lower end of the income scale are much more likely than more affluent mothers to say they'd like to work full-time. Women who work part-time but would rather work full-time are more than twice as likely to be poor.[24] The Pew Research Center finds that 40 percent of mothers with annual family incomes of less than $50,000 would prefer to work full-time (this is known as involuntary part-time employment). This is compared to 25 percent of mothers who have incomes of $50,000 or higher (who are voluntarily employed part-time).[25] Organizations that allow employees to work part-time treat this as a benefit, but there are very few women who have the luxury of being able to view it in this way. Part-time work is not a benefit, but because it is treated like one, it makes it easy to ignore the various ways it limits women's career advancement.

GIRL UP: The Case for Co-Leadership

Job sharing is a good way to overcome some of the penalties women face with part-time work. Anna Blue and Melissa Kilby, coexecutive directors of Girl Up, an organization founded in 2010 by the United Nations Foundation, are working mothers who decided in 2018 to share leadership responsibility for their organization.

In a post they cowrote for LinkedIn, Blue and Kilby outline why sharing leadership roles makes a lot of sense for parents[26] and argue that companies need to create more opportunities for parents to lead. Job sharing is one way to do this because it enables two capable employees to manage a senior leadership role. Companies effectively get two employees for the price of one. It's also good for working parents who want to dial back their hours without sidestepping their careers.

While some organizations might worry about potential downsides of job-sharing senior leadership roles, such as concerns about who is in charge or confusion over accountabilities and who employees need to follow, Blue and Kilby recommend that organizations trial role sharing to see if it can work well for them. Enabling opportunities for employees to lead together encourages women and men to advance while managing their interests outside of work. Blue and Kilby state that companies like Oracle, Warby Parker, and theSkimm have all found success with co-CEOs. If workplaces want to support working parents, they need to be willing to rethink traditional approaches and try new ways of doing things.

More and more organizations like Microsoft, Airbnb, and Twitter are providing employees with access to maternity and paternity leave, which can range anywhere from sixteen to fifty-two weeks in some cases. There is just one catch. Often these policies only apply to full-time, salaried employees. While policies like this one are extremely generous, they are not helping all women. Family-friendly policies and programs are often linked to an employee's salary and job status, which means that part-time or temporary workers don't qualify, even though part-time workers often need these benefits the most.[27]

It is not just the benefits women stand to lose. Working part-time carries with it a wide range of career-limiting penalties. For example, when women transition into part-time work, they are often demoted to a lower-level role, carrying out tasks that are well below their capabilities. Part-time workers regularly earn less per hour for the same work as their full-time counterparts and are often denied promotion opportunities.[28] All of the penalties associated with part-time work often go unnoticed in organizations. If companies want to remove the barriers to women's advancement at work, they need to start by providing similar levels of support to their part-time employees—the majority of whom are women.

THE FIX: Get the Basics Right

The penalties associated with part-time employment in workplaces today are a significant barrier to women's advancement. The basic biological fact is that most working women and men are likely to have children at some point. Workplaces were not designed to accommodate this, which is why valuing all employees in the same way starts with getting the basics right. This includes providing part-time employees with the same access to family-friendly policies as their full-time counterparts.

While not every organization can offer unlimited parental leave, those that can should commit to extending this benefit to part-time employees. At a minimum, all companies can agree to treat and value mothers like they do all employees—regardless of the hours they work. Removing the stigma associated with part-time employees requires that leaders revalue part-time workers, which can include any of the following actions:

✔ Pay part-time employees the same hourly wage as full-time workers for undertaking the same work.
✔ Provide the same benefits (pro-rated or not) to full- and part-time workers.

✔ Put checks in place to ensure part-time workers' capabilities are being fully utilized.

✔ Provide opportunities for part-time workers to job share to enable career development.

✔ Provide part-time workers with career development planning and support.

✔ Provide opportunities to change role requirements to reduce working hours.

✔ Create meaningful career advancement opportunities for part-time employees.

These actions ensure that part-time employees are equally utilized, developed, and rewarded as their full-time counterparts.

Barrier #10: The Motherhood Tax

When I became a mother for the first time, I was given access to a maternity coach through my company, which is a bit like a career counselor who helps mothers transition back into the workplace. In our first meeting, the counselor asked me what difficulties I anticipated experiencing returning to work. All I said was "Confidence." I had never lacked self-assurance in this way before, but I was struggling with it after becoming a mum. When I asked my coach why I was experiencing this crisis of confidence, she assured me this was a challenge all working mothers face with going back to work. Six years and two children later, and it's clear to me the crisis of confidence mothers face is less about our own insecurities and more about how to endure the constant management of motherhood and working life.

In hindsight, my lack of confidence coming back from maternity leave makes complete sense; my new identity was incompatible with my workplace. How can mothers be confident working in an environment that doesn't value motherhood? There are a limited number of ways mothers can respond to this challenge. The first is to simply hide motherhood. Literally. According to research, pregnant women often feel unwelcome at work.[29] Consequently, many women try to hide the effects of pregnancy, by presenting themselves as physically well even when they are tired or unwell. Women invest a lot of time and effort hiding their pregnancy behind loose-fitting clothes to try to fit into work cultures that never valued their womanhood to start with. When it comes to motherhood, women face an unwritten rule: workplaces will tolerate pregnant women deviating from the ideal worker if they continue to try to live up to the ideal by hiding their pregnancy. This rule applies throughout motherhood, as workplaces want men and women to work as though they don't have children. However, society requires that working mothers raise children as though they never work.

> *This rule applies throughout motherhood, as workplaces want men and women to work as though they don't have children.*

Another strategy that women can adopt is to simply work harder than anyone else. Research finds that pregnant women often feel the need to do more and prove themselves after announcing their pregnancy.[30] Women need to work extremely hard to overcome negative gender stereotypes regarding their capability. However, when women become mothers, they need to double these efforts to overcome unfair, negative perceptions of their performance. These assessments are unjustified, as research shows that mothers are more productive before and long after childbirth.[31]

In fact, a recent study by the Federal Reserve Bank of St. Louis investigated this by analyzing the productivity of ten thousand academic economists through assessing the amount of research they published as a measure of performance—a common benchmark for academics. Over the course of a thirty-year career, mothers consistently outperformed women with no children at nearly every career stage. Mothers with two children were the most productive,[32] which is evidence that mothers are indeed performing at a higher level.

> *In the United States, mothers suffer a per-child wage penalty of approximately 5 percent per child, on average, after controlling for the usual factors that affect wages.*

Working harder than everyone else is particularly difficult for working mothers to maintain given the demands they face at home. As of 2015, dual-income households made up 66 percent of families with children under the age of eighteen, and there were only 28 percent of families where fathers were the only breadwinner.[33] Despite this, women continue to manage the majority of household and childcare responsibilities. When it comes to primary breadwinners in married households, working mothers who are the primary breadwinners are three times more likely than working fathers to manage children's schedules.[34] Working mothers must manage the roles of mother and worker, even when they are the primary breadwinner. As hard as this is, even if women succeed and manage the dual roles with no overlap, their managers will *still* believe that they struggle to manage work and family because the two are simply incompatible.[35]

Mothers are stigmatized, which reduces their opportunities for promotions and advancement.

Mothers who manage to fulfill both roles are also unlikely to be rewarded for their efforts. A great example of this is the motherhood penalty. In the United States, mothers suffer a per-child wage penalty of approximately 5 percent per child, on average, after controlling for the usual factors that affect wages.[36] According to the National Partnership for Women and Families, in 2019 the wage gap for mothers is larger than for women overall.[37] Mothers with full-time, year-round jobs are paid 71 cents for every dollar paid to fathers—a gap that has not changed in more than thirty years.[38] The motherhood penalty exists for all women regardless of their education level, and on average this costs every woman $16,000 a year in lost wages, according to an analysis of census data by the nonprofit advocacy organization National Women's Law Center in 2018. For example, fathers who earn a master's degree or a doctoral degree are typically paid $100,000 and $115,000, respectively. Conversely, mothers with these same degrees are typically paid no more than $90,000 annually.[39] The reason for this persistent gap is discrimination.

> *Mothers with full-time, year-round jobs are paid 71 cents for every dollar paid to fathers—a gap that has not changed in more than thirty years.*

Research investigating this issue compared the outcomes of fictitious job applicants who had the same qualifications, background, and experience.[40] The only item that differed was their parental status. Participants making the hiring and salary decisions discriminated against mothers, believing they were less competent and committed than non-mothers.

Men did not experience the same discrimination. In fact, fathers were perceived as more committed and were offered higher starting salaries. The "motherhood penalty" may account for a significant proportion of the gender gap in pay, as the pay gap between mothers and non-mothers could in fact be larger than the pay gap between men and women.[41]

It's also important to understand that not all women experience the motherhood penalty in the same way. According to one study, the motherhood wage penalty is proportionally largest for the lowest-paid workers.[42] The wage penalty for every child of preschool age is almost five times greater for women in low-wage brackets compared to women in the high-wage brackets. In addition, women working in low-paying jobs tend to have less access to benefits and support from their organizations, which makes it harder to manage the demands and financial constraints of motherhood. While the motherhood penalty is an issue for all women, mothers who need the most financial support tend to face the largest wage penalty.

When it comes to pay discrimination, overall, mothers are likely to be worst off, especially the lowest paid workers. But the challenges do not stop there. The pay gap widens the more women differ from Don. While the motherhood penalty is an issue for all women, imagine how challenging it must be for mothers who are already having to overcome the pay gaps (as outlined on page 139) related to their race, ethnicity, sexual orientation, gender identity, and physical or mental ability.

While parenthood can be challenging for both working mothers and fathers, women face many more obstacles to overcome. This isn't only about paying mothers more; if it was that simple this issue would have been solved a long time ago. This is about creating work environments that celebrate, support, and encourage women and men to share their identities as parents. We can't achieve this if there is only one ideal worker image everyone is encouraged to live up to. Family-friendly policies, like maternity leave, flexible work, and dependent care enable mothers and fathers to manage their dual roles, but the workplace culture determines whether these efforts will succeed. Only by creating family-friendly cultures will we stop penalizing mothers financially and start to remove the various barriers they face at work.

THE FIX: Recognize the Mothers in Your Workplace

While recognizing all employees is important, this really matters when it comes to working mothers, given all the ways their contributions are undermined. Each of us can take action to shift the cultures in our teams when it comes to valuing the contributions of working mothers. This can include small actions, like telling your coworker they did a good job or recognizing their contribution at a team meeting. It can also include more impactful actions, like telling a coworker's manager when they did a good job or nominating your colleague for an employee award (if your company has that kind of program in place).

Leaders can also take the time to recognize the contribution mothers make by ensuring they are paid the same as their colleagues for undertaking the same work. As discussed on page 140, a policy of pay transparency can help achieve this. But managers can also commit to measuring and rewarding employees based on the quality of work they produce, rather than the time spent producing it. Given that mothers are very productive, this approach has the potential to solve a range of barriers working moms face when it comes to hours, performance, promotions, and pay.

Barrier #11: Carrying the Mental and Emotional Load

It's nearly impossible for mothers to feel like they are doing their best at work and at home. Being a good employee requires putting in long hours, which takes away from time at home and being a "good mother." When working mothers need to miss work for family reasons, they feel as if they are letting down their company or not living up to the ideal worker standard. Trying to succeed in each of these roles invariably means not fulfilling one of them—there is no win-win.

Nevertheless, women persist in trying and this adds to women's mental and emotional load, which is the mental and emotional labor associated with thinking, planning, organizing, and balancing the integration of work and home life. In 2018, U.S. childcare provider Bright Horizons conducted research investigating the mental and emotional load motherhood creates for women. In 2018, I interviewed Maribeth Bearfield, chief human resources officer for Bright Horizons, about the findings.[43] "While women are trying to advance their careers," Bearfield said, "they are still expected to be the leaders of the household. So even while women are holding similar jobs as men, they are being asked to do so much more outside of the workplace. The interesting thing is that year over year, mental load has increased for women, not decreased." Bearfield explains how the mental load has significant implications for career success, as women are often faced with a choice between their two roles, which is not really a choice at all. Mothers will always put their children first, and workplaces often perceive this as a sign working mothers are somehow less committed to work. This ultimately reduces opportunities for development and advancement.

IT'S NOT YOU:
Gillian Anderson on the Real Cost of Doing It All

Gillian Anderson, known for her role as FBI special agent Dana Scully on The X-Files, *wrote the book* We: A Manifesto for Women Everywhere *in 2016 with broadcast journalist and activist Jennifer Nadel.[44] I interviewed both Anderson and Nadel about their book, which aims to redefine work and success for women. Anderson, a mother of three, says the challenges women face at work are different from men's because women are expected to flawlessly juggle all the different (and often incompatible) responsibilities associated with work and home life.*

Women are expected to be everything to everyone, which comes at a great cost to their mental and emotional health. "We have been striving to have it all and we can indeed have it all, but once we do, we realize that it can be at the expense of quite a lot, including our sanity. We therefore have such high expectations of ourselves that we can find it hard to admit when we struggle under the weight of all the different parts of ourselves," Anderson says.

Anderson believes that part of the problem is how women have been socialized to relate to one another. "We have been taught to have a competitive edge over other women as we've fought for the limited female roles in the workplace, and over time, among other things, it has translated into harsh judgment and criticism of each other," she says.

To combat this reality, Anderson says women can begin to recognize and relate to one another in a more sympathetic way. This includes having more empathy for themselves and recognizing the heavy load they carry. "We are our own and each other's harshest critics and yet our very nature is in fact to be collaborative and compassionate. Now, more than ever, we need to work together," she says. Every woman can commit to a new way of relating to one another *and themselves—one that recognizes the different loads we carry and how remarkable we are for carrying them.*

In addition to managing the greater mental load, mothers also oversee the emotional needs of their dependents. A 2019 study, published in the journal *Sex Roles*, finds most of the middle-class American women surveyed maintain primary responsibility for managing their children's well-being and emotional happiness.[45] This is stressful because mothers don't have a lot of control over these challenges, and the potential consequences are significant. When women carry this load, on their own, it can lead to feelings of distress and emptiness, as well as marriage and life dissatisfaction.

This study only investigated this issue for married or partnered mothers. But what about single mothers? Imagine carrying the mental and emotional loads as well as the financial responsibility associated with raising children on your own. This heavy load disproportionately affects black and Hispanic women who make up 56 percent and 26 percent, respectively, of all single mothers in the United States. This combined load comes at a cost, as it negatively impacts employees' mental and emotional well-being.

Employers can play an important role in overcoming this. "The average person has over one hundred and fifty undone tasks on their mind at any given time. When the mind is trying to resolve these tasks and remember all of the things that we need to do, this increases stress and absenteeism, which is costing organizations billions of dollars," Bearfield says. To overcome absenteeism, organizations need to encourage employees to share their identities outside of work and practice family-friendly leadership behaviors that support all employees with integrating their work and home lives. This starts with being honest about the invisible load women carry.

THE FIX: Carry Your Share of the Load

When people ask me how I balance motherhood and work, I always say the same thing: "I don't, but we do. My husband and me." Turns out this is in fact the key to achieving balance for all working parents. A recent study found that when men and women are equally committed to managing both aspects of home and work life, it increases marriage satisfaction and feelings of balance.[46]

Both men and women have a role to play in this, as each of us needs to get comfortable with not conforming to prescribed gender roles. At home, this means keeping track of the various domestic responsibilities and determining who is going to carry the associated mental and emotional load. This is something I regularly have to do. My husband is a full-time senior executive. At the time of this writing, I was not only holding down a job, I was also completing a PhD. We both have two small children—and a dog for good measure. The only way we survive all the competing responsibilities is by talking about them. Every week, we discuss what the activities are and who can take on what. Generally, this involves writing things down on a white board for clarity. Every week looks different, but one thing is always the same: we treat our responsibilities inside the home as shared and outside the home as equally important. When the white board looks uneven, we talk about it. If someone is feeling things are unfair, we talk about it. There is no perfect solution to sharing the load or a prescribed list of tasks men and women can do because the only solution is to decide what makes sense for you. But I do know that the only reason you are able to read this book now is because my husband and I made having this weekly conversation a habit.

This also needs to happen at work. Both men and women can commit to stepping outside of prescribed gender roles by doing small things like being transparent about leaving the office early to go to the dentist, a parent-teacher meeting, or any activity outside of work. This is how we take the "ideal worker" mask off, and when we do this, it makes it easier for others to do the same. This is how we all can reset expectations and norms at work. While both men and women can do this, men are better positioned to bring about change through this one act, as they are the dominant group at work and don't face the same stigma when they become parents as women do. This puts them in a much more powerful position to change this standard, through small daily intentional acts.

As is hopefully clear by now, at this stage of a woman's career, the barriers really begin to take a toll. The cumulative impact of overcoming these challenges, often multiple times, negatively impacts women's mental and emotional health. Over time it starts to become clear that no matter how motivated, dedicated, and resilient women are, career success to a large extent is dependent on managers, colleagues, and leaders in organizations. As well as spouses and life partners who are willing to practice equality.

I distinctly remember reaching this point in my career, after the birth of my second child, when the inequality moments became innumerable and increasingly difficult to manage. I started to reevaluate my career and the same question kept coming up: If I was going to lead, despite these challenges, would it all be worth it? Would I get to engage in meaningful work and lead? This is a question that a lot of women ask themselves as they approach the third and final phase of their careers, when they want to make a contribution but still encounter barriers trying to do so.

7.

The Contribution Phase
Six Invisible Barriers Women Leaders Face

Imagine working for an organization where all women feel respected, valued, and supported. Where all employees believe the organization supports gender equality and that the CEO is personally committed to this. In this workplace, increasing the number of women leaders is not a public relations effort, but a natural outcome of every leader's commitment to equality. Despite operating in a male-dominated industry, the organization has achieved near parity across all levels of leadership, including the executive level, where nearly 40 percent of leaders are women.[1]

While this might sound far-fetched or impossible to achieve, this organization exists. Ultimate Software is a technology company that has consistently been ranked as the number-one place to work, especially for women. More importantly, employees openly share how much they love working for the organization, describing it as "An amazing place to work with a lot of great women to look up to," and "An extraordinary company for women" as well as "An organization and culture for all."[2]

We all deserve to work in organizations like this. Women deserve to lead in this type of workplace. But most never will. From around age forty-six to sixty women enter the third and final phase of their careers—the contribution phase. For many women, this coincides with taking on a senior leadership position. One of the key assumptions often made about women leaders is that they have managed to break through the glass ceiling, and they are now free to lead. But the barriers women experience do not disappear once they become leaders. In fact, women are more likely to be confronted with gender inequality when they lead because they are exposed to discrimination and marginalization at every level of the organization, as women leaders work in leadership teams and manage departments that are likely to be dominated by men.[3]

Women leaders do not have access to the same quality leadership positions as men do. They must also grapple with trying to lead workforces that don't see or treat them as leaders. Women must find a way to reconcile the Don Draper leadership ideal with their own leadership style. And worst of all, women leaders are often isolated, marginalized, stereotyped, and discriminated against. The fact that women lead despite all these challenges makes them remarkable. But what truly makes women exceptional is that despite spending their entire careers battling gendered workplaces, in the final phase of their careers, women want to give back. They want to make a difference. Women leaders want to contribute to their organizations, families, and communities. Women will work around the numerous barriers in this phase and continue to manage all the barriers from previous phases just to have the opportunity to do so. Imagine the impact women leaders could make if workplaces enabled them to succeed.

Barrier #12:
Access to Quality Leadership Opportunities

"It's all about bums on seats at the end of the day, Michelle. Women just want a place at the leadership table, so men need to give up theirs. That makes it hard for men to get behind all this gender stuff." This is an actual quote from a male leader I worked with following a presentation I had given on the different barriers faced by women leaders.

I was disappointed that this male leader continued to limit his definition of equality to giving women a seat at the table, as if this is effort enough and women are less deserving than men. Leaders love boiling equality down to a number, as if getting an arbitrary number or percentage of women in leadership positions means you've ended inequality once and for all. It makes things simple and it focuses everyone on achieving the same outcome, even if this does nothing to change behavior. Often these numerical aspirations are followed up with blanket statements like "Our business and employees need to reflect the communities we operate in." This seems like a strange thing to say, given that men continue to dominate nearly all positions of power in society. Equality is bigger than any number—especially when it comes to leadership.

One of the biggest challenges women leaders face is simply accessing the same types of leadership opportunities as men. Women leaders are often presented with lower-quality leadership opportunities because organizations don't value women's contributions and capabilities in the same way they do men's. According to 2005 research by Professor Alexander Haslam from the University of Queensland and Professor Michelle Ryan from the University of Exeter, women are more likely than men to be recruited for precarious, high-risk, and extremely challenging leadership roles.[4] This is known as the glass cliff phenomenon, and examples of it are everywhere, such as in the case of Mary Barra, who took over the position of CEO of General Motors in 2014 during the crisis over faulty ignition switches. Or Marissa Mayer, who took over as CEO of Yahoo!, the struggling web portal, in 2012. And Anne Mulcahy, who was promoted to CEO of Xerox in 2001 when the company was on the edge of bankruptcy.

These precarious leadership positions set women up to fail. Female leaders are often forced or compelled to take riskier roles because they don't have other leadership opportunities to choose from. Making the most of these opportunities tends to be the only option, but it's difficult to turn around the performance of a failing organization. Consequently, women leaders are often used as scapegoats to justify the lack of improvement, even though this was the most likely outcome to begin with. This then reinforces the idea that women leaders are just not as competent as men.

Riskier roles are often considered a good fit for women, even though the chances of failure are higher. One study found that women experience the glass cliff because people think they are better equipped to handle crisis situations.[5] Women can manage difficult situations because they know how to assume the caretaker role and manage a lack of social support. I recently interviewed Professor Haslam on his research findings, and he said one of the other reasons these roles are considered a good fit for women is because their careers are viewed as "expendable."[6] Women can afford to take risks and even fail because gender stereotypes ensure their perceived primary roles are still mother and housewife, unlike men, whose roles as breadwinners are core to their identity.

Leading a gendered, high-performing organization is extremely challenging for women, as they are defying the standard for what leadership looks like. When these high-profile women don't survive the glass cliff, their downfall serves to reinforce negative stereotypes people hold about their leadership capabilities. Consequently, women are often replaced with a white male leader, a phenomenon that happens often enough to have a name: the "savior effect." Even if women manage to survive the glass cliff by staying employed or turning things around, their performance is usually not rewarded. Research finds that regardless of the firm's performance, female CEOs are 45 percent more likely than male CEOs to be dismissed.[7] While male leaders are more likely to be retained when an organization's performance is high, the same is not true for women. When it comes to the glass cliff, it seems no matter what women do, they face the risk of being driven off.

Riskier roles come with greater penalties for failure, as a 2013 report by the management consulting company Strategy&, found that over a ten-year period, 38 percent of women leaders were forced to leave their positions as CEOs compared to 27 percent of male CEOs.[8] Despite taking on riskier roles, women have no opportunity to fail and simply fall off the cliff. For example, Jill Abramson was fired in 2014 from her position as executive editor of the *New York Times* after trying to lead the organization through the downturn in print media. Her departure sparked a national debate about gender bias and the glass cliff in organizations.[9] Or consider Marissa Mayer, who faced personal and professional scrutiny during her time leading Yahoo! as a working mother, and eventually left the organization.[10] Women don't have the same access as men do to quality leadership opportunities, opportunities to succeed or take risks.

This issue is even more challenging for racial and ethnic minority women. As of 2018, women of color made up only 4 percent of C-Level positions, which is significantly less than white women, who comprised 19 percent of these roles.[11] Women of color are expected to perform to a higher standard than white men and women, while at the same time they are less likely to have their achievements recognized and promoted by leaders. They also receive less support from managers with navigating organizational politics and internal networks. Women of color simply lack the sponsorship needed from leaders to get ahead.

IT'S NOT YOU:
Michelle Cowan: How to Pay It Forward at Work

Michelle Cowan is an Australian rules football coach and one of the few women to make it as a professional coach at the highest level of the Australian Football League. In 2019, I interviewed Cowan for my podcast to better understand what enabled her success.[12] "I was fourteen years old when I decided that I wanted to be a professional coach at the highest level in Australia. From that moment forward, I did everything possible to learn, grow, and be successful in that field," says Cowan.

She wrote to more than sixteen football clubs expressing interest in coaching. "There was one club that gave me an opportunity. This guy sat down with me and said, 'Michelle, we don't have any coaching vacancies at the moment, but I'm going to create something for you. I want to get you on board,'" she said. This enabled Cowan to break into the male-dominated industry and eventually coach men at a state level.

This is how male leaders can play a key role in enabling women's success. This is often a lot simpler than people realize. It starts with providing access to that first career opportunity, supporting women when they get it, and enabling women to advance into a leadership position. This is something that every leader can do.

The better leadership opportunities are reserved for men—something researchers refer to as the "glass cushion." As men make up dominant positions in organizations, they have access to a wide range of informal (predominantly male) networks, mentors, and sponsors who support them. This social support protects men from riskier positions, and, more importantly, provides men with access to better leadership opportunities.

But the reverse is also true. Men can play a key role in dismantling the glass cliff. A 2018 study, examining all women CEO succession events in the largest firms in the United States over twenty years, found that male predecessors play a critical role in determining the success of women leaders.[13] Generally, women leaders thrive in high-performing organizations when male leaders, who have been with the organization for a long time, sponsor them to take on the role. This often happens when the woman has also been with the company for a long time or has worked with a leader for many years, and this leader mentors, encourages, and even possibly nominates them for a leadership position. The same is true for poor-performing companies. This partnership effectively sets women up for success.

However, when women leaders are new to an organization, they tend to be less successful at turning a poor-performing company around, especially if inherited from a male leader who has been with the organization for a while. Male leaders play a critical role in coaching, mentoring, and grooming the next generation of women leaders because this ensures women have the social support and employee buy-in needed to lead. When men actively support women in this way, they reduce the negative effects associated with not fitting the male success prototype. Women successors who are given the same leadership support as their male counterparts are just as successful as them. Interestingly, while men benefit from most scenarios, their success was most pronounced when they took up leadership positions in new organizations. Being an outsider gave men an opportunity to distinguish themselves, as they naturally fit the success prototype.

THE FIX: Succeed Women into Your Job

When I worked for a male CEO of a large multinational organization, one of my tasks was to support him with his succession planning process. While we discussed his team members and their potential opportunities within the organization, he remarked how important this process was. He said the first task the board gave him was to find his successor and groom them to take over his role. This was an integral part of his success and legacy with the organization. The problem was, only white male candidates ever made it to the short list. Imagine, for a moment, if this CEO had committed to developing and preparing two or three women to take on his role. Or, better yet, if every male leader committed to mentoring at least one woman as a successor. How many male leaders today are doing this? Both men and women can make a commitment to advance at least one minority successor and invest time, energy, and social capital to find, retain, and develop these candidates. We need to afford underrepresented groups at work the same encouragement to lead as we do their white male counterparts.

Barrier #13: Stereotypical Typecasting

When people think of a woman leader, they often draw on the mental images society holds of women. The problem is that most of the labels used to describe women are gendered. Terms like "ice maiden," "bitch," "sweetheart," "slut," and "princess" are all used to describe gender stereotypical roles society holds for women. They represent the narrow way society views both women and women leaders.

In patriarchal societies, women leaders are forced to choose between fitting the male success prototype or the gender stereotypical role for women. Often senior women leaders must adopt more masculine behaviors to fit in, even though engaging in these behaviors separates them from other women. When women leaders reject behaviors associated with gender roles, they distance themselves from other women and men. Unfortunately, both options can be a lose-lose for women leaders, which results in their being typecast and labeled according to a gender stereotype. This can include describing women leaders as "soft" but nice, or "bitchy" but competent.

Typecasting matters because it distorts people's perceptions of women, which limits how they are perceived as leaders. When women leaders are stamped with a gender stereotypical label, it limits their effectiveness at work. All of this happens because women were never afforded the opportunity to define what leadership looks like for them. Instead they are given a label.

Patriarchy made it normal for men to be in positions of power, and women to be in subservient positions. Women who are ambitious or take on leadership roles upset this hierarchy and consequently encounter negative reactions from both men and women. These reactions often include undermining behaviors that are all attempts by employees to restore the status quo.[14] This can include things like mocking women leaders, devaluing their achievements, excluding them, and dismissing their ideas, direction, and contributions.

Men and women are used to engaging with male leaders but are often unsure of how to adjust their behavior to interact with women leaders. The combined impact of these challenges is the isolation of women leaders, who are subsequently labeled "queen bees" (for women who don't support other women) or a "bitch" if they come across as too assertive (a trait seen as a positive in male leaders). Once women leaders are labeled, it can be difficult to break free from these pejorative terms, which further limits their leadership effectiveness and advancement.

These terms are fundamentally sexist. There isn't a correlating term like "ice queen" for senior-level men.[15] Labeling women leaders is unhelpful and often perpetuates untruths. Take for example the "queen bee" label, which is frequently used for women leaders and which describes women who do not support other women at work. This label exists because senior women leaders are held accountable for advancing women in lower levels of the organization through mentoring, coaching, and remodeling. The label implies they aren't living up to this duty. But research shows this is something that women leaders actually do. A 2018 study found that despite the "queen bee" label, women in senior executive positions do in fact help women in lower levels of the organization to advance.[16] These labels are simply sexist myths that are used to marginalize women leaders.

IT'S NOT YOU:
Australian Politics as a Case of Stereotypical Typecasting at Work

In October 2012, Australia's first female prime minister, Julia Gillard, delivered a speech to Parliament during a debate about whether the speaker of the house, Peter Slipper, should resign for sending sexist text messages.[17] Gillard was addressing criticism from Tony Abbott—leader of the opposition party in Australia—about her support for Slipper. Gillard had endured many instances of sexism from Abbott over the course of her career, and her speech highlighted some of these moments. 'I was offended when the Leader of the Opposition went outside in the front of Parliament and stood next to a sign that said 'Ditch the witch.' I was offended when the Leader of the Opposition stood next to a sign that described me as 'A man's bitch.' I was offended by those things. Misogyny, sexism, every day from this Leader of the Opposition." Irrespective of your political views, Gillard is one of the few world leaders to publicly confront misogyny in politics.

Here Gillard so clearly captures the stereotypical typecasting that women leaders are forced to endure. Such labels dehumanize women and typecast them, further limiting their leadership effectiveness and making it extremely hard to be perceived in any other way.

I interviewed Gillard in 2019 and we discussed this experience.[18] She said the reason some people were taken aback by her speech is because at the time it was unusual to hear a very direct allegation of misogyny. "I think for many women it's come to be a speech that represents what they would have liked to have said themselves in a moment when they experienced sexism. I think that that speech helps deal with those frustrations and unlock a sense of power that it is possible to stand up and name and shame sexism and misogyny," says Gillard.

One of the strategies Gillard used to cope with these challenges was to develop a strong sense of self. "I think as women, in particular, we often sort of contract out our sense of self. How good or bad we feel about ourselves depends on how we think others see us. I think it's very important to have a sense of self that is stronger than that," she says.

Stereotypical typecasting is further compounded by labels associated with race, class, sexual orientation, ethnicity, religion, and disability. In a journal article published in *Advances in Developing Human Resources*, Professor Christine Stanley, from the Department of Educational Administration and Human Resource Development at Texas A&M University, writes that the lived experiences of black women are positioned within an interlocking system of race, gender, and class.[19] Society holds historical stereotypes of black women, which distort perceptions of leadership effectiveness. According to researchers Janis Sanchez-Hucles and Donald

Davis, racist labels people use include historical images like "Mammy," "Sapphire," and "Jezebel."[20] Consequently, racial minorities experience the compounded effect of racist and sexist labels, which further reduces their credibility, authority, and institutional support.

Stereotypical typecasting is often invisible because labeling women leaders is so commonplace but the impact differs depending on the labels used. Therefore, it's critical for leaders to unpack how stereotypical typecasting shows up differently for all women. A 2016 study investigating the intersectional effects of stereotyping found that white women were mostly described as arrogant, rich, and ditzy;[21] black women were branded as having an attitude, being loud, confident, and assertive; and Asian women were viewed as intelligent, quiet, and shy. These different labels lead to different negative outcomes for women. For example, the labels associated with white women meant that they were assumed to be more communal and likable but lacking in leadership qualities. Black women more closely matched the required leadership attributes but were believed to be less likable, while Asian women were perceived as more competent but lacking the necessary leadership attributes. The labels we apply to women leaders determine the way we expect them to behave and how we view them as leaders. If we want to ensure that women's individual identities and capabilities are recognized at work, then we need to start by creating environments, norms, and behaviors that enable this.

THE FIX: Mind Your Language

In 2017, Mayim Bialik, the actress perhaps best known for her role as Amy Farrah Fowler in *The Big Bang Theory* and Blossom Russo on *Blossom*, released a video blog in which she shared why it's important not to refer to women as girls. The video went viral with more than nine million views, and it sparked an online debate about the importance of language in shaping sexism and bias. I interviewed Bialik, who also has a PhD in neuroscience and a background in academia, to better understand how sexist language limits women at work.[22]

"I experience it in my workplace. To me the most disturbing set of comments I have gotten is from women who say 'Don't you have better things to think about?' That is how deeply ingrained this is. That we have even been taught language doesn't matter or that women or men who kick up a fuss about this are troublemakers," Bialik said.

Language matters. It reflects the values and beliefs we hold as well as how we view each other. Calling a woman girl, sweetheart, princess, darling, or ice queen are all labels that will determine the way other people see and value them. "Language shapes how we frame things in our brain and how we behave. I worked in academia, as a minority, as a woman, in the sciences and that [language] was profoundly disturbing in many ways. The way that males speak about female professors and students would shock a lot of people," says Bialik.

Language creates and reinforces cultures of inequality at work because often what is accepted becomes the norm. Most people are blind to the power of stereotypical typecasting. Only by examining the words we use to describe minorities at work will the impact language has become clear. For many leaders, doing so might be as simple as taking time to consider the way they talk about women and if these terms are ones they would use for men. For example, if leaders wouldn't call men "dear," "love," or "sweetheart," then they shouldn't refer to women in these ways—even if they believe they are being respectful. Outside of blatant labels, each of us can consider the terms we use for men and women at work and how this serves to diminish them. For example, calling women leaders "bossy," "difficult," or "bitchy" for speaking up or asserting themselves are all sexist depictions of them. To really understand the impact of our words, it is worth asking women you work with to share examples of how these terms are used at work and the impact it has on them. While this might be a brave conversation to have, as Bialik says, "We have to properly address things to get through the discomfort. It is up to all of us to start having these conversations."

Barrier #14: Identity Conflict: Leading like Women

What does it mean to be a woman today? The standards we all have for how "proper women" should behave were first developed in the nineteenth and twentieth centuries, when women learned to follow social rules related to how they dress, behave, and look.[23] Women who could live up to these standards were valued, liked, and respected.

Today, women are still required to live up to ideal standards of femininity, especially at work. Research finds that while male leaders are judged on the quality of their work, women are judged on their performance and appearance.[24] Women leaders need to "look the part" and strike a very careful balance to ensure they are not too feminine or masculine. How do women dress the part? By wearing fashionable clothes, manicuring their nails, maintaining a slim figure, and ensuring their hair looks just right. Women who don't live up to this standard are treated negatively by both men and women. Specifically, women who don't conform are met with disapproval, disgust, and loss of status, dignity, and respect as both leaders and women. However, women who manage to get it just right are rewarded and viewed as more powerful and in control.

Women's appearance plays an important role in how they are evaluated as leaders. Research finds that women who wear makeup, pants, and jewelry will be rated as more competent than women who wear a skirt without makeup and jewelry.[25] However, being liked is also important for women, and for this, women need to have loose hair and no makeup. If women leaders want to be perceived as both competent and warm, then the ideal look is no makeup, loose hair, jewelry, and trousers. Matching this standard is one way all women leaders can ensure they won't be penalized for their appearance.

The fix-the-women approach to overcoming this challenge might be to suggest all women should follow the ideal dress code at work, regardless of their individual differences. However, if workplaces want people to be their authentic selves, then they need to accommodate difference. We cannot penalize women for ignoring this misogynistic standard. Men's performance is not defined by how well they manage their appearance, so why is this a key criteria for women leaders? (Even though it can be argued that men are encouraged to wear a suit and tie, their appearance is not directly linked to assessment of their competence or performance. If it was, Mark Zuckerberg and entrepreneurs like him would have to ditch the hoodies.)

The challenges associated with managing the conflicting identities of womanhood and leadership do not stop at appearances. Gender is a core part of an individual's identity. It's something people enact at work through language, behavior, and even dress. Regardless of whether women leaders choose to adhere to the dress code or not, they all need to manage their conflicting identities. For example, when it comes to showing emotions at work, women leaders are penalized for even minor displays compared to men—especially when expressing anger or dominance.[26] For men, the ideal is to be emotionally restrained, but there is no similar strategy for women leaders. If women are cold and unemotional, they violate gender roles, as women are expected to be warm and softhearted. Managing this creates significant psychological strain as women are required to constantly regulate their emotions and reactions to prevent backlash.

Women leaders are extraordinary. They have to walk a tightrope of behaviors in order to lead. This makes women leaders the hardiest of survivors, as they have had to overcome one invisible barrier after another. This is supported by research, which found successful female managers are perceived differently than women in general.[27] They are in their own category as people view them as having fewer stereotypical attributes associated with women and more attributes associated with men. Women leaders are less likely than male leaders to be married or have children and they are more willing to sacrifice non-work-related interests in the pursuit of career success. Women leaders are exceptional, which makes them the exception not the norm. Because of this, women leaders are not representative of all women and shouldn't be used as examples of how equality has been achieved.

IT'S NOT YOU:
Jennifer Fountain on Being a Woman at Work

Over the course of a year, Jennifer Fountain transitioned from male to female while working as a senior leader in the financial services sector. Fountain had to grapple with the potential challenges and fall-out associated with transitioning in a traditionally masculine work environment. This was a risk worth taking, as she says Jennifer is her authentic self.

"Over the last year, I came out to most of my friends, family, and then finally to everybody in the workplace. I'm coming to work two, three days a week as Jenny. I need to build confidence in being able to be Jenny in the workplace before I can become Jenny in front of clients," says Fountain.

In experiencing the organization as a woman, Fountain noticed the heightened focus on her appearance. "Everybody looks me up and down rather than listening to what I say. The first thing they do when they meet me is look me up and down first and then 'Oh, yeah, what did you say your name was?'" Women are not only required to dress a certain way, Fountain says women also must learn how to be like men. "In our female career accelerator programs, we're trying to teach women how to be men, and basically speak Martian. The whole basis of everything that we do is to make women manlier rather than to liberate men to be who they are," she says. Living up to outdated leadership prototypes and gender stereotypes negatively impacts both men and women.

Fountain believes that most men have identities outside of work that they would never reveal in the office, and this conformity ultimately creates a dull, stale workplace. To change this, Fountain says workplaces need to be far less judgmental when it comes to their employees. This starts with educating people about difference. "They're so ill prepared for something that they don't know. When I came out to my boss (who knew nothing about being transgender), I was disappointed when a few months later, I was talking to him again about it and he still knew nothing," she said. Every leader can educate themselves, by reading, researching, and engaging people to understand different identities. "If one of my employees had come to me, I would have asked Human Resources for materials and support. I would have asked the person, 'Are you okay? Can I help?' I'd have made sure that support was available," she said.

Whether born out of necessity or choice, women leaders are encouraged to distance themselves from traditional womanhood and align themselves with the leadership ideal. However, the key reason many women pursue leadership roles is to change the status quo and advance future generations of women leaders.[28] Everyone stands to benefit from this. Research finds that women who view their gender identity in a positive light experience less conflict with their identity as a leader.[29] Women enjoyed leading because they didn't feel the need to suppress stereotypical behaviors women might engage in. Overall, this reduced stress, fatigue, and strain. However, gender is just one of many identities. When individuals perceive conflict between their identity at work and identities related to gender, race, ethnicity, nationality, and ability, they reported lower levels of well-being. This even extends to social roles, as conflict between motherhood and working life carries with it a range of negative outcomes.

SCOPE: Why Our Differences Shouldn't Be Barriers to Overcome

Scope is an organization that works to achieve everyday equality for fourteen million disabled people in the United Kingdom. Their strategy for realizing this is based on the social model of disability, which is a way of viewing the world developed by people with different mental and physical abilities.[30] It's the idea that society disables physically impaired people by assuming everyone experiences life in the same way. By not accounting for people's differences—one of which is physical impairments—we inadvertently exclude people from fully participating in day-to-day activities. This can include structural barriers, like not having access to handicap-accessible toilets, or social barriers, like holding negative attitudes and behaviors toward people with impairments.

In other words, Scope's strategy is to change the conversation by saying that people are disabled by the barriers they encounter in society, and not by their differences. By viewing disability in this way, we can begin to tackle ableism and start to identify all the barriers that prevent people with impairments from having equal opportunities in life. Creating equality and valuing each other in the same way begins with how we view the problem. This is the same issue we face when it comes to gender inequality at work. Men and women might work in similar environments and stay in organizations for the same amount of time, but they face very different barriers. None of us want to be discriminated or marginalized against because of who we are. A large part of achieving this starts with how we view inequality.

When employees' identities are not valued, it reduces their confidence, self-worth, self-esteem, and career satisfaction. For too long, women have had to change, hide, or adapt their identities to fit into the man-made world of work. If workplaces want to advance all women, they need to value women's identities in the same way they do men's identities.

THE FIX: Identify, Enable, and Embrace Different Identities at Work

More equal workplaces benefit everyone's careers and helps workplaces to attract talent as employees want to work for these organizations. For example, the consulting firm Bain found that the number-one factor that affects employee engagement is pressure to fit the ideal worker stereotype.[31] Employees who work for companies that embrace different types of workers and career paths are substantially more engaged than average—that is, they have a positive attitude toward their work and the organization. Using employee surveys to measure engagement, Bain found that men's engagement in these companies is two times the male average and women's is three and a half times the female average.

The bottom line is that it's in a corporation's best interest to work toward equality. White male leaders alone cannot provide the innovation and creativity needed for the future. Workplaces need to harness the multiple identities people have if they want to survive. Some workplaces are already doing this. For example, the management consulting firm EY[32] is seeking out people with autism, attention deficit hyperactivity disorder, and other disabilities, precisely because of the unique talents these employees have to offer.

To empower employees and work toward equality, we need to create different career paths that meet employees' different needs. This includes understanding employees' different ambitions, challenges, and career aspirations rather than adopting a one-size-fits-all approach. To do this, both employees and leaders need to be willing to try new approaches to work—like job sharing. This also includes advancing employees who contribute to the organization in new, innovative, and meaningful ways rather than simply rewarding individuals who fit a management standard that only serves themselves or a select few.

Barrier #15: Backlash: Influencing Without Authority

From a young age, we are taught what the appropriate behavior is for boys and girls. Through repeated exposure over the years we come to know how men and women are meant to behave. These beliefs are then used to make judgments about women at work. When women succeed in traditionally male-dominated roles, they defy the expectations society has for women and they are punished for it. One study found that when women lead teams with only male employees or teams with a mix of male and female employees, their status as a woman leader activates gender stereotyping, which negatively impacts how they are perceived as leaders.[33] These penalties can include social rejection, personal affronts, reduced rewards, and limited career progression.[34] When research participants were told that a woman was successful, without providing any further information, they assumed this woman was selfish, deceitful, manipulative, and cold. Women who do not conform to the feminine stereotype are more likely to be sexually harassed. One study even found that while 35 percent of all women experience sexual harassment, this issue disproportionately impacts women leaders and lesbian women.[35] This is backlash. Women don't have to do anything to create these negative outcomes. Simply being successful and occupying a role normally held by men will trigger social penalties. This is the backlash women face for defying gender roles by simply being leaders.

Successful women often disregard gender roles, which makes people uncomfortable. For female leaders, managing this is critical. Having people support you determines how well you can build relationships and influence people—in other words, how well you can lead. Leading through backlash can be an incredibly difficult thing to do, as it takes a toll on women's self-esteem and relationships. Backlash results in people disliking successful women and preferring male leaders. As society doesn't associate women with power, employees don't either, which is why it's acceptable to push back on women leaders and question their legitimacy. Not only does this limit women's ability to lead, but it also increases women's stress levels and anxiety and affects mental health. Fix-the-woman solutions encourage women leaders to try to be more communal and engage in stereotypical feminine behaviors to counteract this.[36] While this may help make women leaders more palatable, it's an incredibly misogynistic fix. We are basically asking women to make everyone feel better about their success. Smile more, speak softer, dress better, and do anything you can to put others at ease with your authority.

Simply engaging in the same behaviors as men at work will not ensure women are treated in the same way as men because of gender stereotypes. For women to lead, they need to influence without the likability or authority automatically afforded to men. And they must do this while managing masculine norms, invisible barriers, inequality moments, gender stereotypes, and backlash.[37] This is what makes women leaders so exceptional. They survive their workplace by developing an ability to interact, speak up, disagree, and engage with men and women in a way that limits their negative reactions. Imagine all the things women leaders could do if these difficulties didn't exist.[38]

THE FIX: Value Different Leadership Behaviors

To change the way employees behave toward women leaders, we need to change workplace cultures. This is something all men and women can do by supporting women to lead rather than undermining their leadership style for being different. It also means challenging gender stereotypical thinking. Statements like "Oh, she will be difficult to work with because she is a woman leader" and "Male leaders are less emotional" not only undermine women in general, but particularly women who are trying to lead in ways that differ from Don Draper.

Individuals in executive positions have a particularly important role to play in supporting women leaders. A 2016 study, titled "Leading at the Top: Understanding Women's Challenges Above the Glass Ceiling," published in *The Leadership Quarterly*, highlights the important role men can play in supporting women leaders, which can include verbally endorsing, advocating, encouraging, and championing them.[39] One participant in this study reported receiving significant backlash to her leadership appointment; however, her boss took a stand and threatened to resign if she did not receive the support needed to lead. Supporting women leaders like this is an intentional and powerful way for male leaders to spend their privilege.

Barrier #16: Isolation: In-group Favoritism

I have delivered countless training sessions in my career. One memorable session was an unconscious bias program I facilitated to more than two hundred leaders within a large multinational organization. Before the session started, we had the entire executive leadership team come up on stage and outline why this initiative mattered to them. As the leaders were all based in different locations, it was unusual to see them all standing together. At first glance, it was clear there is an equality issue given that there were only two women on stage—the remaining eleven leaders were all white, straight, able-bodied, middle-class men.

As the session went on, I noticed that not only was there a lack of gender diversity, but alarmingly six out of the eleven male leaders had the same first name: John. We were all so used to calling them by their last names no one had ever questioned why this was. There were literally more Johns on stage than women, which made me wonder how many women were even in the audience. So, I started counting the number of women at the session, which wasn't difficult given the sea of white male faces. There were about thirty. As the session ended, two male leaders seated next to me remarked how tired they were of all this "diversity stuff." They were not even sure why it was needed and argued the organization should do a better job of outlining the business case.

Sadly, this didn't surprise me. Based on my research, I knew this is something that a lot of men think, which makes sense. When everyone in your workplace, including those in positions of power, look, think, and act like you, there is only one way to be. Imagine for a moment what it must have been like for the two women leaders on stage who were not only numerical minorities in their own leadership team, but also within the entire organization.

A woman's experience of leading is a lonely one. Women leaders often express isolation as a significant barrier to overcome.[40] Women leaders struggle to fit in with male leaders and other women at work, which limits their chances of forming networks and alliances and generating the support needed to effectively work, manage, lead, or run a business. It also makes for a terrible work experience.

What about stepping out of traditional corporate America and forging your own way as an entrepreneur? There is a general belief that women business owners have more of an opportunity to escape the barriers that women working in male-run organizations in corporate America can't. Entrepreneurship is supposed to offer woman an opportunity to rewrite the rules and have greater flexibility and increased support. However, research indicates women who run their own business or work in the gig economy are often more excluded from accessing informal networks to secure work.[41] Men support other men, but do not support women in the same way. This in-group favoritism affects all women leaders. However, the more fluid and informal a work environment is, the more inequality is likely to go unchecked, which can further isolate women.

As discussed throughout this book, while it is difficult for white women to access male-dominated groups at work, it's a lot harder for women of color. White men are more likely to accept white women than black women at work.[42] For example, a 2003 study investigating the issue found that women of color have less access to informal social groups compared to men of color and white women, resulting in lower promotion rates and increased pressure to assimilate.[43] When it comes to the support, mentorship, and alliances that leaders offer one another at work, there is a pecking order that is built to favor the familiar. As men make up the dominant group at work, they are more likely to receive help and support from other men, compared to white women. However, white women are more likely to receive support and mentorship from white men and women when compared to women of color. This in-group favoritism serves to isolate all women leaders at work. But for women of color, this barrier limits their ability to progress and lead to a much greater extent than their white female counterparts. This issue is further compounded for women with disabilities who receive even less support and sponsorship from their managers than other groups of women. One in seventeen women in corporate America have a disability, and they experience more invisible barriers, like a lack of managerial sponsorship, mentorship, career development, and support.

In 2018, Pixar released a short-animated film titled *Purl*, which received more than ten million views on YouTube. The film highlights the in-group favoritism women working in male-dominated organizations experience. In the film, Purl, a pink ball of yarn (a representation of women), is excluded by her male colleagues (actual men) who prefer to engage with one another. Purl tries to fit in with actual men in the organization by dressing like them (in a dark suit), changing her appearance to be more masculine, and being more aggressive in meetings to match their style. This works until more balls of yarn join the organization, at which point Purl realizes she is perpetuating the very same inequality she has experienced. Purl then decides to change back to the way she was by dressing how she originally did, being less assertive, and more inclusive of the other balls of yarn. Soon the office has many more balls of yarn, creating a diverse workplace. This short film perfectly captures everything that is wrong with existing solutions aimed at tackling inequality in workplaces today.

Purl is excluded and marginalized at work, so she changes who she is to fit in, but in the process of doing this she loses her sense of self. To create a more inclusive workplace, Purl is the only one to change. Throughout the story Purl modifies the way she dresses, behaves, and interacts with her colleagues—to ensure everyone feels included. No one else changes. This short film places 100 percent of the onus on Purl to overcome inequality. It also fails to address all the reasons Purl was encouraged to change in the first place—she had to do this to be accepted.

If the solution to inequality is as simple as women choosing to be themselves at work, then gender inequality would have been solved years ago. If women choose to be themselves at work, they are unlikely to be accepted, included, valued, and rewarded in the same way as men. This is inequality. And this cannot be solved by women alone.

THE FIX: Dismantle the Favoritism You Create

In workplaces today, resources, support, politics, alliances, and power all revolve around the dominant group—white male leaders. As you know, the way to be accepted into this group is to make yourself as much like the ideal worker prototype as possible. Even the term *diversity* is problematic because it is used to describe people who are different from the white male standard, but why is there one standard that everyone else revolves around? And why, like Purl, are minority employees expected to solve inequality on their own? This is not how inequality works. It is not something people can create in isolation; it's built into our day-to-day interactions. That means each of us can take steps to dismantle the favoritism we engage in. Here are some ways to get started:

✔ Women and men can commit to engage and include a wide range of colleagues at work—in all aspects of corporate life, from meetings, to networking, mentoring, and social activities—rather than a select few who are similar to you.

✔ Men can model behaviors that value women and ensure the people working with and for them follow suit. This includes things like not participating or tolerating behavior that demeans women or ensuring your networks and social activities at work include a wider range of people.

✔ Leaders can also take extra effort to develop and include minorities at work by making sure they are given adequate opportunities, coaching, and support.

Despite her best efforts, Purl is only ever going to be included when her colleagues decide that she will be. Until we own that, nothing Purl does will fix the inequality in her workplace.

Barrier #17: Legitimacy: From Token to Trophy

One of the common beliefs people hold about gender equality is that it's simply a matter of time until women are equally represented in positions of power. We hold on to the idea that women will eventually catch up to men, despite numerous research studies showing this is not going to be the case. For example, the Global Gender Gap Report 2017, published by the World Economic Forum, found that based on current trends, the global gender gap will be closed in 100 years, which is an increase from their 2016 prediction of 83 years. Worse, the economic gender gap will not be closed *for another 217 years*. Women shouldn't have to be this patient. Waiting out inequality is not a solution, it's a cop-out. The tokenistic efforts companies are making—with quotas, targets, and blatant showcasing of women leaders—do not create sustainable change. Once organizations appoint one woman to a senior leadership role, the chances of them appointing a second women leader in a high-profile position reduces by about 50 percent.[44] This is because workplaces have an implicit quota in place for hiring minorities. Having one female leader in place is evidence that your organization is supportive of gender equality. So, ironically, when organizations appoint a woman leader, they are less likely to appoint any more.

These efforts give women leaders a token status. And tokenism reduces women's legitimacy, as they were hired because of their minority status not their capability. It also means they are often tasked with being the company mascot for the marginalized. Women leaders are generally encouraged to take on a "trophy status," by speaking at events and leading external communications or internal diversity efforts. Showing off token women leaders is a way for companies to highlight their achievements in diversity. This also makes women leaders some-how responsible for advancing the interests of all women within their organization. This is particularly true for women of color, as research finds they are often sought out to take on the role as representatives for diversity.[45]

While senior women leaders are aware of the barriers to women's advancement, it's not their responsibility to lead the path to change even though they often do—as a report found that 73 percent of female mentors help other women, compared with 30 percent of male mentors.[46] When women assume a high-profile position, they are also tasked with advancing more women, even though their presence as a token reduces the company's appetite for more women leaders. Why should women leaders accept this trophy status? Especially when this only serves to further limit their legitimacy.

A 2016 study found when women and racial minorities support diversity efforts, their manager and coworkers perceive them as less competent and they receive lower performance ratings.[47] When white men engage in this same behavior, it leads to high performance ratings. Minorities who advance because of other minorities are perceived as succeeding through nepotism and, importantly, these actions remind people of their token status, which triggers negative stereotypes. To overcome this, we need those in positions of power to take up the fight because they have the power, authority, and privilege to affect change.

THE FIX: Own the Problem

If we want to achieve gender equality at work in our lifetime, then we need to move beyond tokenistic efforts. This is not a public relations activity. We need to stop parading minority employees at work because it is disingenuous and makes things harder for the individual. Assigning women leaders or employees with a trophy status is unhelpful because their legitimacy is already questioned by the mere fact that they are a woman. Taking on any additional labels only serves to further delegitimize their authority at work.

There is one very simple solution to this problem that each of us can commit to: stop asking women to become trophies and instead eliminate the inequality they experience. For leaders, this means take accountability for advancing women and equality within their teams, departments, and organizations. Every leader should be able to identify the key actions they are taking to support the advancement of women in their workplaces rather than simply achieving arbitrary diversity quotas—and chapter nine provides leaders with key actions they can take.

Additionally, every man and woman at work can take ownership by committing to implementing one action, or fix, outlined in this section, and thereby contribute to the advancement of equality in their workplace. This might include learning about the barriers women face, calling out inequality when it happens, recognizing the mothers in your workplace, being conscious of the language used and how this marginalizes women, or simply valuing different leadership behaviors. We need to speed our efforts if we ever hope to achieve equality, and this starts with each of us owning the problem, recognizing our role in creating it, and taking action.

Create a Workplace That Works for Women

Ultimate Software was founded nearly thirty years ago, and despite growing to more than five thousand employees, the organization has maintained an equal gender representation since day one. This company never focused on targets; the aim was to create a workplace where difference could thrive. Given the organization's success in creating a culture of equality, it is worth unpacking how they did so.

To better understand how they achieved this, in 2019 I interviewed Cara Pelletier, director of diversity, equality, and belonging for Ultimate Software.[48] "Ultimate has an incredibly strong culture of people first. It's not just a slogan, but something that we actively try to live. As it turns out, when you hire people who care about people, then the type of people they bring into the organization tends to include women and other typically underrepresented groups in technology," she said. Here are the three things that Pelletier says the leadership team did to create an environment that supported people's different identities at work.

The first thing they did was establish a clear set of values for the organization. Pelletier says that this is a critical first step because it sets the standard for what is important to leaders in the organization. "One of the biggest functions of our executive leaders is they telegraph what values the rest of the organization should be trying to live up to," she said.

Only by having this standard in place can you begin to set expectations for employee behaviors, which Pelletier says is the second important step for leaders to take. "I think people have this idea that corporate culture exists as its own separate entity, that it's out there, and corporate culture is continuously created and co-created by virtue of the conversations that we have with each other." For Pelletier, workplace culture is really the way employees behave, which is why the aim of all leaders should be to align these behaviors with the organization's values. "When we built our leadership development program in house a few years ago, we were really conscious of teaching our leaders how to have conversations that show our values and demonstrate what we want the culture to be."

It's not enough for organizations to want a culture of equality, leaders need to demonstrate the right kinds of behaviors to create it. Pelletier says Ultimate Software made an intentional decision to create a leadership style that serves, supports, and enables all employees. "When you ask leaders to lead in that way and to really be servants of the people that they're leading, then I think it allows leaders to create those open and trusting environments with their people, where their people do feel comfortable bringing their whole selves to work." This is something the organization encourages leaders to practice daily. For example, Pelletier says that how leaders respond to employees' different needs, like requests to take time off or accommodate personal needs, is critical because these moments are where culture is created.

Leaders need to make people feel safe at work if they want them to share their identities. Therefore, the third part of building a culture of equality is to cultivate trust at work. This encourages people to be themselves. "There was a study that I was just reading about not too long ago that shows that LGBTQ people, when they feel safe to be out at work, they will give up to 30 percent more discretionary effort. This squares with my own experience as a queer woman. If I don't have to expend all the emotional energy and effort to try to hide who I am I can put it into being innovative and creative," she says.

It took me a long time to realize just how remarkable women are. In reviewing the invisible barriers and how they impact women at all stages of their careers, one thing becomes crystal clear: the challenges women face at work are because of their workplaces, not them. Seeing all these barriers makes it clear how incredible women are for surviving workplaces and eventually leading them. Women persist, despite a system set up to ensure they don't. With every stroke, women swim against the current until they reach the shoreline. Women don't need to learn to lean in, they are already doing this simply by showing up every day and overcoming one barrier after another. Women must persist against the odds just to do their job, be treated fairly, get paid equally, and access leadership opportunities. Imagine what women could do if none of the invisible barriers existed. We need to create a work environment where women don't have to lean in, because the organization already works for them.

> *Women persist, despite a system set up to*
> *ensure they don't.*

Given all the ways workplaces are rigged against women and the toll this takes, we need gender equality in our workplaces now. So the question we should all be asking ourselves is this: How soon is now? Inequality costs all of us. While women have to navigate inequality, men do too. As we turn to Part III of this book, we focus on how each of us can use our awareness and understanding of inequality to take action and remove the barriers women face. This is an invitation to all men and leaders, who arguably have the most to gain from creating cultures of equality at work, as the following chapters will reveal.

Part III
ACTION

Equality is a practice. It is how employees behave, leaders lead, and workplaces work.

8.

Breaking Up with Don
Why Men Need Gender Equality
Just as Much as Women

I have a male friend who ticks all the boxes associated with an ideal leader. He plays the part of Superman every day by putting on a metaphorical cape and conforming to people's notions of what it means to be the brave male leader, which includes engaging in masculine behaviors, working long hours, taking risks, not showing emotion or displaying any weaknesses. He also works hard to hide his identity as a father by not mentioning his children or taking time off to care for them.

Men are expected to be the hero at work by emulating the success prototype. As touched on in previous chapters, patriarchy doesn't only ensure that masculinity is valued more than femininity, it also upholds the white, middle-class, heterosexual, able-bodied male as supreme. Engaging in masculine behaviors is a way to access and maintain power and privilege. At work, men do this by controlling, favoring, competing, conforming, dominating, and supporting one another.

Masculinity is not inherently toxic, and neither is femininity. These labels are really just the shared mental images and standards we hold for what it means to be a man or woman. What makes these constructs toxic is the value we associate with living up to them. To be considered a "real man," men need to follow a rigid set of behaviors—and doing this comes with benefits. Men who conform can access white male privilege, associated with automatically fitting the success prototype. This privilege also ensures it is easier for men to develop relationships with other men and work long hours, even if they have dependents, because men have someone managing the home front so they can dedicate themselves to work. With this comes access to informal mentoring, social support, and powerful networks. However, it is important to remember that to access all the benefits white male privilege has to offer, men need to fit the prototype by engaging in the associated behaviors. This is how men live up to their privilege, rather than spending it generously by using their dominant position and power to tackle the inequality minority groups experience at work, as discussed in chapter three.

Given the benefits associated with white male privilege, it's easy to assume that there are no downsides for men. While men and women might be able to name a couple of the barriers women face at work, very few would be able to share how gendered workplaces create challenges for men. But when men put the cape of masculinity on, they lose themselves. Workplaces are set up to reward this conformity and hide any challenges this creates for men—and there are many.

> *Workplaces are set up to reward this conformity*
> *and hide any challenges this creates for men—*
> *and there are many.*

Invisible Masculinity: An Obstacle to Men's Identity at Work

Organizations simply don't acknowledge how masculinity plays out at work, which is denial in its purest practice. To become aware of it, we need to put the man back into management, so to speak, and understand all the ways workplaces don't work for men. The terms *managing* or *leading* are believed to be gender neutral, but they are synonymous with men and masculinity. The *think manager–think male* phenomenon, identified by Dr. Virginia E. Schein as briefly discussed in chapter one, clearly demonstrates that both men and women continue to describe leadership with masculine attributes like assertiveness, arrogance, and dominance. Most of us take this for granted, which makes it hard to understand how the ideal way of leading is masculine. We need to see how one type of masculinity dominates nearly every aspect of working life and how there is still a requirement for all leaders to conform to it. Men are more likely to interrupt others, speak first, display dominant behavior, take the lead (even when not asked to), and value the contributions of men more than women. Even if not all men engage in all these behaviors, by endorsing them, men are complicit in setting the standard for workplace norms.

Despite how pervasive masculine leadership is, gender isn't usually considered an important part of men's experience of working life. But if you consider that men have been conditioned to equate their self-worth with living up to the masculine ideal by focusing on power, success, achievements, and status, you can begin to see how this can affect them as much as it does women. Men get to feel good about themselves *only* if they fulfill these requirements, but the trade-off is there are almost no limits to achievement, success, and financial gain. Even when men have this status, they need to maintain their masculinity by consistently engaging in behaviors associated with the ideal worker. This often includes behaviors that marginalize and exclude others.

Gendered standards for behavior are imposed on men and women from the moment they are born, so it is taken for granted as the way things are. Consider the following masculine standards men are expected to live up to, and how this prevents them from being themselves at work:

✔ To be accepted, men are expected to engage in masculine behaviors. Consequently, they may experience backlash for displaying "feminine" behaviors like expressing their feelings or raising concerns about inequality in the workplace or work-life balance. Men also face pressure to go along with behaviors that exclude or marginalize others, even if they don't agree with them.

✔ To be perceived as tough and strong, men are encouraged to display a lack of empathy with others and themselves. Therefore, men may have trouble expressing feelings or seeking out emotional support at work.

✔ Male leaders are expected to have all the answers, take risks, and avoid admitting mistakes. This isolates men, who then lack the emotional and social support often needed to deal with challenging situations.

✔ To be perceived as powerful, men are encouraged to display aggression, dominance, and physical strength. Men are urged to work long hours or engage in discriminatory office banter and bullying.

✔ Men are expected to be the primary breadwinner, therefore succeeding at work is intrinsically linked with men's self-esteem, value, and identity. This requires that men hold down a steady job, conform to the ideal worker image, advance at work and make sure they prevent their home life from interfering.

Asking men to champion gender equality is really an invitation for men to take their capes off and decide for themselves what it means to be a man—at home and at work.

In contrast, men aren't encouraged to take on feminine attributes at work. Men don't have the freedom to explore or choose how to engage at work and instead follow the default standard. This conformity gets rewarded. Take, for example, marriage, which fits the Don Draper prototype. Leaders who best fit the ideal are married, heterosexual males, because that lifestyle conforms to the stereotypical masculine breadwinner image. Research finds that marital status is consistently associated with higher earnings for men. For example, unmarried men face a 33.9 percent reduction in earnings relative to married men, and divorced men face a 19.2 percent earnings penalty.[1] Adhering to one standard of masculinity creates challenges for all men.

From a young age, men are socialized to engage in competitive, aggressive, and dominant behaviors, which then play out in how they behave at work and lead. These behaviors themselves are not intrinsically bad, which is why labeling masculinity as "toxic" is not helpful. We have been sold one version of masculinity for so long, we believe that this is all there is. But masculinity is diverse and multifaceted. It's shaped by the environment and interplays between an individual's race, class, sexual orientation, culture, religion, ethnicity, ability, and any other identity. For example, research finds that men from lower social status backgrounds engage in masculine norms by displaying their physical strength and endurance at work to make up for their social status. Engaging in traditional masculine behaviors is a way for men to reclaim their value.

But labeling masculinity as toxic makes it difficult to see why individuals engage in this behavior. Labels also make it seem like the aim of equality is to do away with masculine attributes, but there are many situations where being assertive, competitive, and tough may be required. It is not that we don't need masculinity, it's that we need to give men the freedom to engage in a range of masculine and feminine behaviors, rather than forcing them to live up to a standard.

Men need this freedom just as much as women do. The more men endorse the masculine ideal, the more likely they will suffer from isolation and negative mental and emotional health. A 2007 study found that men who hold strong beliefs about conforming to traditional masculinity were more likely to engage in unhealthy behaviors like heavy drinking, tobacco use, and a tendency to avoid vegetables.[2] Hallmarks of masculinity are an ability to be tough and go it alone, but this only leads to more solitude. Despite male dominance at work, which brings with it things like solidarity groups, all male networks, and homosocial practices, men are still encouraged to keep their emotions to themselves because sharing this is not what "real men" do. It is easy to blame men for gender inequality, if you ignore all the challenges they encounter conforming to the masculine standard, but every man needs the opportunity to define this standard for himself. The single most important thing men can do to support gender equality is to reflect on what it means to be a man at work.

> *The single most important thing men can do to support gender equality is to reflect on what it means to be a man at work.*

Workplaces stand to benefit from this too. The consulting firm BCG found when men are actively involved in gender diversity efforts,

96 percent of organizations report progress with these efforts compared to only 30 percent of companies when men are not involved.[3] The case for change put forward to date has largely been made with facts and figures all showing how gender diversity leads to better operational and financial performance. According to the World Economic Forum, those organizations with more women on leadership teams outperform those that don't. On average these organizations will have a 48 percent higher operating margin, a 42 percent higher return on sales, and a 45 percent higher earnings per share.[4] The benefits of equality are clear for organizations but not for men.

Cultures of equality help men advance, but they do so much more than that: they give men freedom to be themselves, which helps to counter the challenges they face at work. In more equal work enviroments, there is no Don Draper to live up to. Men get to decide for themselves how they want to show up at work and lead: the ultimate freedom and privilege we all stand to gain from gender equality.

THE FIX: Accept the Invitation

According to Justin Baldoni, the actor best known for his role as Rafael Solano in *Jane the Virgin*, many men are ready to revisit outdated notions of what it means to be a man. I interviewed Baldoni in 2017 to discuss his online show *Man Enough*, which tackles issues surrounding traditional masculinity and gender inequality.[5] Baldoni said men need to think about how masculinity has shaped today's standards before they can tackle gender equality.

The following questions can be a helpful starting point for

thinking about how men are required to live up to the ideal masculine standard at work.

✔ Do you feel the need to comply with the dominant success prototype at work?

✔ Are you aware of the challenges that living up to this standard creates for men at work?

✔ Are you aware of how this limits minorities at work because they are unable to conform to this standard?

✔ Do you feel comfortable playing a supporting role? Or taking direction from people who do not look, think, and act like you?

✔ Is your identity closely tied to your career achievements?

✔ Are you willing to do whatever it takes to succeed, regardless of the impact it has on others, or is it just as important how these results are achieved?

✔ Do you have close relationships with people at work? Do you feel comfortable sharing your feelings or concerns with trusted colleagues?

✔ Do you feel pressure to engage in behaviors that don't always align with your values at work?

✔ When you see colleagues being marginalized or discriminated against at work, do you feel comfortable speaking up and advocating for them?

✔ Do you hide aspects of your identity or home life from colleagues at work?

Baldoni says one of the difficult things about privilege is that those who have it are often blind to it. "I am someone that has it, and I guarantee throughout my life no matter how well-intentioned I have been, I have said and done things that have been sexist and chauvinistic."

Sometimes the best way for men to realize their privilege and how they use it, is to talk about it with the women they work with. This is how men can really begin to understand how their behavior affects minorities and, crucially, how to be an ally to women at work and encourage other men to follow. "It is so important for men to use their louder, more privileged voices to amplify the voices of women who are not being heard." Rewriting the rules for men and women at work starts with understanding how each of us are complicit in creating, reinforcing, and perpetuating inequality.

The Masculine Double Bind

I am raising my son to be a man who practices equality at home and work, which is no easy task because the world is also raising him and not always to support equality. Boys learn what it means to be a man from each person they encounter at school, work, and in their community. We teach boys how to speak and behave, which determines what they will be like as men.

At first glance, gender roles appear to serve the interests of men, who have a higher social status than women. However, when you scratch beneath the surface, it's evident that men face hidden costs for conforming to their prescribed gender role. Could men unlearn these rules and create their own standards of behavior? Not without backlash, like the Femininity Stigma outlined in chapter one. Men and women who do not conform to prescribed gender roles face social and economic costs. They are considered less competent, likable, and capable of leading than individuals who do conform. Men are essentially confronted with a double bind at work. If they live up to the ideal standard of masculinity, it comes at a personal cost to their mental and emotional well-being—even though they have greater access to power and privilege. If men try to engage in a different way, they won't reap the same benefits and will likely face criticism.

> *Men face hidden costs for conforming to their prescribed gender role.*

For example, men are often typecast depending on how much they fit the masculine ideal, and this is evident in the labels we assign to them like "fighter," "sissy," "player," "winner," and "hero." These labels carry different challenges for men. Men need to be the fighter and hero, therefore if they ask for help or provide their colleagues with care and support, they are considered too soft to lead. Men need to be seen as the winner, so when they downplay their achievements at work, they are typecast as weak and perceived as less competent and likable. These labels ultimately highlight the limited ways men can behave at work and lead.

Some jobs are strongly associated with masculinity, like firefighters, construction workers, miners, and oil rig workers. Men working in these environments have traditionally been portrayed as strong, brave, and independent. One of the ways men live up to this image is by taking risks, which can be detrimental given how important safe workplace practices are—especially in these potentially hazardous environments. To avoid life-threatening, unsafe behaviors, men must deviate from the ideal by avoiding risks, asking for help, and being honest about their failures and misgivings. To adopt safe work practices, men need to learn a new way to practice masculinity—which is possible.

The 2010 research paper entitled "An organizational approach to undoing gender: The unlikely case of offshore oil platforms," published in the journal *Research in Organizational Behavior,* reviewed more than twenty years of empirical research on the topic as well as two case studies of men working on oil rig platforms. In both cases, men adopted safe working practices, no longer living up to gender roles.[6] Men didn't reject traditional masculine behaviors, rather they were no longer required to prove themselves by engaging in these behaviors.

For example, the study found that in dangerous situations men typically try to be brave and emotionally detached, which can encourage men to take unsafe risks or avoid asking for help when they need it. In these two cases, however, men were free to share their vulnerabilities and concerns as well as ask for help. Men no longer had to worry about showing everyone how tough they were, but instead they were encouraged and rewarded for calling out unsafe behaviors and confiding in their colleagues when they felt unsure. Men felt free to ask for what they needed in order to conduct their work safely—regardless of whether these needs were viewed as masculine or feminine.

These behaviors were not just limited to safety. Men were also encouraged to share their identities and emotions related to home life. Since home life can often create emotional stress, men were encouraged to seek support from colleagues by sharing aspects of their personal lives. This social support reshaped how men defined masculinity as well as their own manhood. Clearly, it is possible to give men the freedom to choose behaviors that serve them, their colleagues, and the organizations they work in.

THE FIX: Three Ways Leaders Can Rewrite Gender Rules at Work

What did the two organizations in these case studies do to enable men to redefine masculinity for themselves? They changed the culture. Specifically, the research identified three things that transformed how men practice masculinity at work. These three practices are something that every leader can implement.

SHIFT THE GOAL POSTS

Men must prove masculinity, especially at work. That's why they become competitive, aggressive, and risky to the detriment of themselves and their organizations. Men are usually rewarded for taking on these traits, which is why they need environments that encourage them to reset these behaviors. In these two case studies, the safety and well-being of all employees was the shared goal, and the only way for employees to achieve it was to work together. Individual displays of masculinity at the expense of safety were not tolerated.

In a culture that promotes individual ambitions, it would make sense for employees to work as many hours as possible and avoid taking on childcare duties. This is, after all, how employees demonstrate performance, ambition, commitment, and competency. However, in a culture that prioritizes safety and employee well-being, an excessively long workday can result in fatigue, stress, burnout, poor work-life balance, and unsafe work practices. Setting a collective goal for safety made regulating working hours a priority and helped to align employees' behaviors toward achieving it.

All leaders can create a shared aim for employees when it comes to equality. It can be as simple as stating that when it comes to equality in your office, the aim is to ensure all employees succeed at work by having their identities, needs, and experiences equally valued. When workplaces shift from individual goals to shared collective aims, they create a true understanding of what equality looks like. Men deserve the freedom to be themselves at work, but this can only happen when everyone else is free as well. This is why a shared goal is so important.

DITCH THE PROTOTYPE

The ubiquitous success prototype hardwires masculine behaviors with competency. Masculinity is the currency of success because this is what organizations value. However, in these two case studies, the link was rewired. Engaging in masculine behaviors was no longer a sign of capability. Instead, men who supported the shared aim of safety by practicing different behaviors like listening, learning, and collaborating were deemed the most competent. Leaders who could make it safe for people to speak up, call out unsafe work practices, and openly discuss their failings were the ones who succeeded. To hardwire behaviors that support equality, organizations need to make this the basis for deciding who gets hired, promoted, and rewarded.

CREATE A LEARNING CULTURE

When leaders are willing to learn and try new ways of working, they make it safe for everyone else to do so. To tackle inequality head on, we need to create a work environment where employees feel safe to share their identities, discover each other's experiences of inequality, and learn how they contribute to this. Men are being asked to join the fight for gender equality, which requires they rethink a core part of their identity. This depends on both a willingness to learn and a work environment that encourages this. For example, when a safety incident happens, no matter how big or small, it's viewed as an opportunity to learn rather than to blame or punish people. When mistakes happen, employees take time out to investigate the causes and identify what can be done differently—the aim is always to learn from these experiences. Imagine if we treated inequality moments like this as opportunities to learn about the different challenges and barriers we all encounter in working life.

Gendered Expectations: From Breadwinner to Bread-Sharer

Don Draper was a provider. He wasn't a particularly good father or husband, but this was generally tolerated because he was a talented ad man who provided for his family. Men's ability to financially support their family is equated with their identity and self-worth. Living up to this requires that men have a job, conform to the ideal worker image, and advance at work. This is the expectation we all hold for men, and it limits men's freedom to explore their identities outside of work.

We need to break up with Don Draper. This starts with letting go of the idea that women's careers are somehow expendable, but men's careers are not. This is not just good for women, it's good for men. For example, a 2016 study found that men are better able to accommodate their dual identities when their wives work because they get to define success outside of just the breadwinner role.[7] Sharing the burden to provide for the family frees men up to rethink their identity.

The greatest challenge men face in straying from the breadwinner role is the risk of losing their self-worth and social status. When men don't work, they forgo their place in society. Men can no longer build their confidence through their work, so they need to find this somewhere else. Research investigating how men deal with job loss finds that not only do men carry a heavy financial and emotional strain when they are let go, but they also struggle with the sense that they are no longer real men.[8] We look down on men who are not breadwinners because they are not fulfilling what society deems men's role should be. Research also finds this can be painful for men, especially if they are stay-at-home dads and their wives take on the breadwinner role.[9] Men may try to rebalance this perceived loss of masculinity by being less supportive when it comes to childcare and domestic chores.

Dr. Michael Kaufman, author of the book *The Time Has Come: Why Men Must Join the Gender Equality Revolution*, has researched men and masculinity for years and argues that feminism only serves to benefit men. He says this is particularly evident when it comes to fatherhood. In 2019, I interviewed Dr. Kaufman and he shared how parenting has changed over the years, with men striving to be equal partners at home.[10] "This is a major change we're seeing all over the world. It's more advanced in some parts of the world than others, but it's happening everywhere. It's a redefinition of fatherhood as women have been prioritizing the development of their education and careers," he said.

> *Feminism only serves to benefit men.*

According to Dr. Kaufman, men only stand to benefit from sharing the load at home. For example, one of his male colleagues makes his children breakfast every morning and takes them to school. "He told me that this was really important to his wife and her career, but also to his relationship with his children. It made him a better leader because his kids taught him to listen and understand the needs of different people," says Dr. Kaufman. Most men see this change as the best thing that ever happened to them. "Whether that has to do with living lives free from the narrow definition of manhood or free to be loving, caring partners and parents. Whatever it might be, this is a really positive agenda for men," he said.

To realize the positive outcomes associated with gender equality, we need to change how we see men's and women's roles at home. For example, men who viewed their spouse's roles or careers as merely supportive of their own careers believed that their work and commitment to the organization was the number-one priority. However, men who prioritized their spouse's careers were more egalitarian in their approach at home. If men want to integrate fatherhood and working life, they can start by considering their relationships at home and identities outside of work.

THE FIX: How to Become a Bread-Sharer

It is often assumed that women are the only ones who struggle with managing the dual identities associated with work and home life. But men struggle too, as they don't have the opportunities to explore their identities outside of work and become more than a provider. Sharing the breadwinner and caretaker roles is how men and women can begin to treat each other as equal partners.

Each of us can begin this process by reflecting on how we value men and women's contributions at home and work. The questions outlined in the following chart may help with this process.

REVALUING MEN'S AND WOMEN'S CONTRIBUTIONS

Equal partners at home

✔ What does the role of bread-sharer mean to you and how is this different from your role as a provider today?

✔ Do you enable your partner to pursue their work and family goals?

✔ Do you consider your spouse's career ambitions to be as important as your own?

✔ How do you ensure a balance in your house between work and family obligations?

✔ What value do you believe your partner's work provides to the household?

✔ If you are married or in a committed relationship how do you construct your identity in relation to your partner, if they work?

✔ What is your identity outside of your role as the breadwinner?

✔ What can you do at home to transition to a bread-sharer?

✔ How do you help carry the emotional load at home by supporting your children's development and emotional well-being?

✔ What tasks and responsibilities associated with domestic and dependent care duties—the day-to-day management of the household and children— can you take on to better manage the mental load?

Equal partners at work

✔ Are you aware of the barriers and experiences of inequality that men and women face at work?

✔ Do you remain alert to the many ways women are marginalized and discriminated against in your workplace?

✔ Do you interrupt sexism, bullying, or harassment when it happens by speaking up?

✔ Do you support and ensure women's equal participation in meetings, social events, and informal networking?

✔ Do you encourage and support the advancement of women by giving them the same informal support men are given?

✔ Are you equally committed to women's career advancement and do you demonstrate this by developing at least one woman to succeed your role?

✔ Do you check your assumptions and those of others regarding men's and women's career ambitions and leadership capability?

✔ Do you ensure that diversity and inclusion policies, programs, and initiatives do not single out women and make inequality women's problem to solve?

✔ Do you ensure men's interests and needs are also represented in diversity and inclusion programs?

Bullying: Silencing Men at Work

"Why can't you invite her though? I don't understand," I said for maybe the tenth time as my husband got ready to go out with his boss and several male colleagues. These men would often meet up to have drinks, but not invite one of the team members—who just happened to be the only woman on the team. My husband sighed in response to my questions. "You just don't get it. If she was there, it just wouldn't be the same, okay?"

He is right. Having women around makes it a little more difficult for men to engage in all the behaviors they normally would in order to bond. Men participate in in-group favoritism, as outlined in chapter seven, as a way of socializing and supporting one another at work. For example, in 2009, Michele Rene Gregory, associate professor of sociology at York College of the City University of New York, published a journal article that examines male socialization in the advertising industry.[11] Men engage in male-only networking, socializing, and behaviors that sexualize or marginalize women as a way to build camaraderie with one another. In this study, these behaviors were most common among white, middle-class, heterosexual males, and they negatively impacted all women and ethnic, working-class, disabled, gay men. When men align with other men who hold positions of power, they are better able to access the privilege associated with that power. This includes things like having direct access to high-profile people, job opportunities, high-profile assignments, and rewards at work. Homosocial behaviors provide men with ways to develop relationships with other men in positions of power, to their benefit.

There are many ways these behaviors show up in workplaces, like *Negative Gender Norms*, as discussed in chapter six, and *Stereotypical Typecasting*, discussed in chapter seven, but they tend to result in employees tolerating and even accepting bullying, sexual harassment, discrimination, and exclusionary behaviors.[12] Organizational banter is a great example of this and generally includes verbally attacking colleagues under the guise of "joking" to maintain dominance over others. It also involves making sexist jokes or derogatory comments based on people's identities that diminish a person's self-esteem and perceived value. When leaders remain silent, they sanction these behaviors, which also validates the people who engage in them. This can create an entire workplace culture that is hostile toward women.

While most people in workplaces struggle to condemn these behaviors, women are more likely to speak out than men. Research finds that women link the barriers to their advancement with masculine cultures and discriminatory treatment such as behaviors that result in male favoritism, stereotyping, and negative attitudes toward women.[13] It is not that men don't want to speak up. In fact, many men would welcome the change, but studies find men feel like they should remain silent. A 2008 study by researchers Isabel Metz from the University of Melbourne and Alan Simon from the University of Western Australia found that both men and women executives felt their organizational culture had been built by and for men, given that it encouraged conformity, command-and-control leadership, a lack of work-life balance, and short-term thinking—with a focus on profits over people.[14]

Both men and women described this environment as mean-spirited and out of date. However, men felt pressured to remain silent because they feared being ostracized or bullied. In many ways, it can be career suicide for men to share personal difficulties and challenge the status quo. Men who take issue with masculine workplace cultures are likely to feel alone, especially if their male colleagues refuse to point out these problems. This in turn makes it harder for minority groups to speak up. This also creates the perception that men are okay with these practices, and women need to overcome this burden alone. The experiences employees have of their work environment predict how engaged they will be with their work, which in turn impacts retention and job satisfaction. When men don't voice their experiences of inequality at work it becomes harder to fix.

THE FIX: Make It Safe for Men and Women to Speak Up

Recently a male colleague asked me what he could do to support women at work, and I told him to start by being an ally. Simply speaking up when someone makes a derogatory comment about women, even if it seems innocent enough, is how men can practice this. When one of his colleagues made a comment to him about the size of their female coworker's breasts, he spoke up. He said, "Don't do that. Don't speak about her like that. It's not cool." While this might seem like a small action, it is really an incredibly powerful way to create equality at work. By speaking up, my male colleague instantly reset the standards for how men speak, think, and interact with each other and the women in that office.

All men can reset workplace norms by simply changing their behavior and challenging other men to do the same. But this is especially important for managers to do. When male leaders share their inequality moments, experiences, and personal identities outside of work, they make it easier for everyone else to. This can be as simple as men openly discussing the importance of work-life balance, putting family needs ahead of the organization's, reducing hours spent in the office, as well as speaking up when banter excludes and marginalizes minority groups at work. When leaders model behaviors they want to see in an organization, it encourages employees to do the same or speak up when these behaviors are not being practiced.

The Invisible Load: The Costs of Living Up to the Masculine Ideal

The invisible load that women carry, which is the strain women endure having to navigate the many barriers inherent in workplaces, takes a toll on their mental, emotional, and physical health (as discussed in chapters five and six). While this shows up differently for men, because their challenges are different and fewer in number, they too experience mental and emotional strain from living up to prescriptive gender roles, as outlined in this chapter. What makes this particularly difficult for men to manage is that masculinity requires they keep silent and deny the challenges they experience at work. When it comes to managing stress, depression, and suicidal thoughts, men are encouraged to play the hero, put the cape on, and hide their feelings.

Masculine norms stipulate how men can think, feel, and respond to the challenges they face at work, and this only serves to make the challenges harder. For example, research investigating college men's experiences of depression found that men who avoid seeking help with emotional problems are at greater risk for depression.[15] Nearly 70 percent of men in this study who experienced mental health issues did not seek counseling services. While men may have lower rates of depression compared to women, this gap is narrowing. Current figures may also not be entirely accurate, given that men tend to underreport their symptoms and are less likely to seek help than women, which is why men have statistically higher rates of suicide and alcoholism.

In masculine workplace cultures men often feel an increased pressure to conform to the ideal standard, and this negatively impacts their well-being. For example, research finds individuals working in male-dominated industries are at higher risk for depression because of factors like working hours, job demands, role conflict, a lack of social support, and emotional demands.[16] This is the invisible load.

Leaders play a powerful role in shaping the work environment and reducing the invisible load for men. A lack of social support from supervisors is associated with mental disorders in both men and women.[17] However, women are more likely to seek out and rely on this support to cope. This isn't surprising given that masculinity requires men to deal with difficulties on their own. Managers are uniquely situated to provide men with a sense of job security, reduce their role demands, help men integrate work and family life, and provide social support throughout the process.

Therefore, leaders need to be more intentional when it comes to supporting men with their mental and emotional well-being.

THE FIX: How to Lighten Men's Invisible Load

It's difficult to head home at five p.m. if all your colleagues work until eight p.m. But each of us can role model better workplace practices like working reasonable hours, taking breaks, and sharing interests outside of work. This also includes being honest about our needs outside of work—something I am still working on with my husband, who is becoming more truthful about taking time off to look after our children. We can all make it easier for men to share their identities outside of work by being transparent about the needs and challenges we face integrating work and home life. If you have to take your son to the doctor, then own it. By doing this you are establishing a new standard for work-life integration. This makes it easier for the men and women you work with to do the same, because they know you will support them.

This is an especially powerful action leaders can take. When male leaders share their inequality moments, experiences, and personal identities outside of work, they make it easier for everyone else to do the same. This can be as simple as men openly discussing the importance of work-life balance, putting family needs ahead of the organization's, reducing hours spent in the office, as well as speaking up when banter excludes and marginalizes minority groups at work. When leaders model behaviors they want to see in an organization, it encourages employees to follow suit.

I wasn't always aware of the various challenges women experience through their careers or how these challenges show up differently for all women. But I have made it my mission to educate myself about inequality at work and it's an ongoing process. Over the years it became increasingly clear that my education had a major blind spot. Like me, a lot of women assume men don't face any barriers at work. This makes sense. As some men are in positions of power and privilege, it is easy to assume workplaces work for *all* men. It is this lack of awareness that keeps the barriers in place and prevents men from truly investing in gender equality. Companies have business cases, documents detailing all ways gender equality will benefit the organization, but these very rarely include the benefits men stand to gain. By understanding the challenges gender inequality creates for men, the business case for men is clear. Changing the status quo will of course serve women, but it will also free all men to pursue new paths to power and identities outside of work.

We all need to break up with Don Draper. This ideal represents a standard that no one can live up to, nor should they. The ideal worker image doesn't serve the interests of men or women—or workplaces. It's not enough for us to ditch Don, we need our workplaces to do the same. This requires a commitment from every leader to take action, and the steps for doing this are outlined in the following chapter.

9.

Equality
A Call to Lead

I t took me a while to adjust to working for organizations in the oil and gas sector. Every aspect of organizational life is built to ensure the health, safety, and well-being of employees. Just to enter the building, all visitors are required to undergo a short health and safety induction. If you want to walk down the stairs, there is a safe way to do it. If you are carrying a hot drink, there are protocols for that. Even if you want to lift a box, there are standards for how to do it in a safe way.

Employees undergo continuous training on safety, which enables them to put it into practice as part of their jobs. Even meetings start with a safety share, where employees take a few minutes to reflect on safety incidents and lessons learned. To visit an oil rig or mine site, there are a whole new set of protocols and behaviors to learn. These are just a few examples of how these workplaces live and breathe safety. Over time, safety practices become ingrained, habitual, and natural.

Safety is not only something these organizations aspire to achieve, it is fundamental to the way they work. It's a part of the company's DNA and it is as much a priority as productivity and financial performance. Creating a safe work environment is something leaders are proud of. If an employee gets injured, leaders are held accountable and they must face an employee's family and explain what went wrong. Leaders use every opportunity to learn from unsafe workplace practices so they can try to improve their awareness and understanding of how to prevent the incident from happening again. A leader's value is intrinsically linked with everyone going home safely.

Health and safety policies, training programs, and systems are treated as tools rather than solutions. They are preventive and proactive, not initiatives that leaders blindly adopt or have no hand in implementing. If employees don't work safely or actively endanger their coworkers, leaders need to manage this. Employees will be fired—there is zero tolerance. In turn, the organization empowers employees to put safety first because not doing so could threaten their well-being and livelihood. If any employee feels that safety is at risk, they can request that all work stops, and work will not resume until the issue has been investigated and resolved. Safety is an employee-lived experience of the workplace.

Now, imagine for a moment if leaders took inequality this seriously.

The reason we know they don't is because most leaders are not accountable for equality. It's a Human Resources problem or the responsibility of the Diversity and Inclusion team. Until equality becomes an integral part of the way leaders lead, women will continue to remain underrepresented in nearly every aspect of corporate life.

Tackling inequality in your workplace isn't an obligation, it's a privilege. As a leader, you are in a position of power because you get to decide how your employees will experience the organization—this is a privilege. Regardless of how many people you manage or level of seniority, you get to decide how women will be valued, how men will engage, and how all minorities will be treated. You also have the esteemed opportunity to enable the men and women who work for you to put equality into practice every day—something that only those in positions of power get to do. This is the definition of leadership: empowering all women and men to meaningfully contribute to their organization by enabling them to use their different talents and capabilities, and valuing them for this. Equality stops and starts with leaders. The call for leaders to advance gender equality at work is really an invitation for them to lead.

Too often, though, managers opt for what they think is the easy way out. I have seen this time and time again in the organizations I've worked for and with. They blame policies, processes, initiatives, Human Resources, or the CEO for the lack of progress when it comes to advancing women, without realizing that the inequality women and men experience every day happens within their teams (remember our old friend denial?). While a lack of CEO commitment to gender equality is frustrating, it doesn't impede how *you* choose to manage every day or what behaviors you accept from your team members.

If you are reading this chapter, and you hold some type of leadership role, or aspire to a leadership position—and you recognize the importance of gender equality and are committed to help bring about change even though your company doesn't have a single diversity and inclusion initiative in place—there are actions you can take to advance equality. Specifically, there are three key steps leaders can take to put equality into practice, which mirror the three parts that comprise this book: awareness, understanding, and action. In my experience, helping managers and leaders like you focus on these three steps helps tremendously to make equality a practice. These steps will help contextualize inequality within your business and help you embed culture of equality into the very DNA of your team, department, and workplace.

1. BECOME AWARE: Leaders can disrupt the denial in their workplace by creating awareness of how inequality reveals itself in their organization. As part of this, managers can create an opportunity for employees to share their experiences and call out inequality moments when they happen at work.

2. UNDERSTAND: Leaders can take steps to understand how the barriers show up for women and men in their teams by actively managing the inequality moments when they happen. This includes managing informal interactions, which create inequality, and using these experiences and opportunities for employees to learn.

3. ACT: Becoming aware of inequality and understanding how this creates challenges for employees and enables leaders to take action. Every leader can practice equality by walking the talk and modeling the types of behaviors they want employees to adopt. Leaders can also enable employees to identify ways they can practice equality as part of their day-to-day job, so that it becomes a fundamental way of working.

Equality is an ongoing journey that every leader signs up for when they agree to manage people. If you are reading this book and have people reporting to you, then you have made a choice. You know the challenges men and women face in your workplace because of the cultures you have a hand in creating. Now it's a matter of changing them. Here's how to begin your rewarding journey toward transforming your workplace.

1. Become Aware

One of the worst cases of sexual harassment and assault I have ever experienced took place in a small department within a large multinational organization. I was working in human resources supporting about six leaders, all of whom were men, with the management of their teams. Leaders who succeeded in this part of the organization had a very similar approach to leading—think Don Draper. This style was encouraged by the senior leader who would reward, develop, and promote leaders that lived up to this ideal. All the while, he was completely unaware and in denial about the difficulty this ideal standard created for all the women on his team.

After a few months of working with this department, I became very familiar with the way these leaders approached the management of their teams, but I also started to notice something else. In nearly every exchange or meeting with these managers there would be a comment, joke, or behavior that carried with it a sexual undertone. This was never explicit. It would be as simple as a remark about how I looked, or who was the most attractive woman on the team. But over time these commentaries escalated. The leaders would regularly try to engage me in their sexist jokes and discussions about women in the office. At first, I wasn't sure if I was overreacting, and I tried to ignore how this made me feel. As the months passed, I got used to the references about my appearance and the sexual innuendos. But these small moments started to add up. I began to feel self-conscious just stepping foot into the department, and I even considered dressing differently at work to hide my body and avoid their comments.

When other women started sharing similar experiences, I decided to raise this issue with the most senior leader, who dismissed my concerns, telling me that I shouldn't be so sensitive and should try to take it as a compliment. I had no choice but to limit my interactions with the leaders from this department as much as possible. Over time my job performance suffered. I hadn't experienced anything like this before and wasn't sure what to do. I questioned, at the time, whether my experiences were real (gaslighting), but I also knew that other women who worked there felt uncomfortable too.

A few months later a whistleblower shared how every single male leader in this department was either blatantly sexually harassing and/or physically assaulting women on the team, both at work and outside of the office. This included the sharing of vulgar emails, including pornography, sexually explicit comments, racist jokes, and instances of sexual assault against several of the women on the team. A full investigation followed, revealing countless instances of sexism and racism. When I read the final report, I felt sick knowing that what I had experienced was just the tip of the iceberg, and I felt even worse for not having been the one to blow the whistle. These leaders only spared me the full extent of their behaviors because I was a member of the Human Resources department.

In hindsight, it's not surprising that this was happening. Following the investigation, every leader in that department was systematically fired, which was the biggest overhaul I have ever seen an organization make. The company had no choice. Even though the most senior leader hadn't participated in any of this, he was the first to be fired. A leader's job is to be aware of what is happening on their team. And there was no denying what was taking place now. Unfortunately, by this point it was too little too late. Women had been gaslighted, abused, and assaulted.

Awareness of inequality is a leader's job. Not knowing what is happening on your team will cost you as a leader, but more importantly it can endanger the employees who work for you.

Disrupt Denial by Undertaking the Inequality Journey Exercise

By the time employees are raising discrimination, sexual harassment, or assault claims, it is too late. The culture of your team, department, and potentially entire organization is broken because someone somewhere thought this behavior was okay or didn't feel safe to speak up or had seen it and chose to look the other way. To identify how inequality is playing out in your office, you need to become aware of it. This starts with making inequality personal, and storytelling is a powerful way to do this.

Leaders can apply this by having employees map out their "inequality journey." Gather your team members together and ask them to draw a career timeline from when they started working in organizations up until the current role they are in today. Then ask them to plot the moments when they witnessed or experienced inequality against their career timeline. Then encourage employees (those who are comfortable doing so) to share these experiences with the rest of the team. Ideally, leaders would kick off this sharing process by relating their own inequality journey. The purpose is to create the space for employees to share how inequality shows up for them at work. When a leader shows vulnerability, it signals to others it is safe to do the same.

When we connect to inequality in this way, we become more empathetic and aware of the marginalization each of us experiences at work. Like the safety share practice of the gas and oil sector, leaders can harness the power of storytelling every day and encourage their team members to share their inequality moments. These efforts will motivate employees to personally invest in creating solutions and owning the implementation process.

The routine behavior we take for granted at work—like inappropriate jokes, comments, or banter—can become normalized if left unchecked. This slowly blurs the lines between what is acceptable and what isn't, until one day no one can see what is right before them: a broken workplace. This is why every manager is accountable for calling out bad behavior when it happens and disrupting denial by unpacking people's experiences of inequality in their teams, departments, and organizations.

Let's imagine if things had unfolded differently at the department I used to work at. What would the senior leader in the organization have discovered if he had simply had personal meetings with all the women on his team to find out how things were going? Sharing your inequality journey is a great way to disrupt denial, but this needs to become a regular practice because inequality isn't a one-off event. Leaders need to create regular opportunities for employees to share their experiences. This serves leaders because it's the only way they will know where inequality exists on their teams and what they need to do to fix it.

Make Awareness a Practice

Mining is overwhelmingly a male-dominated industry. Tackling gender equality in these environments can be particularly hard. As there are so few women, leaders need to increase women's representation and ensure that the few women on the team are given an equal voice at the table.

To understand how leaders are tackling this, in 2018 I interviewed Bruce Cleaver, chief executive officer of the diamond producer De Beers.[1] De Beers has committed to achieving gender parity in senior appointments across the business by 2020. "When I took on the role of CEO for De Beers, we took a serious look at our gender profile and the speed at which the profile was changing. I was shocked to find that at the rate we are going we won't reach gender equality in De Beers for another forty or fifty years. For me that was an ah-ha moment. I realized that we need to do something differently to achieve gender equality," says Cleaver. This was the starting point in Cleaver's ongoing efforts to raise his own awareness of the challenges women face in his workplace.

To better understand the barriers women encounter in his organization, Cleaver implemented a reciprocal mentoring program, which gives women at all levels of the organization the opportunity to share their challenges, needs, and identities with male leaders. As part of this process, leaders encouraged women to speak up by making it safe for them to voice their concerns and share their experiences. "We started a whole series of programs to get women to feel more confident to speak up. One of the things we do is a reciprocal mentoring program, where men and women meet with more junior female employees. It is a powerful way to get senior men in the organization to stop and listen to what women have to say," he says. Taking the time to listen to women is a small act that all leaders can take to demonstrate their commitment to advancing women in their workplace.

To solve inequality, we need leaders to listen more, think differently, and take action to disrupt the status quo. Programs like reciprocal mentoring help leaders identify how they contribute to the inequality women experience and what they can do to change this. Managers can even formalize this process by asking women to mentor them on a regular basis and provide ongoing advice about the organization's equality efforts. "You don't want people to be different from what they are. This is about people feeling comfortable with who they are, wherever they come from, and making sure they are comfortable to speak up," says Cleaver. Reciprocal mentoring isn't only for male leaders; white women can engage women of color to reverse mentor them. All of us can do our part to understand the different ways people experience inequality.

This starts with making awareness a practice. Every leader can begin to do this by implementing an upward mentoring program in their organization. Outside of this, all leaders can build awareness into their day-to-day management practices by regularly checking in with employees in weekly one-on-one meetings so as to understand what barriers, inequality moments, or difficulties employees are experiencing. This can also include understanding how employees are experiencing the team culture and what behaviors might be happening that they feel uncomfortable with—like the *Negative Gender Norms* outlined in chapter six.

To do this well, leaders need to regularly make time for one-on-one conversations with the managers and employees on their teams. They also need to build trust by promising confidentiality and reassuring the employee that any actions taken are created in partnership with them. This will ensure employees feel heard and valued, because the organization is taking steps to remove the barriers they encounter. This is how managers and employees maintain an awareness of the inequality problem that's in their office.

If we want to build workplaces that work for everyone, we need leaders who are willing to work for everyone—who are committed to become aware, understand, and act on the issues of inequality that affect their co-workers, their organization's culture, and ultimately their own livelihoods. This is something that every leader can do regardless of whether they lead a startup, multinational, or public-sector organization.

For managers, this starts with creating a team environment where employees feel safe sharing the hazards of inequality. That's right. We need to acknowledge that inequality, as discussed throughout this book, poses all kinds of harm to people's lives—from our emotional stress to our confidence levels, mental stress, and even physical health, inequality costs all of us. Inequality is like any other safety hazard because it creates an environment where people are not safe to be themselves. The first step to overcoming this starts by becoming aware of the hazards in your workplace.

Supervisors, managers, and senior executives are the gatekeepers of inequality in corporations. The problem is only solved when leaders own the inequality that employees experience in their teams, departments, and organizations. For example, research conducted by the consulting firm Accenture in 2018 found that women are more than twice as likely to reach executive-leadership levels at organizations where leadership teams are held accountable for achieving equality.[2] Once leaders are aware of the challenges faced by their employees, they must work with their teams to solve it. This is how leaders treat inequality like the business priority that it is.

Treat Inequality Like a Business Problem

In 2017, Mike Gamson, when he was still senior vice president for LinkedIn Global Solutions (the sales division within the company), set out to increase the number of women on his leadership team, but the status quo solutions, which included off-the-shelf initiatives like unconscious bias training, didn't seem to be working.

I interviewed Gamson in 2017 to find out how he was tackling this issue differently.[3] "I think we were wearing ourselves out and patting ourselves on the back for being such enlightened men, trying harder. As we looked around, nothing had changed. This is not working. Trying harder is not how you solve a business problem," said Gamson. Frustrated, he decided to take matters into his own hands and approach the challenge of gender inequality like any other business problem. So, he engaged the leaders on his team to solve it.

Rather than dictating a rigid path forward or relying on the latest diversity initiative, Gamson wanted his team to identify why women were not advancing at the same rate as men and what creative solutions they could implement to change this. "We started with investing and leading from within . . . bringing together voices from a range of backgrounds and perspectives to develop and lead the initiative, our vision, and actionable plan for a more representative organization," he said. As a result, the LinkedIn Global Solutions team came up with a leader-driven program that identified very specific solutions their teams wanted in place to change the culture and improve the way they recruit, promote, and advance women. In just a few short years, Gamson increased the representation of women in his team from around 6 percent to 30 percent. What made this approach so effective is that the leaders on his team owned the problem.

Like safety, leaders were active participants in making their workplace culture more inclusive and supportive of everyone, which is rare. Gamson took ownership of gender inequality, made it personal, and then encouraged employees to do the same because he knew it was fundamental to LinkedIn's success. After all, it's really hard to sell your company's services to a diverse range of customers with only one type of employee or set of behaviors.

Every leader can follow Gamson's approach. This starts with becoming aware, framing equality like any other business problem and engage your team to solve it, like Gamson. Leaders need to facilitate open conversations with their teams about how inequality plays out day to day and what they can do collectively to tackle it. This is easier than you might think. Every leader can facilitate team conversations to identify and agree on the main problems with the following three steps:

1. Open the session by sharing, as a leader, how inequality shows up for you in the team, or by outlining examples of barriers you have witnessed women experience within the team, like *Negative Gender Norms* outlined in chapter six or the *Lack of Access to Quality Leadership Opportunities*, as outlined in chapter seven.
2. Encourage employees to share their observations. When leaders

openly discuss their observations, this gives team members permission to do the same. Leaders can ask men and women to share inequality they have witnessed or experienced within the team. This might include sharing examples of sexist behavior, jokes, or exclusionary behaviors. Not all employees will feel comfortable doing this or sharing specific instances. One way to combat this is to encourage women to simply name the barriers they have witnessed or experienced within the team or organization without giving specific details.

3. Work collaboratively to identify and implement solutions. The final part of facilitating these sessions is to encourage your team to identify strategies for solving the challenges workplaces experience. Depending on your team's size, this might involve an initial brainstorming session where employees are encouraged to share ideas, followed by a second session to identify the key actions the team will take by specific dates. The aim is to leave this session with a clear sense of what actions are going to be taken.

These three steps largely follow what Gamson did to make his teams accountable for tackling inequality. When leaders treat inequality like any other business problem, they ensure their employees are motivated, engaged, and committed to solving it.

2. Understand the Barriers

Why do so few leaders approach equality in this way? It's thanks to our old friend denial. As part of my work, I regularly review and advise organizations on their diversity and inclusion efforts. Several years ago, I was working on a project where I had to present results from a culture survey to more than twenty male and female partners in a law firm. The results clearly showed the organization's culture was perpetuating inequality. There were countless comments written by employees detailing examples of discrimination, harassment, and even sexual assault. Many of the example's employees shared in the survey involved leaders who either condoned the behavior or engaged in it themselves.

As soon as I finished presenting the results, the leadership team went straight into solution mode, looking for a quick fix the Human Resources team could implement. They wanted anything that would make this fluffy "culture stuff" go away—ideally an initiative that someone else would be accountable for. Not surprisingly, this included the same old tired programs, like diversity targets and unconscious bias training. If these leaders didn't start to own the problems on their teams, it's likely I would be presenting these exact same results the next year and the year after that.

These leaders had been given the gift of feedback and insight about how their leadership (or lack thereof) was negatively impacting the men and women who worked for them. Their workplace was broken and the only way they could see this was to spend time examining the countless examples women and men had shared, of how managers, employees, and even some of the leaders in the room marginalized, discriminated, and devalued them. Only by seeing things for what they are would these leaders realize the golden opportunity they had been given to make their mark and define how their workplace was going to function from that point onward. These leaders could do better than a list of initiatives, which was really just more of the same, a proposed solution that required no investment or involvement from them. What they needed to do was manage the inequality moments employees were experiencing, which is actually a part of their job.

Equality requires commitment from leaders. It takes effort to manage the inequality moments every day, something Donna Carpenter, CEO of Burton, the global manufacturer of snowboards, knows all too well. Burton was founded in 1977 and experienced tremendous success early on with triple-digit growth in just a few short years. However, the culture quickly became problematic, which Carpenter detailed in an interview with me in 2019.[4]

"I think this happens to a lot of companies that grow quickly, the culture becomes a male culture, sort of without us realizing it," said Donna Carpenter. In 2003, the Carpenters first realized the extent of the problem when they were in a meeting with twenty-five global directors from the business and only two out of the twenty-five were women. "It was actually Jake (cofounder of Burton) who turned to me and said, 'We've got a problem here, and we need to do something about it.' He knew at a gut, entrepreneurial level that we were not going to succeed in the long term if we didn't have more diversity in the room," said Carpenter. Through planned, systematic effort and commitment to manage her organization differently over fourteen years, Carpenter has transformed the culture and increased the number of women in leadership positions to 42 percent.

How did she do it? By managing the inequality moments in her organization. This started as soon as she became aware that she had a problem. "I started by interviewing about sixty women, former and current employees, and men as well, and saying, 'Hey, what are the challenges, what are the opportunities?' And several women described the culture to me as a frat house or high school locker room," said Carpenter. By having these one-on-one conversations, Carpenter soon realized the organization had made it harder for women to thrive and advance.

Consequently, Carpenter made it her mission to manage the inequality moments employees had shared. For example, when women reported struggling with a role conflict and a lack of role models and career development, support, and advice, Carpenter focused on improving the career paths and opportunities for women to advance in the organization. She also ensured employees had access to parental leave and the support needed to take it.

While it's highly likely women will directly experience inequality during their time in the workplace, it's almost guaranteed all of us will witness inequality moments in our workplaces. A survey of 851 managers in the United Kingdom, conducted by the Chartered Management Institute in 2018, found that 85 percent of women and 80 percent of men have witnessed discriminatory behavior at work.[5] This included things like inappropriate remarks, gender bias in recruitment and promotion decisions, and gender inequality in pay and rewards. These moments are what make or break cultures of equality. So, when Burton's culture began to change, Carpenter says she had to ensure that leaders sustained the changes. "You can have all the great strategies in place, and you can state what your values are, but if people aren't behaving that way, and if you're not incentivizing people to be inclusive, then you're not going to see real change," says Carpenter.

All managers experience opportunities to build cultures of equality every day. This can be as obvious as a colleague sharing how they are being bullied or sidelined. Or witnessing your team members engaging in office banter that verges on sexual harassment. Or it can be as subtle as a parent on your team asking to change their working hours to accommodate school drop off. There will never be a policy long enough to account for how leaders need to behave in every one of these moments. And there shouldn't be, because these moments are an opportunity for leaders to lead. When any manager speaks up against harassment or supports parents with integrating their dual identities, they are demonstrating what equality looks like in their workplace, which then sets the standard for all employees to live up to.

Manage the Inequality Moments

Inequality is a practice—it's something employees do, which is why leaders need to continuously manage it. This includes handling the informal interactions in your teams that make employees feel devalued. When leaders see behaviors that are sexist, discriminatory, and exclusionary they need to call it out by addressing the issue directly with employees in the moment. This includes giving employees direct one-on-one feedback outlining how their behavior marginalizes other employees—whether they intended this or not—and the impact this has. This is also an opportunity for the employee to identify how they will commit to change. Every manager can support their employees in practicing equality by providing continuous one-on-one coaching, mentoring, development, and feedback. This also includes holding employees accountable for changing their behavior.

When inequality moments happen in a group setting, this gives leaders an opportunity to reset the team's norms. When colleagues openly share sexist jokes, dismiss women's contributions, or speak over them, it's an opportunity for leaders to take a moment to stop the meeting and point out what is happening. This can be as simple as calling out the behaviors and explaining the impact and what needs to change. Transforming the behaviors, norms, and cultures in your team begins with paying attention to the inequality moments and managing them.

Likewise, when employees practice equality, leaders can use this as an opportunity to publicly recognize these behaviors and encourage employees to make them a habit. For example, one of the managers I used to work for would start each team meeting by asking all team members to share a recent example of how colleagues had behaved in a way that was supportive and inclusive. This simple routine made equality relevant and reminded all employees of what "good" looks like when it comes to equality.

It's not enough to manage the inequality moments. To get more women into leadership positions, we need managers to actively enable women's advancement, which is, after all, what most of us think a leader's job is. A 2018 study by the Chartered Management Institute also found that 75 percent of managers believe that it is senior male leaders' responsibility to support women's career development.[6] While a lot of leaders have career development conversations with their employees on a semi-regular basis to understand their career interests and ambitions, this isn't enough when it comes to women. As you now know very well, men's and women's careers unfold in different ways, and they experience different challenges because of gender inequality. To get more women into leadership positions, we need managers to manage women's careers and any barriers they face. This starts with understanding the career objectives women on your team have, knowing what current and anticipated barriers they are likely to encounter, and working with them to remove these impediments so they can in fact advance.

Support Women's Career Ambitions by Removing the Barriers

To advance women managers it's not enough to simply know what their career aims are, leaders need to know what challenges women are experiencing and put solutions in place to overcome them. This is something leaders can do from the moment a woman joins the organization.

In 2018, I interviewed Arianna Huffington, founder of Huffington

Post and CEO and founder of Thrive Global, to discuss how companies can better support employees with their individual needs and career aims. In the interview, Huffington shared an important practice she undertakes with every new employee within Thrive Global: entry interviews.[7] These are informal conversations new hires have with their managers shortly after they first join an organization. The aim is for managers to get to know their employees and what matters to employees outside of work. It's also an opportunity to get to know their new hires, to understand their career ambitions and any difficulties they face in achieving these goals—like integrating work and home life.

Typically, organizations only understand the importance of these conversations once an employee has resigned. This normally takes the form of a traditional exit interview where employees are asked about their reasons for leaving, but by this point it's too late. Conducting entry interviews is something every single leader can do; by taking the time to meet with new employees, and in particular women, the leader can come to understand how to best support them to succeed.

In our conversation, Huffington shared an example of when an employee told her that dropping her daughter off at school every morning was really important to her, but she worried about managing this with the morning team meetings. Knowing this, Huffington made sure team meetings were rescheduled to later in the day. Engaging in meaningful dialogue gives managers the opportunity to identify how they can take small steps like this to remove the invisible barriers.

Conducting entry interviews is a great way for leaders to demonstrate that they value women from the get-go. But career conversations are never a one-off event. As women's careers progress, they enter different phases, and are likely to experience different barriers. Career conversations should be an ongoing dialogue that starts with an initial entry interview but continues with regular one-on-one meetings to review the different challenges women are encountering. In these conversations leaders could include the following questions:

- ✔ How would you describe the organizational or team culture?
- ✔ Do you have any needs that are not being met at work?
- ✔ What aspects of the team do you enjoy?
- ✔ Do you feel leaders in the team demonstrate behaviors that are aligned to corporate values? Can you share an example?
- ✔ What is the most challenging aspect of your job?
- ✔ Have you witnessed or participated in an inequality moment recently that you feel comfortable sharing?
- ✔ Do you see a career path for yourself in this organization and what does this look like? What career aims do you have for the next six to twelve months?
- ✔ What are some of the barriers that you experience or anticipate experiencing in the next six to twelve months?
- ✔ What solutions do you think could be put in place to overcome these challenges? Is there anything I can do to remove some of these barriers?
- ✔ How do you think the team can make more of an effort to value the contributions of everyone?
- ✔ What is the one thing you would change about the culture if you could?

These one-on-one exchanges provide rich information that leaders can use to not only help women advance but also to track opportunities for improving the culture. This practice is a meaningful way to support women's career advancement and it sends a message to all employees that leaders take equality seriously.

There will always be employees who resist equality efforts. This comes up every time employees deny, roadblock, or disengage with the process of change.

Carpenter experienced this firsthand at Burton. "We had a backlash where the men said, 'Hey, what's going on? Are there going to be quotas?' And then they realized that because we were becoming a better company for women, we were becoming a better company for them," she says. When men at Burton understood why the changes were needed and how this actually benefited them—by introducing new benefits like paternity leave and childcare subsidies—they championed the change.

While resistance is a normal part of any change in management process, it often signals a lack of understanding or denial. When employees don't know why changes are needed or what is being asked of them, it's easy to resist. But when employees understand the difficulties their colleagues face this makes it harder to disengage from the change efforts and what is being asked of them.

Manage Resistance Through Allyship

Overcoming resistance starts with giving employees opportunities to educate one another about their different experiences of inequality. This can be achieved with allyship programs. These are programs that are generally employee run that seek to enable employees to advance equality in their workplace. Scott Beth, chief diversity and inclusion officer at the software company Intuit, is tackling the challenges LGBTQ employees face at work through an allyship program, which aims to educate employees about difference through empathy, advocacy, and leadership.

In 2019, I interviewed Beth to understand how this program worked

and if it could be applied to all areas of difference.[8] "Our program begins with education, basic terminology—like what is the difference between gender identity and sexual orientation? What is a lesbian? What is
a transgender person? We educate our allies on the gay rights movement
beginning in the U.S., and the challenges that LGBT citizens face around
the world," he said. By using the power of storytelling and including interviews and testimonials with leaders and employees, allyship programs
are a powerful way to disrupt denial and educate employees about how
they can take action to support equality.

By unpacking individuals' different experiences of inequality, Beth
says leaders can also learn how to create a culture where everyone can
bring their full selves to work. "This is advocacy, standing up and saying
what needs to be said in support of your LGBTQ employees. Helping to
correct people with the use of pronouns, calling people out when they say
'Oh that's so gay,' and learning how to call out hurtful behavior," he says.
Education is the key to building allies and creating work environments
where different perspectives are truly valued. "When you allow people to
bring their whole selves to work, then they are focused on solving challenges for each other, for customers, and ultimately shareholders—it's
freeing. When we can create this diverse environment, which embraces
curiosity, that's when innovation is unleashed," Beth said.

To date, Intuit's allyship program has reached more than four hundred employees, but it's only the beginning. "This [allyship] applies to
all dimensions of diversity like ethnicity, gender, or military. We are embarking upon an education program around disabilities in the workplace.
We're also working in the space of mental wellness. Many of us battle
with depression, and anxiety, and other elements that we need to be able
to talk about and fully include that piece of the human experience into the
workplace," he added. Every manager can encourage employees to start

an allyship program in their workplace and ensure they have the support needed to make it a success.

While it is critical for leaders to raise employees' understanding of the barriers by managing the inequality moments, supporting women's careers, and enabling employees to become allies, these changes alone—while meaningful—won't guarantee lasting change. When managers leave, they take their equality building behaviors with them. This can often result in a loss of employee interest and motivation, which stalls progress. To create sustainable change equality needs to become a mainstream part of organizational life, which means making it a part of the way work gets done. This is really the whole point of equality: having employees approach their work in a way that values the contributions, needs, and interests of everyone equally. If every employee did this, not only would more women rise to senior leadership positions, but they would stay there.

This is really the whole point of equality: having employees approach their work in a way that values the contributions, needs, and interests of everyone equally.

3. Take Action

At the time Jacinda Ardern was elected prime minister of New Zealand in 2017, she was the world's youngest female leader, having taken office at the age of thirty-seven. In 2017, I interviewed Ardern, shortly after she had assumed her role of prime minister.[9] In our interview I wanted to understand what Ardern hoped to achieve. I was surprised to learn that one of her key ambitions was to leave people with a sense that the government was kind. It's not every day a world leader makes kindness their main priority.

Intrigued by this response, I asked her if she could share an example of how she plans to achieve this. Ardern said that throughout her career she saw decisions being made by the government that didn't consider the human experience. "Yes, we want a strong economy and our markers do show that we're making progress. But they don't take into account well-being. Whether we're housing all of our people. Whether or not children are growing up without enough food to eat," she says. For Ardern, kindness was a value she wanted her government to practice in all aspects of their work, which included not only the policies, programs, and initiatives they put in place, but how her leaders lead.

A key part of this work for Ardern was to encourage leaders to practice empathy and understanding. "For me it's about having a government that sees beyond just crude measures and looks at the human experience and well-being of people. And I guess I sum that up with kindness," she says.

This isn't just something Ardern wants leaders to practice, it's something she is willing to live by, which the whole world got to witness firsthand on March 15, 2019, when New Zealand faced a gruesome terrorist attack against the Muslim community, where fifty-one people died and forty-nine were injured.[10] During these dark days Ardern reached out to the Muslim community, displaying compassion and empathy. She was praised worldwide for the way she embraced the community following the attack, which included covering the funeral costs of the victims, spending time with the families, and wearing a hijab to honor the victims. Through her actions, Ardern showed the world what it means to lead with empathy, understanding, and, above all, kindness. This is now what her government will be known for, not just in New Zealand, but worldwide.

Anyone can blindly follow a policy or implement a diversity program, but when it comes to equality, real leadership is about being brave and dealing with difficult situations that don't always have a readymade answer. Just like kindness, equality is a value that every leader can live up to. The key to doing this well, like Ardern, starts with defining what equality means to you. How will you know when your culture supports equality? What does "good" look like? Defining this is how leaders begin to make equality the way they lead, and, in turn, the way employees behave. Over time, this becomes what the organization is known for.

Lead with Equality: Define What "Good" Looks Like to You

The first time I shut down an office I was in my late twenties. Working in human resources, it was my job to meet with every employee and their manager to explain why the office was closing. Over a month I met with more than two hundred employees. The meetings were tough. Employees cried, shouted, called me every name you can imagine, threatening both me and the company in the process. By the end I was broken. This experience made me question who I was and if corporate life was even for me.

When the managing director for the organization called me into his office to find out how the office closure was going, I struggled to speak. I was fighting back tears. Eventually I composed myself and asked him, "As a leader, how do you know if you are doing the right thing? By closing down this office we are affecting hundreds of people's lives—so, how do you know?" He looked at me, nodding knowingly, then opened his desk drawer and pulled out a copy of the company's values. "Whenever I don't know what to do, I read the company vision and value statement. I think about the impact of the difficult decisions I have to make and whether these are supported by what we value. Then I use that to guide my own behavior as much as possible. Most of the time no one really knows. There isn't a policy or straightforward answer. Being guided by our shared mission and values is how we get through it," he said. This experience changed my entire view of leadership.

We need leaders to make their commitment to equality a fundamental part of how they lead. The way managers hire, promote, reward, include, and develop their employees should all reinforce equality. The only way for leaders to know if they are living up to this is to define what "good" looks like for them. Ardern had a very clear take on what kindness meant to her government, not only in how they lead, but also in the day-to-day aspects of their work. Every leader can define what equality means to them. This starts with answering the following questions:

- ✔ What do you want your leadership to be known for? How will practicing equality support this?
- ✔ Why does inequality matter to you as a leader and how can you practice this day to day?
- ✔ How can you integrate equality into the different aspects of your team's work?
- ✔ What behaviors will help create a culture of equality in your team and how can you demonstrate that you value these actions?
- ✔ When it comes to achieving equality in your current role as a leader, what does "good" look like for you?

Every leader should take time to answer these questions for themselves and use the answers to come up with a personal definition of what equality means to them. Like a mission statement or set of values, this is a useful reference point for leaders to understand if they are meeting their own measures of success. It can also be used to help guide manager's decisions day to day, like whether to change meetings to accommodate school drop off or whether to have an uncomfortable conversation with an employee about their borderline sexist comments. Knowing what equality means to you as a leader will make it clear what the right answer is.

In my work as a researcher, I have heard many men's and women's accounts of inequality at work. In analyzing these experiences, it is clear that there are three conditions that create inequality at work: ambiguity, inconsistency, and a lack of transparency. When employees are not clear on how equality can be put into practice it is unlikely that they will enforce it. If employees are not sure what behaviors get rewarded, then they are unlikely to consistently behave in a way that is inclusive. If it's not clear what equality looks like as a set of behaviors, norms, and routines, it won't be achieved—even if companies have an equal number of male and female leaders. To create cultures of equality at work, it's not enough for leaders to walk the talk—they need employees to do the same. This is how cultures of equality really begin to take hold in organizations. This starts with making it a part of the way work gets done.

Make Equality Part of Every Employee's Job

For equality to become a mainstream part of organizational life, it needs to matter to employees—and for most employees doing a good job is the main priority. How do you know if you are doing a good job? For most employees, they get told at their annual performance review, when their manager reviews their achievements against the key performance indicators (KPIs) established at the beginning of the year. Based on this assessment, employees are given an overall performance score, which impacts their bonus and promotability. Every leader and employee can make equality part of their day-to-day work by working with employees to make equality part of their annual KPIs or targets.

Leaders can facilitate this process by encouraging employees to think about each of their key objectives and how these tasks can be completed in a way that includes and values all of their colleagues. This could include asking employees to think about any of the following in relation to their KPIs:

✔ How do you demonstrate equality in your day-to-day behaviors at work? For example, can you share how you support women's advancement in this organization? Or how you practice inclusive behaviors?

✔ How do you practice equality in the day-to-day tasks you carry out? For example, have you created an opportunity for both women and men to have equal input and contributions to the work? When you work on teams do you ensure there is a diverse mix of people and that everyone is given an opportunity to contribute?

✔ How are you educating yourself about the different experiences men and women have of working life, to ensure that gender stereotypes, blind spots, and assumptions do not negatively impact the quality of your work?

✔ How do you include both women's and men's perspectives when making major decisions? For example, how do you ensure that you collaborate and engage men and women you work with equally to better understand their different perspectives on projects, decisions, and key business issues?

✔ How can you achieve your KPIs in a way that supports the organization with advancing equality? For example, can you identify one action you can take to make the team more inclusive, collaborative, and supportive of both men and women, like starting an allyship program?

When leaders encourage employees to consider how equality can be integrated in their day-to-day work, projects, or behaviors, it helps employees think differently about the very nature of their jobs. It also makes employees commit to practicing equality as part of their day-to-day responsibilities at work. This is how equality becomes a practice, which is sustained over time, regardless of who is leading the team.

How do organizations become known for equality in the same way that oil and gas companies are known for safety? They build equality into the way business gets done. When leaders and employees practice equality in their day-to-day behaviors, it transforms people's experiences of work because you removed the barriers. Over time, this changes the culture in entire teams, departments, and workplaces. But the benefits don't stop there. As organizations mature in their equality efforts, they often look for opportunities to integrate these practices in all aspects of the business.

Make Equality the Way Workplaces Work

The final action every leader can take is to look for ways to integrate equality into their business practices. This can include every aspect of working life, like only choosing to work with service providers who have at least 30 percent of women on their leadership teams and are taking action to create a culture of equality. Or thinking about the way your company advertises its products and considering whether this reinforces gender stereotypes or roles. Or whether the causes your company supports or sponsors represent the diverse needs of your community. Regardless of your department or teams' function, every leader can engage their teams to think about how to integrate equality into their business practices.

This will look different for every organization, but it starts with encouraging employees to think differently about the way the business works. A great example of this is the global L'Oréal Group, which in 2010 created a program called "Solidarity Sourcing," where the company used their purchasing power to select suppliers who shared their focus on inclusion.[11] Specifically, L'Oréal chose to conduct business with small- and medium-sized suppliers who hire disabled and disadvantaged employees, are minority-owned, and engage in fair trade practices. While this program is applied in all L'Oréal purchasing centers worldwide, within the United States the company specifically focused on supporting their supplier relationships with women- and minority-owned businesses. L'Oréal decided to work with companies who shared their commitment to progressing minorities at work.

> *This is what "good" looks like. This is what it means to lead.*

This is how equality evolves from an isolated internal practice to a fundamental way of doing business. Not only does this transform company cultures, but much like safety and environmental sustainability, it simply becomes the way workplaces work. Every leader can take time with their teams to think about how they can make equality a fundamental way of doing business. When leaders do this, they also put pressure on their peers and partnering organizations—as L'Oréal did with its suppliers—to do the same.

This is a game changer. Imagine if every company, in every area of business, did this. We would transform entire industries and eventually society. This is how equality gets achieved.

The Bottom Line

It doesn't matter whether your company, board, CEO, senior vice president, or human resources team support gender equality or only want to pay lip service to it. What matters is that you support it. You understand how inequality and gender denial keep your employees blind to the inequality they witness, experience, or create. You now know the barriers women and men face in your workplace. You also now understand the great privilege and opportunity you have been given as a leader—and how to put that privilege to good use. When you practice equality as a leader, you are working to create an environment where the women and men who report to you feel respected, valued, and free to be themselves and to use their talents at work. This is what "good" looks like. This is what it means to lead.

10.

It's Our Workplace

So, Let's Fix It Like Our Futures Depend on It

Remember Sarah and the difficulties she faced year in and year out trying to get promoted? Eventually, she did get promoted; the hair clip and glasses never prevented her from becoming a highly effective leader. Despite the invisible barriers Sarah had to overcome, she got her seat at the leadership table because she is fantastic. As a leader, Sarah is collaborative, creative, authentic, engaging, and supportive. She has a knack for championing her team members and empowering them. Sarah supports employees with their careers, encouraging them to try new things, take risks, and develop their capabilities. She makes people feel included, valued, and respected. In short, Sarah's the kind of leader most people want to work for—and in these ways, she represents the future of leadership.

Over the next five to ten years, jobs will change due to technological advancements like artificial intelligence, robotics, the Internet of Things,

3-D printing, and nanotechnology. While these advancements will create a range of new jobs in industries yet to be created, many of today's jobs will still exist, they will just look a little different and probably involve working with machines. Consider the field of medicine, where medical doctors are primarily responsible for correctly diagnosing and treating patients. In the future, it may be algorithms making these diagnoses with remarkable accuracy. Computers could be used to make recommendations about the best treatment. Artificial Intelligence could replace pharmacists, and, in some cases, robots could even carry out surgery.[1] Doctors won't disappear, but they won't diagnose or prescribe medicine in the same way they do today. Their role will change as they will need to comfort and manage patients to a greater extent.[2]

Just like this example, in the immediate future, advancements in technology won't necessarily replace all jobs, but it will alter the way most of us work. The parts of our jobs that are routine, administrative, and repetitive will likely be replaced by technology. According to the consulting firm McKinsey, for 60 percent of all jobs at least one-third of the activities can be automated.[3] Like doctors, employees will be freed up to undertake new tasks in new ways, which will require new skills.

The World Economic Forum's 2016 report, "The Future of Jobs," states that overall social skills, like persuasion, emotional intelligence, and teaching others, will be in higher demand across all industries compared to technical skills, like programming. Just like Sarah, whose leadership skills stood out for her interpersonal talents, employees will need to future-proof their employability by developing their interpersonal capabilities.

As part of my role with UN Women, I led many of the programs related to gender equality in the domains of innovation and technology. It was part of my job to stay up to date with which skills might be needed when technological advancements are introduced, and how the acquisitions of new "softer" skills might affect men and women differently. One of the arguments for why we need more women in leadership positions is that men tend to adopt a more command-and-control style of leadership—like Don Draper; women, on the other hand, tend to have a more communal and democratic approach to leadership—like Sarah. Arguably, Sarah's leadership style is more suited to the changing world of work, which requires social skills like persuasion, collaboration, and emotional intelligence.

To test the strength of this argument, I voluntarily conducted a survey with a hundred and two women and men from a professional services firm. The survey contained thirty questions, three of which focused on women and men and the future world of work, as outlined in the chart on page 282 titled "What Are the Skills We Need in the Future?" The first question asked respondents to select the top five skills out of a list of eleven that they think are necessary for the future. These were the key social skills participants selected: adapting to change and managing ambiguity; managing people to achieve outcomes; achieving results and outcomes; demonstrating emotional intelligence; and demonstrating resilience.

In the second question, I asked participants to identify the top five social skills that women possess. The third question asked participants to identify the top five social skills that men possess. Both men and women who responded to the survey stated that women have four out of the five capabilities needed for the future (as detailed in the chart).

According to this, women today already have 80 percent of the skills and capabilities needed to succeed in the future. Interestingly, these same participants only attributed one out of the five capabilities needed in the future to male leaders.

WHAT ARE THE SKILLS WE NEED IN THE FUTURE?

Question 1.

What are the top five capabilities (out of a list of eleven) that you think will be most needed in the future world of work?

- ✔ Adapting to change and managing ambiguity
- ✔ Managing people to achieve outcomes
- ✔ Achieving results and outcomes
- ✔ Demonstrating emotional intelligence
- ✔ Demonstrating resilience

Question 2.

What are the top five capabilities (out of a list of eleven) that you think women bring to the workplace?

- ✔ **Adapting to change and managing ambiguity**
- ✔ **Managing people to achieve outcomes**
- ✔ Leading inclusive environments
- ✔ **Demonstrating emotional intelligence**
- ✔ **Demonstrating resilience**

Question 3.

What are the top five capabilities (out of a list of eleven) that you think men bring to the workplace?

- ✔ Taking risks
- ✔ Achieving strong task performance
- ✔ **Achieving results and outcomes**
- ✔ Demonstrating courage
- ✔ Managing the social and political aspects of work

Even though this was a small one-off study that I undertook, larger studies also support this argument. Several studies have investigated the differences in men's and women's leadership styles. In the 2003 paper "The Female Leadership Advantage: An Evaluation of the Evidence," researchers Alice Eagly from the Department of Psychology at Northwestern University and Linda Carli from the Department of Psychology at Wellesley College examined sex differences in leadership styles by conducting a meta-analysis, which included examining more than 162 studies of leadership.[4] Their research found that women managers overall had a more democratic leadership style compared to men—women were more collaborative, participative, and inclusive. This style of leadership is often described as "transformational," as it includes mentoring and developing employees to do their best and ensure they engage in meaningful work.

This is further supported by research published in 2013 by the journal *Industrial and Commercial Training*, which also found that women adopt a more transformational leadership style overall, including demonstrating compassion, care, concern, respect, and equality.[5] In contrast, men had a more transactional approach, which included a more task-focused, achievement-oriented, and directive style of management. As the nature of jobs change and therefore alter the way organizations function, leaders who are able to perform a transformational style of leadership will be necessary to manage disruptive changes, develop employees' skill sets, and solve complex problems by engaging different perspectives.

This is good news for Sarah, as the 2019 *Harvard Business Review* article titled "Research: Women Score Higher Than Men in Most Leadership Skills" found that based on an analysis of 360-degree reviews of women and men in leadership positions, women were rated as more effective than men on the vast majority of leadership competencies.[6] Across every level of an organization, women were perceived by their managers, and particularly male managers, to be more effective than men. Importantly, this included traditionally male functions like information technology and operations.

The bottom line is Sarah's leadership capabilities are what make her exceptional today, but they will make her extremely valuable and indispensable to organizations in the future.

While there is a clear link between the capabilities that women have, and the skill sets workplaces will need over the next ten years, this isn't a straightforward case of women are better leaders. Remember that most men today are still required to conform to gendered roles, which restricts their leadership styles. Living up to the Don Draper ideal is costing men. It limits their effectiveness because the way we work is changing. Organizations require leaders who can not only drive results and focus employees on achieving outcomes, like Don, but they also need leaders who can do all of this in a way that is inclusive and collaborative, like Sarah. Men who have been boxed into masculine ways of leading may have benefited up until now, but this success prototype won't continue to serve them in the future. This is precisely why men have the most to gain from cultures of equality. It's the permission slip they need to take on different ways of engaging, working, and leading, so they are the ones who do not get left behind.

As enticing as it is to believe that women alone represent the future of leadership, this narrative ignores how we got into this mess in the first place. Success prototypes that leaders are expected to live up to helped Don succeed, because his leadership style matched the ideal standard for leaders in his company. To date, women have worked in environments where the ideal leadership standard is stereotypically masculine. But in the future, men will work in environments where the ideal leadership standard is arguably more stereotypically feminine. Neither of these options serve women or men. They are handcuffs. Gender stereotypes and success prototypes force women and men to behave in certain ways to get ahead, favoring those that can best fit in. This is evident in both the *think manager–think male* phenomenon and the *femininity stigma*. Forcing men and women to fit one standard at work prevents them from effectively leading because they cannot use, adapt, and evolve a diverse range of skills.

We learn how to lead from the world around us. Leadership is a practice. It is something people do to motivate, inspire, and engage employees to achieve the organizational goals. We put leadership into practice by responding to our environment and the people in it. A 2013 study found the most effective leaders draw on a range of leadership traits, depending on their environment.[7] In the future, the best leaders won't be restricted to one way of leading by outdated stereotypes, rather they will be ambidextrous, as they can flex their wide range of capabilities depending on what the situation requires. These leaders will encourage employees to display cognitive, emotional, and behavioral flexibility to best achieve the organization's aims. Not every office environment needs either a transactional or transformational leadership style. Some may require both or a mix. When we force leaders to conform to one way of leading, we prevent them from being able to effectively adapt their skills to meet the needs of any given moment, situation, or environment. Versatility is critical to effectively lead and respond to the changes and increased complexity coming our way. The goal for organizations shouldn't be to make male leaders more feminine or female leaders more masculine. The aim should be to create an environment where women and men can apply their capabilities in new, innovative, and creative ways to solve the problems at hand and enable employees to do the same.

We cannot expect employees to develop different skill sets if workplaces don't value differences. For employees to thrive in the future, they need to know that their unique talents, capabilities, skill sets, identities, and perspectives will be valued—this requires a culture of equality. In 2019, the consulting firm Accenture surveyed eight thousand employees in twenty-seven countries and found that employees are six times more likely to adopt an innovation mind-set—they are willing to innovate, problem solve, and create—in workplaces that have a culture of equality.[8] Their findings conclude that if employees feel a sense of belonging and feel valued by their employers for their individual identities, they will be more empowered to innovate. Inequality not only creates barriers to women's advancement, it creates barriers to employees who want to share their diverse perspectives, collectively problem solve, and work together. Companies that have a culture of equality will be able to outcompete their peers.

> *Companies that have a culture of equality*
> *will be able to outcompete their peers.*

Creating this type of workplace requires leadership. As outlined in chapter nine, we need leaders to take the first step in the journey to creating cultures of equality at work. Every supervisor, manager, and leader deserves a copy of this book. It's their invitation to lead, to disrupt denial, manage inequality moments, and make equality the essence of how their businesses work. It's time for leaders to begin the journey of removing the barriers that women and men experience at work so they have the freedom to use their identities, backgrounds, and skill sets to innovate, create, and meaningfully contribute in their organizations.

This book puts every leader on notice. We now know how inequality, patriarchy, and the invisible barriers work in organizations. This makes these challenges impossible to deny. We know the fixes men and women can use to navigate inequality in their workplaces today. We know what actions leaders need to take to dismantle it.

The time has come. We can no longer afford to work in environments that marginalize, discriminate, diminish, and devalue women or men because of their different identities—our futures depend on it. Equality is no longer a nice thing to have, it is the only way companies will survive the inevitable changes to come. It is a way for leaders to thrive in the future world of work. And it is an opportunity for all of us to finally recognize and value our different identities and talents. The best part about undertaking this work is that everyone wins. Equality is in each of our best interests because we all want to thrive at work and home. Men. Women. Leaders. Businesses. It's time to fix our organizations so they work for everyone—and it's time for men and women to do this together.

Acknowledgments

The journey I have taken in writing this book has been a long and deeply personal one. Along the way I have been supported by incredible people, who like me believe in the fight for freedom. This entire book would also not have been made possible without Leila Campoli, my literary agent at Stonesong, who has the amazing gift of helping new writers to find their voice. Thank you for believing in me enough to listen to my story.

One of the difficulties writers have is to break a complicated idea down into concepts that are easy for readers to understand and apply in everyday life. This is what makes editors so important, which is why I am so grateful to Sarah Pelz, executive editor, Simon and Schuster Inc., Atria Books, for helping me tell my story. I am also extremely grateful to Arijeta Lajka and Michele Matrisciani, who supported me with reading and editing the words in this book to help bring them to life. For this I am eternally grateful.

To Jennifer Nadel and Gillian Anderson, thank you for taking the time and effort to support and amplify this book with your words—I am eternally grateful to you both.

The writer's process is a lonely one. Every day you are on your own, staring at a computer with nothing but your ideas, research, and stories for company. Even though the process can be isolating, mine was filled with so many incredible people. I had the patience and loving support of my husband, Mark Johnson, and our two children, Milly and Rex.

There were also all the remarkable women who supported my career over the years. This includes my sister, Emma King, and friends Thea Dunlap, Charlotte Biering, Daphne Yap, Marie McNaull, the Rangi Rangers (George Selby, Florence Hartigan, Carmel Stef, Sarah Edwards, and Alex Nealon), Dr. Jennifer Gardner, Jodie Hazeley, Jenny Dalalakis, Sarah Boden, Liezel Strauss, Jennifer Koury, Claudia Chan, Belinda Riley, Arianna Huffington, Meredith Walker, Maggie Chieffo, Dr. Cindy Pace, Dr. Nina Ansary, and Camille Laurente. I have also been lucky enough to have the encouragement of so many remarkable men, including Nigel Barker, Nate Hurst, Justin Baldoni, Wade Davis, and Maverick Aquino.

There is also a long list of people (too many to name here) who have at one point or another supported my work by saying yes to interview and research requests, endorsements, and reviews. Thank you for helping me share my story with the world.

This journey started because women were brave enough to share their experiences of inequality with me. This helped me see myself and the inequality I have experienced, which led me to research and write this book. That's why this book is for you. It has been my great privilege to have the opportunity to research, write, and tell the story of gender inequality at work. My only hope is that this book might one day encourage each of you to see all that you are and fight for the freedom to be yourself at work.

Notes

Introduction: It's Not a Woman Problem, It's a Work Problem

1. Soohan Kim, Alexandra Kalev, and Frank Dobbin, "Progressive corporations at work: The case of diversity programs," *NYU Review of Law & Social Change* 36 (2012): 171.

2. "Quick Take: Women of Color in the United States," Catalyst, November 7, 2018. Accessed January 8, 2018, at https://www.catalyst.org/research/women-of-color-in -the-united-states/.

3. "The World's Women 2015: Trends and Statistics," United Nations. Accessed January 7, 2019, at http://unstats.un.org/unsd/gender/worldswomen.html.

4. "Four Imperatives to Increase the Representation of Women in Leadership Positions," CEB Corporate Leadership Council, November 2014. Accessed January 10, 2016, at https://www.cebglobal.com/human-resources/corporate -leadership-council/women-leaders.html.

5. "United States: Indra Nooyis Pepsi Exit Means Another Female CEO Replaced by a Man." MarketWatch. August 7, 2018. Accessed February 28, 2019. https:// www.marketwatch.com/press-release/united-states-indra-nooyis-pepsi-exit-means -another-female-ceo-replaced-by-a-man-2018-08-07.

6. Benjamin Artz, Amanda Goodall, and Andrew J. Oswald, "Research: Women ask for raises as often as men but they are less likely to get them," *Harvard Business Review*, June 25, 2018. Accessed January 7, 2019, at https://hbr.org/2018/06/research-women -ask-for-raises-as-often-as-men-but-are-less-likely-to-get-them.

7. Kim Parker, "Women in majority-male workplaces report higher rates of gender discrimination," Pew Research Center, March 2018. Accessed January 7, 2019, at https://www.pewresearch.org/fact-tank/2018/03/07/women-in-majority-male -workplaces-report-higher-rates-of-gender-discrimination/.

1: Who Broke the Workplace?

1. Alice H. Eagly and Linda L. Carli, "The female leadership advantage: An evaluation of the evidence," *Leadership Quarterly* 14, no. 6 (2003): 807–834.

2. Steven H. Appelbaum, Barbara T. Shapiro, Katherine Didus, et al., "Upward mobility for women managers: Styles and perceptions: Part two," *Industrial and Commercial Training* 45, no. 2 (2013): 110–118.

3. "Global Gender Gap Report 2016," World Economic Forum, 2016. Accessed

January 7, 2018, at http://reports.weforum.org/global-gender-gap-report-2016/files/2016/10/GGGR16-GenderParity.pdf.

4. Yuval Noah Harari, *Sapiens: A Brief History of Humankind* (New York: Random House, 2014).

5. Wendy Wood and Alice H. Eagly, "A cross-cultural analysis of the behavior of women and men: implications for the origins of sex differences," *Psychological Bulletin* 128, no. 5 (2002): 699.

6. Maria Alexandra Lepowsky, "Fruit of the motherland: Gender and exchange on Vanatinai Papua New Guinea," (1982): 5174–5174. PhD dissertation, University of California, Berkeley.

7. "How Americans Describe What Society Values in Men and Women," Pew Research Center's Social & Demographic Trends Project, July 24, 2018. Accessed January 7, 2019, at http://www.pewsocialtrends.org/interactives/strong-men-caring-women/.

8. "On Gender Differences, No Consensus on Nature vs. Nurture," Pew Research Center's Social & Demographic Trends Project, December 5, 2017. Accessed January 7, 2019, at http://www.pewsocialtrends.org/2017/12/05/on-gender-differences-no-consensus-on-nature-vs-nurture/.

9. Julie Coffman and Bill Neuenfeldt, "Everyday Moments of Truth: Frontline Managers Are Key to Women's Career Aspirations," Bain Brief, Bain & Company, July 17, 2014. Accessed January 7, 2019, at https:// www.bain.com/insights/everyday-moments-of-truth; "Global Gender Gap Report 2016," World Economic Forum, 2016.

10. Ibid.

11. "Global Gender Gap Report 2016," World Economic Forum, 2016.

12. Coffman and Neuenfeldt, "Everyday Moments of Truth."

13. Laura Guillén, Margarita Mayo, and Natalia Karelaia, "Appearing self-confident and getting credit for it: Why it may be easier for men than women to gain influence at work," *Human Resource Management* 57, no. 4 (2018): 839–854.

14. Stewart R. Clegg and Mark Haugaard, eds., *The Sage Handbook of Power* (Thousand Oaks, CA: Sage, 2009).

15. Allen C. Bluedorn, "Scientific Management (comprising Shop Management, The Principles of Scientific Management, and Testimony Before the Special House Committee)," *Academy of Management Review* 11, no. 2 (1986): 443–447.

16. Clegg and Haugaard, *The Sage Handbook of Power*.

17. Bluedorn, "Scientific Management."

18. Jane Sturges, "What it means to succeed: Personal conceptions of career success held by male and female managers at different ages," *British Journal of Management* 10, no. 3 (1999): 239–252.

19. Virginia Schein, "A global look at psychological barriers to women's progress in management," *Journal of Social Issues* 57, no. 4 (2001): 675–688.

20. Ibid.

21. Robyn C. Walker and Jolanta Aritz, "Women doing leadership: Leadership styles and organizational culture," *International Journal of Business Communication* 52, no. 4 (2015): 452–478.

22. Alexis Nicole Smith, Marla Baskerville Watkins, Jamie J. Ladge, and Pamela Carlton, "Interviews with 59 Black Female Executives Explore Intersectional Invisibility and Strategies to Overcome It," *Harvard Business Review,* May 10, 2018. Accessed January 7, 2019, at https://hbr.org/2018/05/interviews-with-59-black-female -executives-explore-intersectional-invisibility-and-strategies-to-overcome-it.

23. Ashleigh Shelby Rosette and Robert W. Livingston, "Failure is not an option for Black women: Effects of organizational performance on leaders with single versus dual-subordinate identities," *Journal of Experimental Social Psychology* 48, no. 5 (2012): 1162–1167.

24. Jeffrey Pfeffer, *Power: Why Some People Have It—and Others Don't* (New York: Harper Collins, 2010).

25. "Press Release," Men's Health Foundation, June 2019. Accessed July 7, 2019, at https://menshealthfoundation.ca/menshealthweek/2019/press-release/.

26. Isabel Metz and Alan Simon, "A focus on gender similarities in work experiences in senior management: A study of an Australian bank builds the case," *Equal Opportunities International* 27, no. 5 (2008): 433–454.

27. Ashlee Borgkvist, Vivienne Moore, Jaklin Eliott, and Shona Crabb, " 'I might be a bit of a front runner': An analysis of men's uptake of flexible work arrangements and masculine identity," *Gender, Work & Organization* 25, no. 6 (2018): 703–717.

28. Laurie A. Rudman and Kris Mescher, "Penalizing men who request a family leave: Is flexibility stigma a femininity stigma?," *Journal of Social Issues* 69, no. 2 (2013): 322–340.

29. Margaret W. Sallee, "The ideal worker or the ideal father: Organizational structures and culture in the gendered university," *Research in Higher Education* 53, no. 7 (2012): 782–802.

30. Scott Coltrane, Elizabeth C. Miller, Tracy DeHaan, and Lauren Stewart, "Fathers and the flexibility stigma," *Journal of Social Issues* 69, no. 2 (2013): 279–302.

31. Robin J. Ely, Pamela Stone, and Colleen Ammerman, "Rethink What You 'Know' About High-Achieving Women," *Harvard Business Review,* December 2014. Accessed January 14, 2019, at https://hbr.org/2014/12/rethink-what-you-know -about-high-achieving-women.

2: Gender Denial

1. Alison Flood, "Gender Pay Gap Figures Reveal Big Publishing's Great Divide," *The Guardian,* March 23, 2018. Accessed January 7, 2019, at https://www.theguardian .com/books/2018/mar/23/gender-pay-gap-figures-reveal-big-publishings-great -divide.

2. J. K. Swim, K. J. Aikin, W. S. Hall, and B. A. Hunter, 1995. "Sexism and racism: old-

fashioned and modern prejudices." *Journal of personality and social psychology*, 68(2), p.199.

3. Jeffrey M. Jones, "Gender Differences in Views of Job Opportunity," Gallup, August 2, 2005. Accessed January 7, 2019, at https://news.gallup.com/poll/17614 /gender-differences-views-job-opportunity.aspx.

4. Alexis Krivkovich, Marie-Claude Nadeau, Kelsey Robinson, et al., "Women in the Workplace 2018," McKinsey & Company, Lean In, 2018. Accessed January 7, 2019, at https://womenintheworkplace.com/.

5. Kim Parker and Cary Funk, "Gender discrimination comes in many forms for today's working women," Pew Research, 2017. Accessed June 22, 2019, at https://www.pew research.org/fact-tank/2017/12/14/gender-discrimination-comes-in-many-forms -for-todays-working-women/.

6. Belle Rose Ragins, Bickley Townsend, and Mary Mattis, "Gender gap in the executive suite: CEOs and female executives report on breaking the glass ceiling," *Academy of Management Perspectives* 12, no. 1 (1998): 28–42.

7. Ibid.

8. Marta Geletkanycz, Cynthia E. Clark, and Patricia Gabaldon, "Research: When Boards Broaden Their Definition of Diversity, Women and People of Color Lose Out," *Harvard Business Review*, October 3, 2018. Accessed March 1, 2019, at hbr.org /2018/10/research-when-boards-broaden-their-definition-of-diversity-women-and -people-of-color-lose-out.

9. Marta Geletkanycz, "Derailed by the Money Train: Governance Reform and the Attenuation of Diversity Gains," *Journal of Management Studies,* Conference on "New Perspectives on Diversity," Babson College, April 2018.

10. Al Norman, "Sex Discrimination Wal-Mart: The 'Bitches' Story That Won't Go Away," Huffington Post, September 17, 2017. Accessed August 1, 2018, at https:// www.huffpost.com/entry/sex-discrimination-t-wal-mart-dthe-biktches-story_b _578bbafae4b0b107a24147d3?guccounter=2.

11. "Road to Inclusion," Wal-Mart, 2017. Accessed August 1, 2018, at https://cdn.corporate .walmart.com/11/0d/f9289df649049a38c14bdeaf2b99/2017-cdi-report-web.pdf.

12. Marla Baskerville Watkins, Seth Kaplan, Arthur P. Brief, et al., "Does it pay to be a sexist? The relationship between modern sexism and career outcomes," *Journal of Vocational Behavior* 69, no. 3 (2006): 524–537. Accessed at https://doi.org /10.1016/j.jvb.2006.07.004 and http://www.sciencedirect.com/science/article/pii /S0001879106000820).

13. Ibid.

14. Arthur P. Brief, Joerg Dietz, Robin Reizenstein Cohen, et al., "Just doing business: Modern racism and obedience to authority as explanations for employment discrimination," *Organizational Behavior and Human Decision Processes* 81, no. 1 (2000): 72–97.

15. T. A. Van Dijk, "Discourse and the denial of racism," *Discourse & Society,* 3(1)(1992): 87–118.

16. Louise Matsakis, Jason Koebler, and Sarah Emerson, "Here Are the Citations for the Anti-Diversity Manifesto Circulating at Google," *Motherboard*, August 7, 2017. Accessed March 3, 2019, at https://motherboard.vice.com/en_us/article/evzjww /here-are-the-citations-for-the-anti-diversity-manifesto-circulating-at-google.

3: Privilege at Work

1. Brittany Packnett, "How to Spend Your Privilege," The Cut, *New York Magazine*, August 1, 2018. Accessed March 3, 2019, at https://www.thecut.com/2018/08/nia -wilson-spend-your-privilege.html.

2. Joanne B. Ciulla, Donelson R. Forsyth, Michael A. Genovese, et al., *Leadership at the Crossroads*. ABC-CLIO (Westport, CT: Praeger 2008).

3. Julie Coffman and Bill Neuenfeldt, "Everyday Moments of Truth: Frontline Managers Are Key to Women's Career Aspirations," Bain Brief, Bain & Company, July 17, 2014. Accessed January 7, 2019, at https:// www.bain.com/insights/everyday -moments-of-truth.

4. Ibid.

5. Bell Hooks, *Ain't I a Woman: Black Women and Feminism* (New York: Routledge, 2014).

6. "Quick Take: Women of Color in the United States," Catalyst, November 7, 2018. Accessed March 3, 2019, at https://www.catalyst.org/research/women-of-color-in -the-united-states/.

7. Janis V. Sanchez-Hucles and Donald D. Davis, "Women and women of color in leadership: Complexity, identity, and intersectionality," *American Psychologist* 65, no. 3 (2010): 171.

8. Michelle King, "NASA's Real Life 'Hidden Figure' on How to Advance Women in STEM," *Forbes*, February 20, 2018. Accessed March 3, 2019, at https://www.forbes .com/sites/michelleking/2018/02/20/nasas-real-life-hidden-figure-on-how-to -advance-women-in-stem/#2e0c4a8f7ab9.

9. Gerald R. Ferris, Sherry L. Davidson, and Pamela L. Perrewé, *Political Skill at Work: Impact on Work Effectiveness* (Boston: Nicholas Brealey, 2011).

10. Ibid.

11. Kate Mackenzie Davey, "Women's accounts of organizational politics as a gendering process," *Gender, Work & Organization* 15, no. 6 (2008): 650–671.

12. Ibid.

13. Michelle King, "How Businesses Break the Glass Ceiling," Huffington Post, March 24, 2017. Accessed March 3, 2019, at https://www.huffpost.com/entry/how -businesses-break-the-glass-ceiling_b_5925a0ebe4b0dfb1ca3a102b.

14. "20 of the Most Memorable Mad Men Quotes," *The Telegraph*, December 01, 2010. Accessed March 3, 2019, at https://www.telegraph.co.uk/culture/tvandradio/8170937 /20-of-the-most-memorable-Mad-Men-quotes.html.

4: It's a Path, Not a Ladder

1. Lisa Belkin, "The Opt-Out Revolution," *The New York Times Magazine,* October 26, 2003. Accessed January 7, 2019, at https://www.nytimes.com/2003/10/26/magazine/the-opt-out-revolution.html.

2. "Raising Kids and Running a Household: How Working Parents Share the Load," Pew Research Center, November 4, 2015. Accessed January 7, 2019, at https://www.pewsocialtrends.org/2015/11/04/raising-kids-and-running-a-household-how-working-parents-share-the-load/

3. "Quick Take: Women in the Workforce Quick," Catalyst, 2019 Accessed January 7, 2019, at https://www.catalyst.org/research/women-in-the-workforce-united-states/.

4. R. W. Griffeth, P. W. Hom, and S. Gaertner, "A meta-analysis of antecedents and correlates of employee turnover: Update, moderator tests, and research implications for the next millennium," *Journal of Management* 26, no. 3 (2000): 463–488.

5. "Women in the Workplace 2018," McKinsey & Company, Lean In. Accessed January 7, 2019, at https://womenintheworkplace.com/.

6. Karen S. Lyness and Donna E. Thompson, "Climbing the corporate ladder: Do female and male executives follow the same route?," *Journal of Applied Psychology* 85, no. 1 (2000): 86.

7. "Ambition and Gender at Work," Institute of Leadership and Management, 2011. Accessed January 7, 2019, at https://www.institutelm.com/resourceLibrary/ambition-and-gender-at-work.html.

8. Janeen Baxter and Erik Olin Wright, "The glass ceiling hypothesis: A comparative study of the United States, Sweden, and Australia," *Gender & Society* 14, no. 2 (2000): 275–294.

9. Deborah A. O'Neil and Diana Bilimoria, "Women's career development phases," *Career Development International* 10, no. 3 (2005): 168–189.

10. Julie Coffman and Bill Neuenfeldt, "Everyday Moments of Truth: Frontline Managers Are Key to Women's Career Aspirations," Bain Brief, Bain & Company, September 12, 2018. Accessed March 3, 2019, at https://www.bain.com/insights/everyday-moments-of-truth.

5: The Achievement Phase

1. Sarah Damaske, "A 'major career woman'? How women develop early expectations about work," *Gender & Society* 25, no. 4 (2011): 409–430.

2. Stephanie Sipe, C. Douglas Johnson, and Donna K. Fisher, "University students' perceptions of gender discrimination in the workplace: Reality versus fiction," *Journal of Education for Business* 84, no. 6 (2009): 339–349.

3. S. R. Sipe, L. Larson, B. A. Mckay, and J. Moss, "Taking off the blinders: A comparitive study of university students' changing perceptions of gender discrimination in the workplace from 2006 to 2013," *Academy of Management Learning and Education* 15, no. 2 (2016), 232–249.

4. Adelina Broadbridge and Ruth Simpson, "25 years on: Reflecting on the past

and looking to the future in gender and management research," *British Journal of Management* 22, no. 3 (2011): 470–483.

5. "Women in the Workplace 2018." McKinsey & Company, Lean In. 2018. Accessed January 7, 2019. https://womenintheworkplace.com/.

6. "Advancing Women and Girls With Disability." USAID. 2019. Accessed September 7, 2019 https://www.usaid.gov/what-we-do/gender-equality-and -womens-empowerment/women-disabilities.

7. "Yomi Adegoke and Elizabeth Uviebinené: Slay in Your Lane," *The Fix with Michelle King,* iTunes, July 23, 2018. Accessed January 7, 2019, at https://podcasts.apple.com /bo/podcast/yomi-adegoke-and-elizabeth-uviebinen%C3%A9-slay-in-your-lane /id1336361820?i=1000428095911&l=en.

8. Alison Mountz, "Women on the edge: Workplace stress at universities in North America," *Canadian Geographer/Le Géographe canadien* 60, no. 2 (2016): 205–218.

9. Stephanie Rader Sipe, Lindsay Larson, Britton A. McKay, and Janet Moss, "Taking off the blinders: A comparative study of university students' changing perceptions of gender discrimination in the workplace from 2006 to 2013," *Academy of Management Learning & Education* 15, no. 2 (2016): 232–249.

10. Kyoko Nomura and Kengo Gohchi, "Impact of gender-based career obstacles on the working status of women physicians in Japan," *Social Science & Medicine* 75, no. 9 (2012): 1612–1616.

11. Rebecca Luzadis, Mark Wesolowski, and B. Kay Snavely, "Understanding criterion choice in hiring decisions from a prescriptive gender bias perspective," *Journal of Managerial Issues* 20, no. 4 (2008): 468–484.

12. Eric Luis Uhlmann and Geoffrey L. Cohen, "Constructed criteria: Redefining merit to justify discrimination," *Psychological Science* 16, no. 6 (2005): 474–480.

13. Gordon Hodson, John F. Dovidio, and Samuel L. Gaertner, "Processes in racial discrimination: Differential weighting of conflicting information," *Personality and Social Psychology Bulletin* 28, no. 4 (2002): 460–471.

14. "Yassmin Abdel-Magied: Smashing Stereotypes," *The Fix with Michelle King*, iTunes, 2018. https://podcasts.apple.com/sg/podcast/yassmin-abdel-magied -smashing-stereotypes/id1336361820?i=1000427604158. Accessed March 1, 2019.

15. Chester I. Barnard, *The Functions of the Executive* (Cambridge, MA: Harvard University Press, 2005).

16. Ann M. Morrison, Carol T. Schreiber, and Karl F. Price, "A Glass Ceiling Survey: Benchmarking Barriers and Practices," Center for Creative Leadership, April 1995. Accessed March 3, 2019, at https://www.ccl.org/articles/research-reports/a-glass -ceiling-survey-benchmarking-barriers-and-practices/.

17. "Research: Women Ask for Raises as Often as Men but Are Less Likely to Get Them." 2010. *Harvard Business Review.* Accessed November 7, 2019. https://hbr.org/2018/06 /research-women-ask-for-raises-as-often-as-men-but-are-less-likely-to-get-them.

18. J. Camille Hall, Joyce E. Everett, and Johnnie Hamilton-Mason, "Black women talk about workplace stress and how they cope," *Journal of Black Studies* 43, no. 2 (2012): 207–226.

19. Paula Nicolson, *Gender, Power and Organization: A Psychological Perspective on Life at Work* (New York: Routledge, 2015).

20. Rosabeth Moss Kanter, *Men and Women of the Corporation*, 2nd edition (New York: Basic Books, 2008).

21. "Report: Emotional Tax: How Black Women and Men Pay More at Work and How Leaders Can Take Action," Catalyst, October 11, 2016. Accessed March 3, 2019, at https://www.catalyst.org/knowledge/emotional-tax-how-black-women-and-men -pay-more-work-and-how-leaders-can-take-action.

22. Isis H. Settles, NiCole T. Buchanan, and Kristie Dotson, "Scrutinized but not recognized: (In)visibility and hypervisibility experiences of faculty of color," *Journal of Vocational Behavior* 113 (August 2019): 62–74.

23. Sonia Liff and Kate Ward, "Distorted views through the glass ceiling: The construction of women's understandings of promotion and senior management positions," *Gender, Work & Organization* 8, no. 1 (2001): 19–36.

24. Isabel Metz and Alan Simon, "A focus on gender similarities in work experiences in senior management: A study of an Australian bank builds the case," *Equal Opportunities International* 27, no. 5 (2008): 433–454.

25. Laurie A. Rudman, "Self-promotion as a risk factor for women: The costs and benefits of counterstereotypical impression management," *Journal of Personality and Social Psychology* 74, no. 3 (1998): 629.

26. Jioni A. Lewis and Helen A. Neville, "Construction and initial validation of the Gendered Racial Microaggressions Scale for Black Women," *Journal of Counseling Psychology* 62, no. 2 (2015): 289.

27. Michelle King, "Body Language Expert Amy Cuddy on the Difference Between Confidence and Arrogance," *Forbes*, May 24, 2017. Accessed March 3, 2019, at https://www.forbes.com/sites/michelleking/2018/05/24/amy-cuddy-shares-why -confidence-trumps-competence-at-work/#502889951070.

28. Wieke Bleidorn, Ruben C. Arslan, Jaap J.A. Denissen, et al., "Age and gender differences in self-esteem—A cross-cultural window," *Journal of Personality and Social Psychology* 111, no. 3 (2016): 396–410.

29. Karen S. Lyness and Donna E. Thompson, "Climbing the corporate ladder: Do female and male executives follow the same route?," *Journal of Applied Psychology* 85, no. 1 (2000): 86.

30. Monica Biernat and Diane Kobrynowicz, "Gender- and race-based standards of competence: Lower minimum standards but higher ability standards for devalued groups," *Journal of Personality and Social Psychology* 72, no. 3 (1997): 544.

31. Settles, Buchanan, and Dotson. "Scrutinized but not recognized.

32. Sheryl Sandberg, *Lean In: Women, Work, and the Will to Lead* (London: W.H. Allen, 2015).

33. Donelson R. Forsyth, Michele M. Heiney, and Sandra S. Wright, "Biases in appraisals of women leaders," *Group Dynamics: Theory, Research, and Practice* 1, no. 1 (1997): 98.

34. Christine Alksnis, Serge Desmarais, and James Curtis, "Workforce Segregation and the Gender Wage Gap: Is 'Women's' Work Valued as Highly as 'Men's'?," *Journal of Applied Social Psychology* 38, no. 6 (2008): 1416–1441.

35. *The Wage Gap: The Who, How, Why, and What To Do,* April 2016. Accessed September 3 https://nwlc.org/wp-content/uploads/2016/04/The-Wage-Gap-The -Who-How-Why-and-What-to-Do-1.pdf.

36. "When She Rises, Getting to Equal 2018—Spotlight on Young Leaders," Accenture, 2018. Accessed March 3, 2019, at https://www.slideshare.net/accenture/getting-to -equal-2018-spotlight-on-young-leaders-119165401.

37. Benjamin Artz, Amanda H. Goodall, and Andrew J. Oswald, "Do women ask?," *Industrial Relations: A Journal of Economy and Society* 57, no. 4 (2018): 611–636.

38. "When She Rises, Getting to Equal 2018—Spotlight on Young Leaders."

39. "Why we made pay transparent," *Verve,* 2018. Accessed March 3, 2019, at https:// verve.co/news/why-were-transparent-about-pay/.

40. Ibid.

41. Edward S. Lopez and Nurcan Ensari, "The effects of leadership style, organizational outcome, and gender on attributional bias toward leaders," *Journal of Leadership Studies* 8, no. 2 (2014): 19–37.

42. Denise Sekaquaptewa, "Discounting their own success: A case for the role of implicit stereotypic attribution bias in women's STEM outcomes," *Psychological Inquiry* 22, no. 4 (2011): 291–295.

43. Georges Desvaux, Sandrine Devillard, Alix de Zelicourt, et al., "Women Matter: Ten Years of Insights on Gender Diversity," McKinsey & Company, October 2017. Accessed March 3, 2019, at https://www.mckinsey.com/featured-insights/gender -equality/women-matter-ten-years-of-insights-on-gender-diversity.

6: The Endurance Phase

1. "Women in the Workplace 2018," McKinsey & Company, Lean In. Accessed January 7, 2019, at https://womenintheworkplace.com/.

2. Jess Huang, Alexis Krivkovich, Irina Starikova, Delia Zanoschi, and Lareina Yee. "Women in the Workplace 2019." McKinsey & Company. October 2019. Accessed November 2, 2019. https://www.mckinsey.com/featured-insights/gender -equality/women-in-the-workplace-2019.

3. Ellen Weinreb, "At work, do women care more than men about sustainability," Greenbiz, February 20, 2013. Accessed March 3, 2019, at https://www.greenbiz.com /blog/2013/02/20/work-do-women-care-more-men-about-sustainability.

4. "Why Work Life Balance Matters for Your Business," CPA Canada. Accessed March 3, 2019, at https://www.cpacanada.ca/en/connecting-and-news/blogs /leadership-innovation/why-work-life-balance-matters.

5. Deborah A. O'Neil and Diana Bilimoria, "Women's career development phases," *Career Development International* 10, no. 3 (2005): 168–189.

6. Jeff John Roberts, "I Was Fired for Being a Woman, Sallie Krawcheck Tells Crowd," *Fortune*, October 8, 2016. Accessed March 3, 2019, at https://fortune.com/2016/10/08/sallie-krewcheck-fired/.

7. Belle Rose Ragins, Bickley Townsend, and Mary Mattis, "Gender gap in the executive suite: CEOs and female executives report on breaking the glass ceiling," *Academy of Management Perspectives* 12, no. 1 (1998): 28–42.

8. British Psychological Society, "Employers prefer male managerial potential to female proven track record," Science Daily, May 2015. Accessed March 3, 2019, at https://www.sciencedaily.com/releases/2015/05/150506164244.htm.

9. Kathi Miner-Rubino and Lilia M. Cortina, "Working in a context of hostility toward women: implications for employees' well-being," *Journal of Occupational Health Psychology* 9, no. 2 (2004): 107.

10. O'Neil and Bilimoria, "Women's career development phases."

11. Eden B. King, "The effect of bias on the advancement of working mothers: Disentangling legitimate concerns from inaccurate stereotypes as predictors of advancement in academe," *Human Relations* 61, no. 12 (2008): 1677–1711.

12. Ivona Hideg and D. Lance Ferris, "The compassionate sexist? How benevolent sexism promotes and undermines gender equality in the workplace," *Journal of Personality and Social Psychology* 111, no. 5 (2016): 706.

13. Seth Stevenson, "Don't Go to Work," Slate, May 11, 2014. Accessed March 3, 2019, at https://slate.com/business/2014/05/best-buys-rowe-experiment-can-results-only-work-environments-actually-be-successful.html.

14. Kim Bhasin, "BEST BUY CEO: Here's Why I Killed The 'Results Only' Work Environment," Business Insider, March 18, 2013. Accessed March 3, 2019, at https://www.businessinsider.com/best-buy-ceo-rowe-2013-3/?IR=T.

15. Ibid.

16. E. Cahusac and S. Kanji, "Giving up: How gendered organizational cultures push mothers out," *Gender, Work & Organization* 21, no. 1 (2014): 57–70.

17. King, "The effect of bias on the advancement of working mothers."

18. Michelle King, "Arianna Huffington and Citi Are Supporting Women to Do Less and Achieve More," *Forbes*, March 8, 2018. Accessed January 7, 2019, at https://www.forbes.com/sites/michelleking/2018/03/08/arianna-huffington-and-citi-are-supporting-women-to-do-less-and-achieve-more/#6d6481d6c128.

19. Heejung Chung, "Gender, Flexibility Stigma and the Perceived Negative Consequences of Flexible Working in the UK," *Social Indicators Research*, November 2018, 1–25.

20. Mark DeWolf, "12 Stats About Working Women," *US Department of Labor Blog*, March 1, 2017. Accessed January 7, 2019, at https://blog.dol.gov/2017/03/01/12-stats-about-working-women.

21. Anne Morrison and Katherine Gallagher Robbins, "Fact Sheet: Part-Time Workers Are Paid Less, Have Less Access to Benefits—and Two-Thirds Are Women," National Women's Law Center, September 2015. Accessed March 3, 2019, at https://www.nwlc.org/sites/default/files/pdfs/part-time_workers_fact_sheet_8.21.1513.pdf.

22. Catherine Hill, Kevin Miller, Kathleen Benson, and Cerace Handley, "Barriers and Bias: The Status of Women in Leadership," NCGS, March 2016. Accessed March 3, 2019, at https://www.ncgs.org/research/database/barriers-and-bias-the-status-of-women-in-leadership/.

23. "Childcare Report Shows That Moms Feel Stuck," Winnie Report, 2019. Accessed January 7, 2019, at https://Winnie.com/blog/2019-childcare-report-shows-moms-feel-stuck.

24. Anna Chu, "Women and Poverty in 2015," NWLC, November 15, 2016. Accessed March 3, 2019, at https://nwlc.org/blog/women-and-poverty-in-2015/.

25. Wendy Wang, "Mothers and Work: What's 'ideal'?," Pew Research Center, August 19, 2013. Accessed March 3, 2019. http://www.pewresearch.org/fact-tank/2013/08/19/mothers-and-work-whats-ideal/.

26. Anna Blue and Melissa Kilby, "4 Reasons Why Co-Leadership Works for Girl Up and Might Be Right for Your Organization," LinkedIn Pulse, March 7, 2018. Accessed January 1, 2019, at https://www.linkedin.com/pulse/4-reasons-why-co-leadership-works-girl-up-might-right-anna-blue/.

27. Jenny M. Hoobler, "On-site or out-of-sight? Family-friendly child care provisions and the status of working mothers," *Journal of Management Inquiry* 16, no. 4 (2007): 372–380.

28. Morrison and Robbins, "Fact Sheet: Part-Time Workers Are Paid Less, Have Less Access to Benefits—and Two-Thirds Are Women."

29. Caroline Gatrell, "Policy and the pregnant body at work: Strategies of secrecy, silence and supra-performance," *Gender, Work & Organization* 18, no. 2 (2011): 158–181.

30. Ibid.

31. Matthias Krapf, Heinrich W. Ursprung, and Christian Zimmermann, "Parenthood and Productivity of Highly Skilled Labor: Evidence from the Groves of Academe," Federal Reserve Bank of St. Louis, January 11, 2014. Accessed March 3, 2019, at https://s3.amazonaws.com/real.stlouisfed.org/wp/2014/2014-001.pdf.

32. Ibid.

33. "The rise in dual-income families," Pew Research Center, 2016. Accessed March 3, 2019, at https://www.pewresearch.org/fact-tank/2019/06/12/fathers-day-facts/ft_16-06-14_fathersday_dual_income/.

34. "Modern Family Index," Bright Horizons, 2017. Accessed March 3, 2019, at https://solutionsatwork.brighthorizons.com/~/media/BH/SAW/PDFs/GeneralAndWellbeing/MFI_2017_Report_v4.ashx.

35. Jenny M. Hoobler, Sandy J. Wayne, and Grace Lemmon, "Bosses' perceptions of

family-work conflict and women's promotability: Glass ceiling effects," *Academy of Management Journal* 52, no. 5 (2009): 939–957.

36. D. J. Anderson, M. Binder, and K. Krause, 2003. "The motherhood wage penalty revisited: Experience, heterogeneity, work effort, and work-schedule flexibility." *ILR Review* 56(2): 273–294.

37. "Fact Sheet America's Women and the Wage Gap" National Partnership for Women and Families. Accessed September 3, http://www.nationalpartnership.org/our-work /resources/economic-justice/fair-pay/americas-women-and-the-wage-gap.pdf.

38. Ibid.

39. Ibid.

40. Shelley J. Correll, Stephen Benard, and In Paik, "Getting a job: Is there a motherhood penalty?," *American Journal of Sociology* 112, no. 5 (2007): 1297–1338.

41. Ibid.

42. Michelle J. Budig and Melissa J. Hodges, "Differences in disadvantage: Variation in the motherhood penalty across white women's earnings distribution," *American Sociological Review* 75, no. 5 (2010): 705–728.

43. "Maribeth Bearfield: Is Your Mental Load Holding You Back?," *The Fix with Michelle King*, Podbean, 2018. Accessed January 7, 2019, at https://www.podbean.com/media /share/pb-2v4z9-95bc56.

44. Michelle King, "Gillian Anderson Is Redefining What It Means to Have It All," *Forbes*, March 27, 2017. Accessed July 3, 2019, at https://www.forbes.com/sites /michelleking/2017/03/27/gillian-anderson-is-redefining-what-it-means-to-have-it -all/#4b8ef1054f20.

45. Lucia Ciciolla and Suniya S. Luthar, "Invisible household labor and ramifications for adjustment: Mothers as captains of households," *Sex Roles* 81, nos. 7–8 (2019): 467–486. Accessed at https://link.springer.com/article/10.1007/s11199-018-1001-x.

46. Kelli A. Saginak and M. Alan Saginak, "Balancing work and family: Equity, gender, and marital satisfaction," *Family Journal* 13, no. 2 (2005): 162–166.

7: The Contribution Phase

1. "Ultimate Software Profile," Fairygodboss. Accessed May 15, 2019, at https:// fairygodboss.com/company-overview/ultimate-software.

2. Ibid.

3. Ibid.

4. Michelle K. Ryan and S. Alexander Haslam, "The glass cliff: Exploring the dynamics surrounding the appointment of women to precarious leadership positions," *Academy of Management Review* 32, no. 2 (2007): 549–572.

5. Michelle K. Ryan, S. Alexander Haslam, Thekla Morgenroth, et al., "Getting on top of the glass cliff: Reviewing a decade of evidence, explanations, and impact," *Leadership Quarterly* 27, no. 3 (2016): 446–455.

6. "Alexander Haslam: Beyond the Glass Ceiling, the Glass Cliff," *The Fix with Michelle King*, iTunes, 2019. Accessed March 3, 2019, at https://podcasts.apple.com/gb/podcast /the-fix-with-michelle-king/id1336361820?i=1000433433749.

7. Ryan, Haslam, Morgenroth, et al., "Getting on top of the glass cliff."

8. "Female leaders are being set up to fail," World Finance, 2018. Accessed March 3, 2019, at https://www.worldfinance.com/strategy/female-leaders-being-set-up-to-fail.

9. Jillian Berman, "A Sexist Explanation for Why the New York Times Just Fired Its Top Editor," Huffington Post, May 15, 2014. Accessed March 3, 2019, at https:// www.huffpost.com/entry/jill-abramson-female-exec_n_5325830?guccounter= 1&guce_referrer=aHR0cHM6Ly93d3cuZ29vZ2xlLmNvbS8&guce_referrer_sig= AQAAAMgnF5yc9_9thTQh6wYoazZPfBT-eNx_YujUUnNbS-ooc_fWeGaLrSkJO oxMLjg36oneKSqLyjy5cKrURovCjXC-2PVnUoKfTtt33o6jROnoPPbEHImF2dc Ofp9I1DX12XneqIwF9UGQjI-Rxg_cBYm9Ify3aWg2GHsrBqaiFzek.

10. Bartie Scott, "Women CEOs Like Marissa Mayer Are Often Set Up to Fall Off the 'Glass Cliff,'" Inc., 2016. Accessed March 3, 2019, at https://www.inc.com/arite-scott /marissa-mayer-women-ceos-glass-cliff.html.

11. "Women in the Workplace 2019." McKinsey & Company, Lean In. 2019. Accessed November 7, 2019. https://www.mckinsey.com/featured-insights/gender-equality /women-in-the-workplace-2019.

12. "Michelle Cowan and Nicole O'Keefe: Women Working in Male-Dominated Industries (Part 2)," *The Fix with Michelle King*, iTunes, 2019. Accessed March 3, 2019, at https://podcasts.apple.com/bo/podcast/michelle-cowan-nicole-o-keefe -women-working-in-male/id1336361820?i=1000444574383&l=en.

13. Priyanka Dwivedi, Aparna Joshi, and Vilmos F. Misangyi, "Gender-inclusive gatekeeping: How (mostly male) predecessors influence the success of female CEOs," *Academy of Management Journal* 61, no. 2 (2018): 379–404.

14. Sharon Mavin, "Venus envy 2: Sisterhood, queen bees and female misogyny in management," *Women in Management Review* 21, no. 5 (2006): 349–364.

15. Ibid.

16. Paulo Roberto Arvate, Gisele Walczak Galilea, and Isabela Todescat, "The queen bee: A myth? The effect of top-level female leadership on subordinate females," *Leadership Quarterly* 29, no. 5 (2018): 533–548.

17. "Transcript of Julia Gillard's Speech," *Sydney Morning Herald*, October 10, 2012. Accessed July 10, 2017, at https://www.smh.com.au/politics/federal/transcript-of -julia-gillards-speech-20121010-27c36.html.

18. "Julia Gillard: Calling Out Misogyny," iTunes, 2019. Accessed March 3, 2019, at https://podcasts.apple.com/bo/podcast/julia-gillard-calling-out-misogyny /id1336361820?i=1000441895297&l=en.

19. Christine A. Stanley, "Giving voice from the perspectives of African American women leaders," *Advances in Developing Human Resources* 11, no. 5 (2009): 551–561.

20. Janis V. Sanchez-Hucles and Donald D. Davis, "Women and women of color in

leadership: Complexity, identity, and intersectionality," *American Psychologist* 65, no. 3 (2010): 171.

21. Ashleigh Shelby Rosette, Christy Zhou Koval, Anyi Ma, and Robert Livingston, "Race matters for women leaders: Intersectional effects on agentic deficiencies and penalties," *Leadership Quarterly* 27, no. 3 (2016): 429–445.

22. Michelle King, "Mayim Bialik on Her Viral Video and Why What We Call Women at Work Matters," *Forbes,* April 10, 2017. Accessed May 15, 2019, at https://www .forbes.com/sites/michelleking/2017/04/10/mayim-bialik-on-her-viral-video-and -why-what-we-call-women-at-work-matters/.

23. Sharon Mavin and Gina Grandy, "Women elite leaders doing respectable business femininity: How privilege is conferred, contested and defended through the body," *Gender, Work & Organization* 23, no. 4 (2016): 379–396.

24. Ibid.

25. Jennifer Klatt, Sabrina C. Eimler, and Nicole C. Krämer, "Make up your mind: The impact of styling on perceived competence and warmth of female leaders," *Journal of Social Psychology* 156, no. 5 (2016): 483–497.

26. Victoria L. Brescoll, "Leading with their hearts? How gender stereotypes of emotion lead to biased evaluations of female leaders," *Leadership Quarterly* 27, no. 3 (2016): 415–428.

27. Karen S. Lyness and Donna E. Thompson, "Above the glass ceiling? A comparison of matched samples of female and male executives," *Journal of Applied Psychology* 82, no. 3 (1997): 359.

28. Patricia Lewis and Ruth Simpson, "Kanter revisited: Gender, power and (in)visibility," *International Journal of Management Reviews* 14, no. 2 (2012): 141–158.

29. Natalia Karelaia and Laura Guillén, "Me, a woman and a leader: Positive social identity and identity conflict," *Organizational Behavior and Human Decision Processes* 125, no. 2 (2014): 204–219.

30. "Everyday Equality: Our strategy 2017–2022," Scope, 2017. Accessed January 7, 2018, at https://www.scope.org.uk/about-us/everyday-equality.

31. Julie Coffman and Bill Neuenfeldt, "Everyday Moments of Truth: Frontline Managers Are Key to Women's Career Aspirations," Bain Brief, Bain & Company, 2014. Accessed March 3, 2019, at https://www.bain.com/insights/everyday-moments-of-truth.

32. Karen Tuaronite, "Neurodiversity: Driving Innovation from Unexpected Places," EY, 2018. Accessed May 15, 2019, at https://www.ey.com/Publication/vwLUAssets /EY-neurodiversity-driving-innovation-from-unexpected-places-may-2018/$FILE /EY-neurodiversity-driving-innovation-from-unexpected-places.pdf.

33. Crystal L. Hoyt, Stefanie K. Johnson, Susan Elaine Murphy, and Kerri Hogue Skinnell, "The impact of blatant stereotype activation and group sex-composition on female leaders," *Leadership Quarterly* 21, no. 5 (2010): 716–732.

34. Madeline E. Heilman and Tyler G. Okimoto, "Why are women penalized for success

at male tasks?: The implied communality deficit," *Journal of Applied Psychology* 92, no. 1 (2007): 81.

35. McKinsey & Company, "Women in the Workplace 2018" 2018. Lean In. Accessed January 7, 2019, https://womenintheworkplace.com/.

36. Ibid.

37. Marla Baskerville Watkins and Alexis Nicole Smith, "Importance of women's political skill in male-dominated organizations," *Journal of Managerial Psychology* 29, no. 2 (2014): 206–222.

38. Ibid.

39. Christy Glass and Alison Cook, "Leading at the top: Understanding women's challenges above the glass ceiling," *Leadership Quarterly* 27, no. 1 (2016): 51–63.

40. Eric K. Kaufman and Pat E. Grace, "Women in grassroots leadership: Barriers and biases experienced in a membership organization dominated by men," *Journal of Leadership Studies* 4, no. 4 (2011): 6–16.

41. Rosalind Gill, "Cool, creative and egalitarian? Exploring gender in project-based new media work in Euro," *Information, Communication & Society* 5, no. 1 (2002): 70–89.

42. Sanchez-Hucles and Davis, "Women and women of color in leadership."

43. Gwendolyn M. Combs, "The duality of race and gender for managerial African American women: Implications of informal social networks on career advancement," *Human Resource Development Review* 2, no. 4 (2003): 385–405.

44. Cristian L. Dezső, David Gaddis Ross, and Jose Uribe, "Is there an implicit quota on women in top management? A large-sample statistical analysis," *Strategic Management Journal* 37, no. 1 (2016): 98–115.

45. Isis H. Settles, NiCole T. Buchanan, and Kristie Dotson, "Scrutinized but not recognized: (In)visibility and hypervisibility experiences of faculty of color," *Journal of Vocational Behavior* 113 (August 2019): 62–74.

46. Jena McGregor, "The Stereotype of the 'queen Bee' Female Executive Is Losing Its Sting," *Washington Post*, June 9, 2015. Accessed May 15, 2019, at https://www.wash ingtonpost.com/news/on-leadership/wp/2015/06/09/the-idea-of-queen-bee-female -executives-is-losing-its-sting/?utm_term=.bea7fc77dd29.

47. David R. Hekman, Stefanie K. Johnson, Maw-Der Foo, and Wei Yang, "Does Diversity-Valuing Behavior Result in Diminished Performance Ratings for Nonwhite and Female Leaders?," Gender Action Portal, Harvard Kennedy School, 2016. Accessed May 15, 2019, at http://gap.hks.harvard.edu/does-diversity -valuing-behavior-result-diminished-performance-ratings-nonwhite-and-female -leaders.

48. "Cara Pelletier: What the Best Place for Women to Work Looks Like," *The Fix with Michelle King*, iTunes, 2019. Accessed March 3, 2019, at https://podcasts.apple.com /bo/podcast/cara-pelletier-what-best-place-for-women-to-work-looks/id1336361820 ?i=1000433929791&l=en.

8: Breaking Up with Don

1. James R. Mahalik, Shaun M. Burns, and Matthew Syzdek, "Masculinity and perceived normative health behaviors as predictors of men's health behaviors," *Social Science & Medicine* 64, no. 11 (2007): 2201–2209.

2. Ibid.

3. Matt Krentz, Olivier Weirzba, Katie Abouzahr, et al., "Five Ways Men Can Improve Gender Diversity at Work," BCG, October 10, 2017. Accessed May 10, 2019, at https://www.bcg.com/publications/2017/people-organization-behavior-culture-five-ways-men-improve-gender-diversity-work.aspx.

4. Belen Garijo, "Gender Diversity Makes Great Business Sense," World Economic Forum, April 29, 2019. Accessed November 10, 2019, at https://www.weforum.org/agenda/2019/04/gender-diversity-makes-great-business-sense/.

5. "Justin Baldoni: Man Enough?," iTunes, 2018. Accessed March 3, 2019, at https://podcasts.apple.com/bo/podcast/justin-baldoni-man-enough/id1336361820?i=1000405240727&l=en.

6. Robin J. Ely and Debra E. Meyerson, "An organizational approach to undoing gender: The unlikely case of offshore oil platforms," *Research in Organizational Behavior* 30 (2010): 3–34.

7. Erin M. Reid, "Straying from breadwinning: Status and money in men's interpretations of their wives' work arrangements," *Gender, Work & Organization* 25, no. 6 (2018): 718–733.

8. Melissa A. Parris and Margaret H. Vickers, " 'Look at Him . . . He's Failing": Male Executives' Experiences of Redundancy," *Employee Responsibilities and Rights Journal* 22, no. 4 (2010): 345–357.

9. Reid, "Straying from breadwinning."

10. "Dr. Michael Kaufman: Why Men Must Join the Gender Equality Revolution," *The Fix with Michelle King*, iTunes. Accessed July 3, 2019 at https://podcasts.apple.com/sg/podcast/dr-michael-kaufman-why-men-must-join-gender-equality/id1336361820?i=1000430552253.

11. Michele Rene Gregory, "Inside the locker room: Male homosociability in the advertising industry," *Gender, Work & Organization* 16, no. 3 (2009): 323–347.

12. Ibid.

13. Isabel Metz and Alan Simon, "A focus on gender similarities in work experiences in senior management: A study of an Australian bank builds the case," *Equal Opportunities International* 27, no. 5 (2008): 433–454.

14. Ibid.

15. Derek K. Iwamoto, Jennifer Brady, Aylin Kaya, and Athena Park, "Masculinity and depression: a longitudinal investigation of multidimensional masculine norms among college men," *American Journal of Men's Health* 12, no. 6 (2018): 1873–1881.

16. Ann M. Roche, Ken Pidd, Jane A. Fischer, et al., "Men, work, and mental health:

A systematic review of depression in male-dominated industries and occupations," *Safety and Health at Work* 7, no. 4 (2016): 268–283.

17. Robert Lundmark, Henna Hasson, Ulrica von Thiele Schwarz, et al., "Leading for change: Line managers' influence on the outcomes of an occupational health intervention," *Work & Stress* 31, no. 3 (2017): 276–296.

9: Equality

1. Michelle King, "De Beers CEO Shares Five Ways to Ensure Women Have an Equal Voice at the Table," Thrive Global, May 9, 2018. Accessed March 3, 2019, at https:// thriveglobal.com/stories/debeers-ceo-shares-five-ways-to-ensure-women-have-an-equal-voice-at-the-table/.

2. Ellyn Shook and Julie Sweet, "When She Rises, We All Rise: Getting to Equal 2018: Creating a Culture Where Everyone Thrives," Accenture, 2018. Accessed March 3, 2019, at https://www.accenture.com/_acnmedia/pdf-73/accenture-when-she-rises -we-all-rise.pdf.

3. Michelle King, "How Businesses Break the Glass Ceiling," Huffington Post, May 26, 2017. Accessed March 3, 2019, at https://www.huffpost.com/entry/how-businesses -break-the-glass-ceiling_b_5925a0ebe4b0dfb1ca3a102b.

4. "Donna Carpenter: When Brands Take a Stand," *The Fix with Michelle King*, iTunes, 2019. Accessed July 3, 2019, at https://podcasts.apple.com/bo/podcast/donna -carpenter-when-brands-take-a-stand/id1336361820?i=1000441134866&l=en.

5. "Research reveals four in five managers have witnessed gender discrimination in past year," CMI, 2018. Accessed January 7, 2019, at https://www.managers.org.uk/about -us/media-centre/cmi-press-releases/research-reveals-four-in-five-managers-have -witnessed-gender-discrimination-in-past-year.

6. Ibid.

7. Michelle King, "Arianna Huffington and Citi Are Supporting Women to Do Less and Achieve More," *Forbes*, March 8, 2018. Accessed March 3, 2019, at https:// www.forbes.com/sites/michelleking/2018/03/08/arianna-huffington-and-citi-are -supporting-women-to-do-less-and-achieve-more/#7b086f946c12.

8. "Scott Beth: How to Be an Ally," *The Fix with Michelle King*, iTunes, 2019. Accessed July 3, 2019, at https://podcasts.apple.com/bo/podcast/scott-beth-how-to-be-an-ally /id1336361820?i=1000436267443&l=en.

9. Michelle King, "Jacinda Ardern, New Zealand Prime Minister's Message to Women: Be Yourself, It's Good Enough," *Forbes*, November 28, 2017. Accessed July 3, 2019, at https://www.forbes.com/sites/michelleking/2017/11/28/jacinda-ardern-new-zealand -prime-ministers-message-to-women-be-yourself-its-good-enough/#5c9e48f032b9.

10. "Christchurch Mosque Shootings," Wikipedia, 2019. Accessed July 7, 2019, at https://en.wikipedia.org/wiki/Christchurch_mosque_shootings.

11. Marjorie Derven, "Diversity and inclusion by design: best practices from six global companies," *Industrial and Commercial Training* 46, no. 2 (2014): 84–91.

10: It's Our Workplace

1. Luke Dormehl, "Algorithm predicts Parkinson's disease by digging through your medical history," Digital Trends, September 20, 2017. Accessed July 7, 2019, at https://www.digitaltrends.com/cool-tech/parkinsons-algorithm-washington/.

2. Ibid.

3. James Manyika, Susan Lund, Michael Chui, et al., "Jobs lost, jobs gained: What the future of work will mean for jobs, skills, and wages," McKinsey Global Institute, 2017. Accessed July 7, 2019, at https://www.mckinsey.com/featured-insights/future-of-work/jobs-lost-jobs-gained-what-the-future-of-work-will-mean-for-jobs-skills-and-wages.

4. Alice H. Eagly and Linda L. Carli, "The female leadership advantage: An evaluation of the evidence," *Leadership Quarterly* 14, no. 6 (2003): 807–834.

5. Steven H. Appelbaum, Barbara T. Shapiro, Katherine Didus, et al., "Upward mobility for women managers: Styles and perceptions: Part 1," *Industrial and Commercial Training* 45, no. 1 (2013): 51–59.

6. Jack Zenger and Joseph Folkman, "Research: Women Score Higher Than Men in Most Leadership Skills," *Harvard Business Review*, June 25, 2019. Accessed July 7, 2019, at https://hbr.org/2019/06/research-women-score-higher-than-men-in-most-leadership-skills.

7. Appelbaum, Shapiro, Didus, et al., "Upward mobility for women managers."

8. "Getting to Equal 2019: Creating a Culture That Drives Innovation," Accenture, 2019. Accessed July 7, 2019, at https://www.accenture.com/us-en/about/inclusion-diversity/gender-equality-innovation-research.

Index